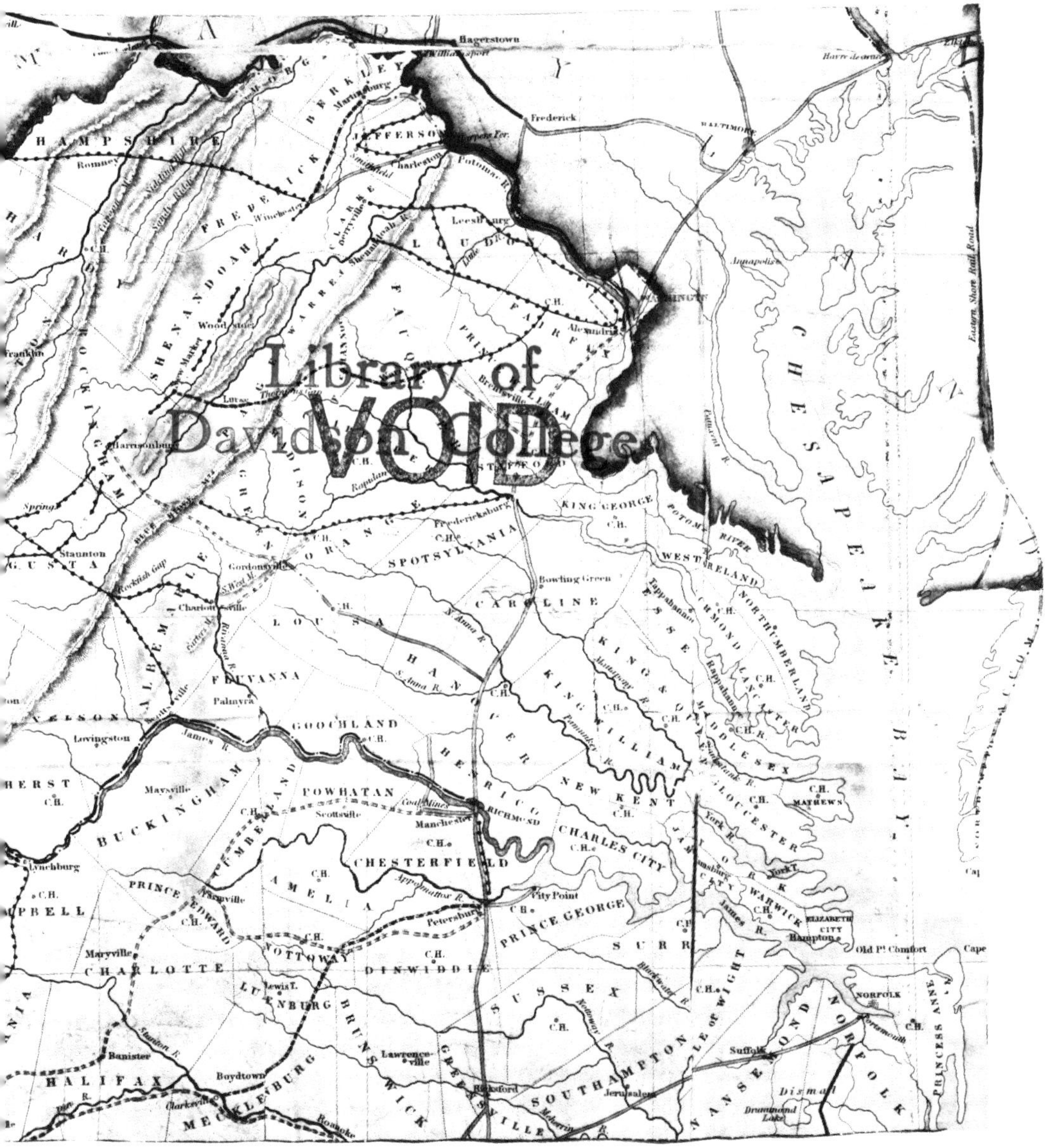
Hagerstown
Frederick
BALTIMORE
Havre de Grace
Annapolis
Eastern Shore Rail Road
CHESAPEAKE BAY
HAMPSHIRE
Romney
BERKLEY
Martinsburg
JEFFERSON
Charleston
Potomac R.
FREDERICK
Winchester
CLARKE
Leesburg
LOUDOUN
SHENANDOAH
Woodstock
WARREN
FAIRFAX
Alexandria
Franklin
ROCKINGHAM
Harrisonburg
New Market
Brentsville
PRINCE WILLIAM
STAFFORD
Rapidan
KING GEORGE
POTOMAC RIVER
Fredericksburg
Staunton
Rockfish Gap
Gordonsville
SPOTSYLVANIA
WESTMORELAND
Bowling Green
CAROLINE
Charlottesville
LOUISA
NORTHUMBERLAND
ALBEMARLE
FLUVANNA
Palmyra
HANOVER
KING WILLIAM
LANCASTER
MIDDLESEX
GOOCHLAND
Lovingston
James R.
HENRICO
NEW KENT
GLOUCESTER
MATHEWS
Maysville
POWHATAN
Scottsville
BUCKINGHAM
RICHMOND
Manchester
CHARLES CITY
Lynchburg
CHESTERFIELD
York R.
York T.
PRINCE EDWARD
Farmville
AMELIA
Appomattox R.
City Point
WARWICK
ELIZABETH CITY
Petersburg
PRINCE GEORGE
Hampton
Old Pt. Comfort
NOTTOWAY
DINWIDDIE
SURRY
Maryville
CHARLOTTE
Lewis T.
LUNENBURG
SUSSEX
NORFOLK
PRINCESS ANNE
Banister
Lawrenceville
Suffolk
HALIFAX
Boydtown
BRUNSWICK
Hicksford
SOUTHAMPTON
Jerusalem
NANSEMOND
Dismal
Drummond Lake
Clarksville
MECKLENBURG
GREENSVILLE
Roanoke
C.H.

Claudius CROZET

FRENCH ENGINEER IN AMERICA

1790–1864

CLAUDIUS CROZET

FRENCH ENGINEER
IN AMERICA
1790–1864

Robert F. Hunter
and
Edwin L. Dooley, Jr.

UNIVERSITY PRESS OF VIRGINIA
Charlottesville

THE UNIVERSITY PRESS OF VIRGINIA
Copyright © 1989 by the Rectors and Visitors
of the University of Virginia

First published 1989

Frontispiece: Portrait of Claudius Crozet by
William Garl Brown. (*Courtesy of VMI Museum,
Lexington, Va.*)

Endpapers: Crozet map of internal improvements
in Virginia, 1838. (*Courtesy of Virginia
State Library and Archives*)

Library of Congress Cataloging-in-Publication Data
Hunter, Robert F., 1921–
  Claudius Crozet, French engineer in America, 1790–1864 / Robert F.
Hunter and Edwin L. Dooley, Jr.
    p. cm.
  Bibliography: p.
  ISBN 0-8139-1222-9
  1. Crozet, Claudius, 1790–1864. 2. Engineers—France—Biography.
I. Dooley, Edwin L., 1942– . II. Title.
TA140.C8H86 1989
620'.0092'4—dc19
[B]   89-5312
                                                                   CIP

Printed in the United States of America

Acknowledgments

The VMI Sesquicentennial Committee sponsored the publication of a new biography of Claudius Crozet as one of its projects in celebration of the 150th anniversary of the Institute in 1989. The authors wish to express their appreciation for the generous financial support of the committee.

The authors also wish to express their appreciation for the time and efforts in support of their research to the staffs of the libraries at the Ecole Polytechnique, the Virginia Military Institute, the United States Military Academy, the Virginia State Library, the University of Virginia, the Library of Congress, Louisiana State University, the College of William and Mary, the University of North Carolina, Washington and Lee University, the Virginia Historical Society, and the Valentine Museum.

Various individuals helped in different ways, in particular Janet J. Aldridge, Henry S. Bausum, Beverly Brannan, George M. Brooke, Jr. and the VMI Sesquicentennial Committee, Marie Capps, Mike Collingwood, June F. Cunningham, Wylma P. Davis, Charles E. Fraley, Emmanuel Grison, Willard M. Hays, Donald D. Horward, Elizabeth S. Hostetter, Jane Hunter, Diane B. Jacob, John W. Knapp, Leonard L. Lewane, Julia S. Martin, Francine Masson, James M. Morgan, Jr., and Joseph D. Neikirk.

Completion of this work would not have been possible without the constant interest, support, and encouragement of our wives, Dorothy F. Hunter and Louise K. Dooley.

Contents

	Preface	ix
1	Early Years in France, 1790–1816	1
2	West Point Professor, 1816–23	16
3	Principal Engineer of Virginia, 1823–31	31
4	Year of Crisis in Virginia, 1831	54
5	Louisiana, 1832–37	85
6	Return to Virginia as Principal Engineer, 1837–43	103
7	The Academic Life Renewed, 1837–49	125
8	The Blue Ridge Railroad and Tunnel, 1849–58	140
9	Virginian to the End, 1858–64	165
	Notes	185
	Bibliography, with a Note on Sources	206
	Index	217

Illustrations
following page 73

College of Navarre, Paris, 1734

Quarters No. 3, U. S. Military Academy, West Point, N.Y.

House at 100 East Main St., Richmond, Virginia

Louisiana in the 1830s

Jefferson College, Convent, La.

North River Canal at James River, near Glasgow, Va.

VMI in 1842

Edmund Randolph house, Richmond, Va.

Crozet in the 1850s

Blue Ridge Railroad and tunnels

West portal, main tunnel

East portal, main tunnel

Interior, main tunnel

Preface

One of the many results of the final fall of Napoleon in 1815 was the departure from France of a number of his former officers. Some left not because they had to but because they wanted to, having been disappointed by the restoration of the monarchy but by no means proscribed by it. One of those who elected to emigrate to America was Captain Claudius Crozet, a graduate of the prestigious Ecole Polytechnique and an experienced military and civil engineer.

Crozet and his new wife sought a home and an opportunity for him to make use of his considerable skills, both in the academic world and in the field—building roads, canals, and, in a few years, railroads. In his academic life, he brought innovative changes in the teaching of engineering and mathematics at West Point, presided over Jefferson College in Louisiana and the Richmond Academy in Virginia, and played an important role in the founding of the Virginia Military Institute. In his life as a professional engineer, he was state engineer in both Virginia and Louisiana, but more importantly in Virginia, where he capped his career by building what was at the time the nation's longest railroad tunnel.

Crozet learned more about the geography of antebellum Virginia, which included West Virginia, than all but a very few of his contemporaries knew and depicted his knowledge on three useful maps of the state. On horseback and on foot, he traversed the state he came to love as his adopted home. He was disturbed by its economic and political decline compared with neighboring states and hoped to reverse that decline by means of a comprehensive transportation network. His views on specific needs were nearly always proved correct by subsequent developments, many of which he foresaw, but they earned the hostility of vested interests who ignored or interfered with his work but never completely curtailed it.

The monuments to Crozet's memory are few and varied in nature. No statue was ever erected, but a town on a railroad line and a building at VMI are appropriately named after him. The story of his life is not one of high drama, but it will interest the reader who enjoys knowing someone who left the world a better place by reason of his skill, integrity, and willingness to put his best effort into every undertaking.

Virginia is properly proud to call Claudius Crozet, an adopted son, one of its own.

Claudius CROZET

FRENCH ENGINEER IN AMERICA

1790–1864

1

Early Years in France
1790–1816

Claude Crozet was born on the second day of January, 1790, in the commune of Villefranche, Department of the Rhône, in southeastern France. His father, François Crozet, was a wholesale wine merchant who traded in Paris. His mother, Pierrette Varion Crozet, was a native of Villefranche. When Crozet was about ten years old, his mother died in Bordeaux, leaving François with two sons, Claude and William, and a daughter, Eliza. A third son, Benoit, had died one month before Claude was born. From all indications, the family was moderately wealthy when the Revolution began and did not suffer greatly by the events of that upheaval. In fact, despite the Revolution, François's wine business survived and probably prospered, and sometime after 1801 he moved his small family to Paris where they took up residence at 15 Rue Saint Marc.[1]

No details are known of Crozet's childhood or early education in Villefranche or Paris, but the extent of his academic preparation is suggested by the list of subjects included in the competitive entrance examination, or *concours*, which he took in 1805 as a candidate for admission into the Ecole Impériale Polytechnique, a school established in Paris in 1794 by the Convention government for the training of all types of engineers, civil and military. The examination was administered on or about 7 September 1805, and it covered arithmetic, the metric system, algebra, the theory of proportion and progression, the use of logarithmic tables, elementary geometry, rectilinear trigonometry and the use of sine tables, the principal properties of conic sections, statics, French composition and grammar, and drawing. His proficiency in the subjects suggests that Crozet may have attended one of the Central Schools authorized by the law of 21 February 1795. These schools, one of which existed in nearly every department of the Republic by 1799, stressed instruction in science and mathematics. Although the instruction provided in them was mostly at an elementary level, the Central Schools did much to prepare talented students specifically for the entrance examination of the Ecole Polytechnique.[2]

The results of the 1805 *concours* were formally reviewed by a jury presided over by the newly appointed military governor of the Ecole Polytechnique, General Jean-Gérard de Lacuée, and the names of the successful candidates were published in order of merit. Crozet's performance on the examination placed him fifty-eighth among the 125 new students admitted on 22 November 1805. It must have been with a sense of accomplishment and relief that he took his place among the 316 young men who constituted the student body that year.[3]

Crozet entered the Ecole Polytechnique at an important moment in its early history. Before 1805 the school was conducted in the Palais Bourbon near the Seine River in Paris, and the students lived separately in private homes or pensions. In 1805, soon after the Empire came into existence and over the objections of the faculty of the Ecole, Napoleon decreed that the school should be reorganized on military lines in order to impose a strict discipline upon the students. By November, he had effected the school's complete militarization by assigning control to a military governor and by housing the students in a barracks at the former Collège de Navarre located in the Latin Quarter. From that time on, the students were considered members of the corps of volunteers (*Corps de vélites*), and they were paid and treated as soldiers. Thus, when Crozet matriculated, he entered an institution governed by a military administration and controlled by a system of military discipline. This structured environment, with its explicit goals and few unpredictable elements, stood in contrast to the turbulence experienced by French society since 1789. Perhaps Crozet's rapid adaptation to the routine of the school reveals a deep-seated need in him for order and stability. Throughout his life, Crozet valued discipline highly, and it became an integral part of his character and personality. In later years, he often said that one could accomplish nothing without discipline.[4]

In addition to the basic organizational changes at the Ecole decreed by Napoleon in 1805, there were changes which had important social implications for the school and which cast light on the financial condition of the Crozet family. From the founding of the Ecole Polytechnique in 1794 until 1805, during which time France experienced a bumpy economic recovery from the first effects of the Revolution, there was little or no cost to students attending the school. In 1805 an economic crisis developed, culminating in a financial panic in Paris which threatened the Bank of France and ruined a number of wealthy financiers. When advisers predicted a shortage of funds to pay the army, Napoleon was driven to adopt emergency measures in many areas, including a new approach to financing the Ecole Polytechnique. By an imperial decree of 8 September 1805, students at the Ecole were informed that henceforth they would be required to pay, in advance, for room and board as well as uniforms and textbooks. The Crozet family's ability to afford the approximately 1,500 francs levied for his first year at the school underscores François Crozet's affluent circumstances in the economic bad times of 1805–7. Not all families were so fortunate, with the result that many talented young men found it impossible to enter the Ecole. When critics expressed fear that the school might become restricted to the wealthy, costs were waived for a few distinguished students who could prove acute need.[5]

The uniform that Crozet purchased became, in a different color, the model for the uniforms of the United States Military Academy at West Point and the Virginia Military Institute at Lexington, colleges with which Crozet would be identified in later years. It consisted of a blue woolen dress coat with blue collar, black pocket flaps, scarlet lining, and buttons with the imperial eagle and the words *Ecole impériale polytechnique*; a white vest and trousers; a blue overcoat; and a black shako with yellow trim. The same uniform as that worn by students of the Ecole Special Militaire of Paris, it was meant to remind the young scholars of their obligations to serve the nation and the emperor.[6]

The military staff of the school (*l'état-major de l'école*) consisted of a governor, General Lacuée, a commandant, a quartermaster/treasurer, two captains and two lieutenants charged with keeping order in the study and living areas of the school, and four drummers. The students were organized into an infantry corps consisting of two divisions of four companies each. They were assigned to sixteen rooms, each of which was under the supervision of a sergeant and a corporal. The instructional staff included a director of studies, an inspector, fifteen professors, eight examiners, a librarian, thirteen assistant professors (*répétiteurs*), and thirty-three support staff. In theory, the professors and the academic program, which extended over two years and emphasized mathematics, physics, and drawing, were supervised by a state-appointed academic council (*conseil de perfectionnement*). In practice, however, the military governor and his administrative council exercised considerable control over every aspect of the school.[7]

By 1805 the course of instruction at the Ecole Polytechnique had been reduced from three years to two, followed by instruction at one of the specialized institutions called schools of applied studies for the public service (*écoles d'application des services publiques*) where students received advanced, practical training in military and civil engineering. Students at the Ecole had no choice in the courses they took, and there were no electives; all students were required to follow a narrow core curriculum. As the demand for engineering officers increased, the administration of the school pressed the faculty to devote more attention to practical instruction in engineering and less to pure mathematics and theoretical work. However, believing that a strong grounding in scientific theory, mathematics, and analysis was essential in the formation of engineers, the academic council successfully resisted these efforts to reduce the stringency of the course of instruction. By 1807 resistance to the administration's efforts was so strong that practical work was altogether abandoned and emphasis was placed entirely on the teaching of science and mathematics.[8]

The list of textbooks used by Crozet in 1805 shows that the intellectual level of the curriculum was high. He studied the subjects contained in Sylvestre-François Lacroix's *Elementary Treatise on Differential and Integral Calculus*, *Descriptive Geometry* by Gaspard Monge, *Analysis Applied to Geometry* by Monge and Jean Nicolas Pierre Hachette, *Treatise on Elementary Mechanics* by Louis Benjamin Francoeur, Antoine François de Fourcroy's *Chemistry*, Jean-François Callet's handbook of *Logarithm Tables*, *Laws of the Movement of Solid Bodies and the Movement of Fluids* by Gaspard de Prony, *Optics* by Nicolas Louis Lacaille, *Architecture* by Jean Nicolas Louis Durand, *Fortifications* by Simon François Gay de Vernon, and *Program of Courses for the Engineer of Bridges and Roads* by Joseph Mathieu Sganzin. Because most of these authors were also professors at the Ecole, the curriculum followed closely the material in their books.[9]

A few of Crozet's professors were engaged full-time at the Ecole Polytechnique, and some even lived at the school. Others held concurrent appointments at other schools, such as the School of Bridges and Roads (*Ecole des ponts et chaussées*), the School of Mines (*Ecole des mines*), and the Ecole Normale, which made it difficult for them to spend much time at the Polytechnique. Several professors, such as the mathematician and senator Gaspard Monge or the chemist and minister of education Antoine Fourcroy, were so deeply involved in the political life of the Empire that they lectured at the Ecole Polytechnique only as their governmental duties allowed. Fortunately for Crozet, Monge was not often called away from Paris in 1805–6, Crozet's first year. Enjoying a brilliant reputation as a mathematician, engineer, and politician, Monge was personally popular with the students and consented several times in 1806 to deliver special lectures at their request. Crozet developed a lifelong admiration for Monge and a serious interest in the subject he founded and taught, descriptive geometry.[10]

Crozet's first year of study (termed the "second division"), which extended from November 1805 to September 1806, included geometry, chemistry, physics, fortification, architecture, public works, mines, mechanics, and drawing. Monthly progress reports on these courses reveal that the class in mechanics was a favorite with the students. Also of special interest was the class in mines, which included several field trips to the School of Mines and the network of tunnels and sewers under Paris. The class in chemistry was not so successful, however, because the construction of laboratories was delayed until March 1806 and essential study did not begin until well into the academic year.

The transfer of the Ecole in 1805 to the site of the College of Navarre caused many difficulties for students and professors. The buildings of the old college were in great disrepair as they had been occupied for nearly a decade by homeless individuals and wandering artists. Stone walls had been pulled down to furnish building materials for other structures. In 1805 laborers were on the scene going about the noisy and dusty business of remodeling the old buildings even as professors tried to conduct classes and the students tried to study. One administrator revealed the frustration that these conditions caused when he reported, "Despite the numerous obstacles resulting from the occupation of a building still filled with workers, and of which many portions are still not completed, instruction is progressing as well as possible." The students managed to put these inconveniences and distractions aside and devoted themselves to their studies. In May 1806 the director of studies was pleased to report,

"There is in the school great zeal . . . many of the students are at work in their rooms from 4 o'clock in the morning." When the academic year ended on 21 September 1806, the director closed his report by saying, "The students of the two divisions have been diligent in their studies and they are to be commended as much for their work as for their behavior."[11]

During the second year ("first division"), Crozet and his classmates studied mathematical analysis, mechanics, descriptive geometry, chemistry, physics, mines, fortification, public works, and drawing. In addition there were courses in belles lettres, map drawing, grammar, and landscape drawing. Monge appeared rarely at the school that year because he was then serving as president of the Senate, and his loss was regretted, but the Ecole retained many other distinguished mathematicians, scientists, and engineers on its faculty.[12]

A brief survey of Crozet's professors in 1806–7 and of their accomplishments up to the time he was a student at the Ecole suggests a stimulating academic environment at the Polytechnique. Siméon Denis Poisson, the outstanding graduate of the Ecole Polytechnique in 1800, was employed as a demonstrator at the school and was assisting the mathematical physicist J. B. J. Fourier at the time Crozet was a student. Another mathematician, Gaspard Prony, was a graduate of the Ecole des Ponts et Chaussées and a noted engineer. He was one of the first professors at the Ecole Polytechnique to teach mathematical analysis applied to mechanics. Jean Hachette, who studied at the royal school for military engineers at Mézières and later taught descriptive geometry there, had been on the faculty of the Ecole Polytechnique for twelve years when Crozet encountered him. In 1807, as Monge's longtime collaborator in descriptive geometry, Hachette took over his lectures at the Ecole when political duties called him elsewhere.

Louis-Bernard Guyton de Morveau, who had worked with the eminent chemists Lavoisier, Berthollet, and Fourcroy, was another member of the faculty who taught Crozet. He was a professor of chemistry at the Ecole Polytechnique from its founding and twice was its director. During Crozet's first year at the school, Guyton de Morveau received the Legion of Honor for his research in chemistry. Also active in this period in the school was Jean Henry Hassenfratz, a mining engineer who was trained at the Ecole des Mines and who had studied descriptive geometry under Monge and chemistry under

Lavoisier. One of the founders of the Ecole Polytechnique, in 1805 he was a professor of general physics, the author of a four-volume work on mining and the processing of iron, and a well-known politician in Paris. Crozet also encountered Joseph Louis Gay-Lussac, distinguished for his work on the laws of gases. A graduate of the Ecole Polytechnique and the Ecole des Ponts et Chaussées, he was an associate of Berthollet and Alexander von Humboldt, and he became a member of the National Institute of Arts and Sciences in 1806. Gay-Lussac lived at the Ecole Polytechnique and taught chemistry there while Crozet was a student.

The final two names on the teaching staff were those of a civil and a military engineer, the two fields of greatest interest to Crozet. Simon Gay de Vernon graduated from the royal school for military engineering at Mézières and became an instructor of fortifications at the Ecole Polytechnique. He was the assistant director of studies there and the author of texts on the application of descriptive geometry to fortification. Joseph Sganzin, an engineer with the corps of bridges and roads, was an instructor of engineering at the Ecole Polytechnique from its founding. He was the author of several texts applying descriptive geometry to engineering problems.[13]

Many years later, in 1843, when Crozet was living in Richmond, Virginia, and contemplating a second move to New Orleans, Louisiana, he offered to sell his entire library to the Virginia Military Institute. Included in the lengthy inventory of books he offered to the superintendent of VMI, Colonel Francis H. Smith, were books written by the scientists and mathematicians mentioned above, with the exception of Guy de Morveau and Gay-Lussac, the two chemists among his distinguished teachers. Crozet's inventory, which was heavily weighted with works on mathematics, astronomy, physics, mineralogy, military engineering and science, machines, and literature, contained only two works on chemistry: Louis Jacques Thénard's *Traité de chimie élémentaire* (1813–16) and a work in English by the American chemist Franklin Bache. Of the three French chemists Guy de Morveau, Gay-Lussac, and Thénard, the last was primarily concerned with the application of chemistry to industry. Crozet's 1843 book list may be taken as evidence that he had little interest or ability in chemistry, except as it was applied to practical problems. The surprisingly poor grade he received in the subject in 1807 seems to confirm this suspicion. The very slow start that chemistry studies had at the new location of the school as a result of delays in completing the chemistry laboratories and a level of instruction in that subject which was consistently inferior to the more advanced work in mathematics and physics may have contributed to Crozet's general lack of interest in chemistry and his poor performance.[14]

Given an environment of assiduous study and brilliant professors, as well as constant reminders that much was expected by the nation from the students and graduates of the Ecole, it is not surprising that life at the school was stressful. The method of instruction reflected the practices of pre-Revolutionary military engineering schools, such as the School of Military Engineering at Mézières and the School of Bridges and Roads, where daily recitation in small class sections was emphasized and frequent examinations were designed to accelerate the production of officers and to weed out quickly those unsuited to the task. Frequent quizzing, especially oral recitations at the blackboard, became a hallmark of the school. Assistants examined students three times each week and at the end of each course, and a final examination was given by the course professor in the presence of the permanent examiners of the school and, at times, eminent scientists of the day. For example, André Ampère, a pioneer in electrodynamics, frequently visited the first-year analysis section to conduct examinations in the school ampitheater, as did Pierre Laplace, the renowned physicist and mathematician. Pressure to succeed was intense, because students who did poorly in their studies or failed to conform to the strict regimen of the school were summarily sent into military service.[15]

The daily routine of these student-soldiers was devoted almost entirely to classes, study, and drill: it was a thoroughly regulated life. Crozet and his fellow students were confined to the grounds of the Ecole most days of the week. They had classes or other duties from 5 A.M. to 9 P.M., six days a week. Only on Wednesday afternoon, from 2 P.M. to 8 P.M., and on Sunday could they enjoy the freedom of leaving the confines of the school to visit in Paris. Some time was allowed for recreation and social activities, such as occasional dancing lessons, but few other distractions were sanctioned by school authorities.[16]

Not unexpectedly, the intense demands of the school did not prevent the students from maintaining a keen interest in the momentous events of the day and the news from the front. The victory of Napoleon at Austerlitz on 2 December 1805 over the Austrians and Russians, for example, resulted in a lengthy letter to the emperor from the students of the Ecole, dated 21 December, expressing their admiration and desire to participate in the achievements of the army. In it they revealed that they had "read and devoured the bulletins of the Grande Armée," which were posted daily in the courtyard of the Ecole Polytechnique. Later in that academic year, on 11 May 1806, as the Grande Armée lay quartered in southern Germany, the battalion of the Ecole Polytechnique paraded for Napoleon at the Tuileries palace in honor of his recent victories across Austria and Germany.[17]

When Crozet advanced to the first division in August 1806, he stood forty-first out of 56 in the examination that marked the promotion of his class. The attrition experienced by his class, which began with 125 members in 1805, is evidence of the stress and severe demands of the program at the Ecole. During his final year Crozet was frequently ill, and school infirmary records reveal that he spent almost thirty days on the sick list. Not surprisingly, his grades suffered. Out of 20 points possible for each subject, Crozet received the following grades in his classes: analysis, 11; statics, 12; physics, 10; chemistry, 3; grammar and belles lettres, 4; geometry, 14; map drawing, 14; figure drawing, 15. One of his teachers wrote that "he applies himself, although he has been sick this year 13 days in January and 14 days in July. In all 27 days."[18]

The number of names on the sick list grew dramatically at the end of the second year as final examinations approached. These rigorous examinations not only determined who would graduate from the Ecole but also influenced the graduate's assignment in the army. Adding to the stress normally associated with final examinations was the practice of appointing special outside examiners to conduct the questioning. For example, in 1806 the final examination in descriptive geometry and physics, Crozet's strongest subjects, was conducted by Etienne-Louis Malus, a captain in the Imperial Corps of Engineers. Malus was a talented officer whose strong interest in physics led him in 1807 to the discovery of the polarization of light. Conducted orally and in front of other students and the faculty, these examinations by eminent scientists and mathematicians were an ordeal dreaded by the students.[19]

Crozet successfully completed all of his final examinations and was graduated from the Ecole Polytechnique in July 1807, ranking twenty-first among fifty-six students destined for the artillery branch. Eighteen years old and having cleared his first hurdle toward a military career, Crozet left Paris amid the military parades and euphoria produced by Napoleon's recent diplomatic success in negotiating the Treaties of Tilsit. Within several months, he passed a qualifying examination for admission into the Artillery Corps and was admitted to the Imperial Artillery School (*Ecole d'application*) at Metz as a sublieutenant. In a letter to Crozet informing him of his appointment, Major General Jean-Jacques Basilien, comte de Gassendi, inspector general of artillery, observed: "I do not doubt that your actions and your work will result in the high distinction which you have earned on entering." Gassendi, an experienced artillery officer who provided sledges on rollers to transport a portion of Napoleon's artillery over the Saint Bernard Pass in 1800 and who had been rewarded for his service with a post at the Ministry of War, was correct in his evaluation of the young man.[20]

After two years of advanced study at the artillery school at Metz, Crozet was commissioned as a second lieutenant in the first battalion of bridge builders (*pontonniers*) of the Imperial Artillery Corps. On 9 June 1809 he entered the service of the Grande Armée and was assigned to Napoleon's headquarters, arriving at his post in time to participate in the battle of Wagram, 5–6 July 1809. Because the emperor's headquarters were located on the island of Lobau, it is conceivable that Crozet had been called there to assist in repairing the key bridges from Lobau to the south bank of the Danube or to construct wing-dams that were piledriven into the river above these bridges. In this battle, bridges played a crucial role in Napoleon's victory over the Austrians. For Crozet, fresh from the classrooms of the Ecole Polytechnique and Metz, Wagram provided valuable practical lessons.[21]

After the battle of Wagram, Crozet remained in Germany for a year before being transferred to Holland upon the annexation of the satellite Kingdom of Holland into the empire. He served there during the years 1810 and 1811 while the great powers of the Continent were at peace and Napoleon concentrated on trying to defeat England through economic blockade and military action in the field in Spain and Portugal. For an engineer whose specialty was bridge building, Crozet must have found excellent opportunities in Germany and Holland to practice his craft and learn new techniques. The Dutch excelled in bridge construction, and as allies of the French, they were recruited in large numbers into the *pontonniers* of the Imperial Guard. The use of jetties to reduce the width of river channels, especially along the Rhine River and in Holland, made a lasting impression on his mind. The three years he spent in Germany and Holland filled his mind with engineering designs and techniques that he would draw upon for many years.[22]

By early June 1812 Crozet had been transferred from Holland to the strategic fortified town of Wesel, located at the confluence of the Rhine and Lippe rivers in the Department of the Rhine. There he became part of the massive buildup of forces soon to be known as the Grand Armée de la Russie. His rank at the time was first lieutenant in the third company of the first battalion of bridge builders attached to the artillery train of the Imperial Guard (*Pontonniers employés à l'équipage d'artillerie de la Garde Impériale à la Grande Armée*). Later, on 22 June, he was promoted to the rank of captain and was assigned to the headquarters staff of General Jean-Ambroise Baston de Laribossière, commander of the artillery of the Grande Armée for the campaign of 1812. The next day, 23 July 1812, the Grande Armée began its invasion of Russia by crossing the Niemen River.[23]

The evidence of Crozet's service in Russia is fragmentary, but it shows that he was assigned to General Louis-Nicolas Razout's Eleventh Infantry Division of Marshal Michel Ney's Third Corps as it marched into Russia. His name appears among the officers of the third brigade, commanded by General d'Hénin. It also appears in the periodic troop reports of the Third Corps throughout its march from the Niemen to the Dvina, and from there along the Dnieper to the vicinity of Moscow. Then, in the report for 1–15 September 1812, his name no longer appears. This report was issued after the fierce battle of Borodino, which took place on 7 September against the forces of General Mikhail Kutusov, and it provides almost certain proof that Crozet was among twenty-three soldiers in the Third Corps taken prisoner during that engagement.[24]

His service at Borodino is unknown, although it is tempting to speculate that this skilled *pontonnier* took part in constructing the bridges over the Kalatsha River, west of Borodino. His capture may have occurred as Marshal Ney's forces attacked the Russian center. Falling into the hands of the enemy at Borodino spared Crozet the worse fate that awaited most of the soldiers of Napoleon's Grande Armée de la Russie as it retreated from Russia during the bitter winter of 1812–13 under the harrying attacks of the Russian army. He spent two years in Russia as a prisoner of war, but no details of this period are known for certain. Tradition has it that Crozet spent this time in the home of a Russian nobleman where he taught French to his captor's children, hunted wolves, and wrote a 113-page *Grammaire Russe* which has survived in manuscript form with his collected papers. One intriguing clue to this period in his life may be found in the name he gave to his second daughter, Claudia Natalia Crozet. The middle name does not appear elsewhere among members of the Crozet family and is clearly Russian in origin. Perhaps it honored someone who, in those dark days of 1812, helped the young French officer.[25]

Crozet was released from captivity after the first abdication of Napoleon on 4–6 April 1814. Traveling from Russia, he made his way back to France, arriving at the city of Metz on 20 August 1814. There he reported to military officials and received orders authorizing his return to Paris, which he reached on 26 August. Much to his relief, he found his father still residing in Paris at 15 Rue Saint Marc, where Crozet took up temporary residence. On 28 August he wrote to the Ministry of War to inform his superiors of his return, and he requested permission to remain with members of his family. Weary from his recent ordeal, Crozet wrote that he would report for duty when he received his orders, "if I am called back to active service." Permission to remain with his family was granted in September.[26]

Shortly thereafter, King Louis XVIII attempted to win the support of selected former Napoleonic officers by authorizing them to receive and wear the "Fleur de Lys," a decoration presented by "his Majesty, full of confidence in [their] fidelity and in [their] devotion to his person." Not a reward for past or present action, it was a weak plea for future loyalty. Crozet accepted the decoration in September—he may have had little opportunity to refuse it—but there is no evidence that he regarded it as significant. Far more important to him than decorations was his status in the army and any pay that might be due him. On 29 October 1814 he received a letter from the Bureau of Personnel of the Ministry of War placing him on the army's inactive list, from 1 October until such time as he might be recalled, and granting him an allowance of half pay. He remained on inactive service for only a short while. In mid-October, Captain Crozet was notified that he was being attached to the central committee of the artillery.[27]

With the coming of spring, Napoleon took advantage of an unpopular royal government and disorganization among the allies to escape from the island of Elba and return to France. On 19 March, as Napoleon drew near to Paris, Crozet received an urgent order from

Baron Dessalles, colonel-director of the bridge building service of the Royal Artillery Corps, to report to Charenton, on the Marne River, where a bridge was being hastily constructed. Crozet was ordered to take command of the entire operation, which included laborers and an attachment of cannoniers, and to send progress reports to Paris every two hours until the bridge was completed. Before the order could be carried out, however, other orders were issued to pull the bridge unit and cannoniers back to Paris.[28]

Events moved swiftly during the next two days. Napoleon entered Paris on 20 March and was joined by many of his former officers. Eight days later, Crozet received orders from the Ministry of War to report on 1 April to the army's general artillery park at Vincennes, on the southeast outskirts of Paris, under the command of Lieutenant General Neigre, director general of artillery parks. While he was assigned to Vincennes, Crozet was sent on temporary duty to Strasbourg, but he was recalled to Vincennes on 13 June by General Neigre and assigned to Colonel Renaud's command with specific instructions to organize the bridge service located there. Several days later, he was ordered to deliver powder and other artillery supplies to the army at Waterloo, but he was delayed by the mud-clogged roads caused by days of pouring rain and failed to arrive in time for the battle of Waterloo on 18 June. Crozet was in Paris when the allies entered the city a few days later.[29]

On 22 June, five months after the second abdication of Napoleon and the second restoration of Louis XVIII, Crozet was once again relieved from active duty and allowed to return to his father's home in Paris, "to wait there for the reorganization of the royal artillery corps and orders." While he waited and watched events unfolding across France, he decided to resign from the army. He wrote to the duc de Feltre, minister of war, on 1 April 1816 saying that it was his intention to quit military service to enter business. At first, officials at the Bureau of Personnel were reluctant to grant him his wish, saying, "This officer is known to be useful to the artillery branch, and if the number of officers available at this moment does not exceed the needs of the service, the request should be denied." In the end, however, Crozet's request was honored, and his discharge became official on 16 April 1816.[30]

Free from further military obligations, Crozet looked forward to a more settled way of life, although not necessarily in Paris or in France. He rented quarters at 18 Rue Chanfereine, in Paris, but gave as his permanent address his hometown of Villefranche. Perhaps he was thinking of joining his father in the wine trade. In the midst of this planning, he was married in Paris on 7 June 1816. His bride, Agathe Decamp, was thirty-three and he was twenty-six, according to documents issued at the marriage ceremony. Her parents were deceased, and she was living in Paris, the place of her birth, with an older sister. Earlier, in October 1814, Agathe's brother, Pierre François Decamp, who had served with the Fourth Hussars, died in Austria after a lengthy illness and left her a legacy, perhaps as much as 2,500 francs. The marriage contract, prepared in Paris on 5 June 1816, indicates that she brought to the union approximately 3,000 francs in savings and 3,000 francs in personal property. To the civil authorities who registered the marriage, Crozet identified himself as a wholesale merchant. His wealth included 15,000 francs in merchandise, perhaps his portion of the family business, 3,000 francs in personal property, and an unspecified amount of undisbursed back pay for his military service in Russia. Their combined assets made them wealthy in the immediate postwar days, and their future appeared secure. With a reassuring amount of capital, they decided to seek a new life across the sea in America.[31]

Why Crozet decided to leave France is not known for certain, but the record clearly indicates that he was not a proscribed soldier or a refugee. There is some evidence that he harbored strong feelings against the restored monarchy for the execution in December 1815 of his old commander Marshal Ney, and it is certain that he was critical of the government's shabby treatment of his admired teacher Monge. When the Ecole Polytechnique was reorganized in 1816, Monge, elderly, in ill health, and criticized for having been an adviser to Napoleon, was excluded from its faculty and expelled from the Académie des Sciences. He died two years later. In the preface to a textbook on descriptive geometry which Crozet published in 1821 in New York, he wrote of Monge: "The republican principles of the great man brought upon him the persecutions of a government hostile to liberal ideas. This and other injuries he received, so wounded his high and generous spirit, as to cause him to fall into a gloomy melancholy that failed not soon to conduct him to the tomb." The prospect of a "government hostile to liberal ideas" chilled Crozet, but perhaps the main reason he decided to leave Europe behind was a feeling of disgust over the excesses of war. Years later, in 1846, he wrote to an associate, "I have had my surfeit of war, I am for peace

... Peace, Peace rises at the top of all my thoughts." In America, he might find the opportunity to devote his thought, energy, and talents to building for a peaceful world.[32]

The last known record of Crozet's activities in France shows that he applied to the minister of war for the back pay owed to him for his military service and, particularly, for his time as prisoner of war in Russia. In his request, he mentioned certain promises made the previous April, before Waterloo, that payments would be forthcoming, and he appealed to the minister's sense of justice to authorize the compensation of one who was "judged worthy . . . [and whose] record of service and favorable recommendations from his commanders [would] justify [the action] to his Excellency." Apparently, Crozet's appeal fell on deaf ears, for the compensation was not paid. Nearly five years later, when Crozet was in the United States, he made another appeal to the Ministry of War. This one was turned down on the basis of insufficient information about Crozet's military service. In the end, it appears that bureaucratic red tape prevented payment of the funds due him.[33]

In the late summer or early fall of 1816, Crozet and his bride sailed to America. Crozet's first biographer, Colonel William Couper, wrote that one of Crozet's fellow voyagers was General Simon Bernard. This engineer met Captain Sylvanus Thayer, the future superintendent of the U.S. Military Academy, in France in 1816 while Thayer and Lieutenant Colonel William McRee were there on a mission for the U.S. Army to purchase books, charts, maps, equipment, and models of fortifications. The Americans persuaded Bernard to emigrate to the United States, where he was commissioned a brigadier general of engineers and assigned as inspector of fortifications at New York and at Fortress Monroe, Virginia. He was also appointed to the Board of Visitors of the U.S. Military Academy. It was possibly through Bernard's influence that Crozet received an appointment to the engineering faculty of the academy in September 1816, for shortly after arriving in the United States, the Crozets took up residence at West Point, New York, to teach cadets destined for the U.S. Army Corps of Engineers.[34]

2

West Point Professor
1816–23

General Simon Bernard, fellow passenger of the Crozets on the westward voyage, was ten years older than Crozet and a fellow alumnus of the Ecole Polytechnique. An officer in the French army from 1797 to 1814, he was Napoleon's aide-de-camp from 1805 and was said to have been the last officer with him at Waterloo. Emigrating to the United States, Bernard became an assistant to Brigadier General Joseph G. Swift, chief of army engineers and, until recently, superintendent of the United States Military Academy at West Point.

According to Swift, Crozet was introduced to him by "Baron Quinet (one of the French Provis. Govt.)."[1] Quinet was apparently one of the party on board the ship that brought Crozet and Bernard to New York in the summer of 1816. The assistant professor of engineering at West Point, Lieutenant Eveleth, wished to resign, and another candidate, Captain Surville, had been considered for the post since March. When Swift met Crozet early in September 1816, news had just arrived that Surville had "been promoted" in France and presumably would not return to the United States. Therefore Swift, on the strength of his personal interview with Crozet, the recommendations of Baron Quereta de Rochmont and General Leraysse, and a letter from the marquis de Lafayette which Crozet presented, decided to go ahead with Crozet.[2]

Swift would have preferred to appoint Bernard to the professorship of engineering at West Point but encountered the determination of President James Madison and Secretary of War William H. Crawford to have Bernard serve in the Army Corps of Engineers, examining the coastal defense works and recommending improvements in them. Swift doubted the wisdom of allowing a foreigner access to such vital intelligence, did not hesitate to tell Bernard so to his face, and pressed Madison and Crawford to send Bernard to West Point as a professor of engineering, but to no avail.[3] Crozet, therefore, received the appointment but did not have in General Swift as staunch a supporter as he believed.

Crozet began his duties as assistant professor of engineering on 20 September 1816. When he and Agathe arrived at West Point, faculty houses were being constructed, and the Crozets moved in March 1817 into one of the first two completed, designated Quarters No. 3. It remained standing until well into the twentieth century.[4] He was hardly alone as a Frenchman teaching in America. Several American colleges and universities, including Harvard, Yale, Columbia, Union, William and Mary, and soon the University of Michigan and the University of Virginia, showed evidence of French influence, but at none of them was it greater than at West Point.[5] In 1816 four of the seven faculty members were French: Christian Zoeller (drawing), Claudius Berard (French), Pierre Thomas (swordmaster), and Crozet (engineering). Shortly before his arrival at the academy, Crozet announced that he intended to follow the methods of the Ecole Polytechnique and that he would use its "authors."[6] He was the first teacher of descriptive geometry in the United States, a subject of elementary importance to engineers, which he taught from a French textbook, probably Monge's. In 1821 Crozet published the first part of his own *Treatise on Descriptive Geometry* in English, but he never completed the second part.[7]

The construction of faculty houses was only a small part of a comprehensive building program under way when Crozet arrived. The United States Military Academy was founded in 1802 and during its first five years admitted an average of sixteen cadets per year, taught by a faculty of three. During the second five years there was an average of forty-three cadets, and in 1812–13 there were sixty. The war with Great Britain demanded expansion to about two hundred cadets between 1814 and 1816.[8] The first superintendent of the academy was Jonathan Williams (1750–1815), a great-nephew of Benjamin Franklin. When Franklin went to France as a commissioner of the Continental Congress, Williams became an agent of the commission at Nantes, responsible for inspecting arms and other supplies being shipped to America. Forced out after becoming involved in the notorious controversy between Silas Deane and Arthur Lee, he remained in Europe, engaged in various business ventures, until Franklin returned to America in 1785. He worked with Franklin in some of his later scientific experiments and attracted the attention of President Jefferson, who appointed him in 1801 inspector of fortifications and superintendent at West Point, with the rank of major.[9] A "rather plump, middle aged, energetic gentleman, who could claim no military experience beyond the translation of a French treatise on artillery," his experience as superintendent was frustrating. Congress withheld funds for faculty, buildings, equipment, books, and everything needed for developing a first-rate school. Moreover, his authority over nonengineering cadets was limited. Williams resigned in frustration in 1803, but Jefferson persuaded him in 1805 to accept reappointment, with the rank of lieutenant colonel and authority over all cadets.[10] Even so, his duties as chief army engineer required frequent travel on inspection trips, during which times the academy "barely continued to exist." To compound the academy's handicaps, William Eustis, secretary of war from 1809 to 1813, was hostile to the institution. "When war came," in the view of historian Edgar Denton III, "the Secretary of War had almost destroyed the Military Academy." In July 1812 Williams resigned, and Brigadier General Swift within a few months took command at West Point.[11]

Joseph G. Swift (1783–1865) had an interesting career. His forebears resided in Massachusetts Bay Colony as early as 1634, and his father was an army surgeon. At age sixteen, Joseph Swift became a cadet in the corps of artillerists and engineers and in October 1801 he was transferred to the new military academy at West Point. He and one other cadet who received their commissions in October 1802 comprised the first graduating class. He rose rapidly in the ranks, and in July 1812, at age twenty-eight, he became a full colonel and chief of army engineers. He was with General James Wilkinson in Canada in 1813 and earned the brevet rank of brigadier general in February 1814. Later in the same year he directed the construction of the defenses of New York City after the British raid on Washington, for which the city showered him with honors.[12]

In the midst of these activities, Swift took charge of West Point in the summer of 1813 and immediately made plans for renovating the existing buildings and constructing new ones to meet the needs of the expanding corps of cadets. Between the spring of 1814 and the close of 1816, Swift directed the construction of three major buildings "of granite and brick, covered with slate," and he reported to Congress on their cost in February 1817. Located in a line at the south end of the "plain" facing north, they were from east to west: first, a cadet barracks of three stories and sixty-six rooms, which Swift commissioned Crozet to assist in designing in its later stages of construction; second, an academic building which included rooms for a library; and third, a refectory of two stories with a separate icehouse behind it, all at a total cost of $94,000. In addition Swift mentioned toward the close of his report, "Three professors houses 2 stories, 27 feet front, by 40 feet; two of these buildings are finished." One of these was Quarters No. 3, into which the Crozets moved the following month. The cost of construction of each house was $4,500.[13]

Performance of the United States Army during the War of 1812, although marked by occasional brilliance on the part of individuals, was, on the whole, disappointing. It was generally agreed that something could be learned from Europe. Secretary of War Crawford observed in a letter to Swift that the English admitted their inferiority to the French in the science of engineering, and "we can hardly suppose that we are superior to the English." With this in mind, Secretary of State James Monroe approved Swift's recommendation to send two army officers of engineers, Lieutenant Colonel William McRee and Captain Sylvanus Thayer, to study in France. They were ordered to Europe "to gain a knowledge of the European military establishment, their fortifications, Military Schools and Military workshops, and also to collect Books, Maps, Plans and Instruments for the Military Academy." The secretary of state was to provide "letters of introduction to our ministers in Europe, and also, to some of the most distinguished military officers in France." They arrived in Europe in the summer of 1815, in the aftermath of Waterloo, and returned to the United States in May 1817, at the end of Crozet's first academic year of service at West Point. There is no clear evidence that McRee and Thayer met Crozet while in France, but they did meet Simon Bernard, who impressed both men favorably.[14]

Lafayette recommended and Congress passed a resolution authorizing the president of the United States to "employ a skillful assistant" to General Swift. Bernard, having been recommended by both Lafayette and Jefferson's former secretary of the treasury Albert Gallatin, was given the courtesy title of brigadier general. Although an assistant to the army chief of engineers in name, Bernard actually was allowed such independence by the president that Swift "found his situation intolerable and resigned from the army in 1818." McRee soon followed Swift, resigning from the coast defense planning board and from the army. Bernard headed that board until he returned to France in 1830, leaving behind a number of excellent works, including an architectural masterpiece in the construction of Fortress Monroe near Norfolk, Virginia. "His work in the United States has been of incalculable value," concluded historian Thomas M. Spaulding, "though it is unfortunate that he was employed in such a way as to force out of the army two of its ablest engineers."[15]

Toward the end of Crozet's first calendar year at West Point, in the summer of 1817, occurred the celebrated confrontation between Captain Alden Partridge and Major Sylvanus Thayer. Most writers of memoirs and narrations of this event have been partial to one or the other, usually Thayer. It is he who is memorialized most visibly at West Point today, while the name Partridge is found in print rather than in granite and bronze. Partridge figures largely in every book written about West Point and has at least one supporter in the current generation of historians.[16]

Alden Partridge (1785–1854) was a native of Norwich, Vermont, who, like Swift, could trace his forebears in New England to the 1630s. He entered Dartmouth College in 1802 but before graduating was appointed a cadet at West Point in 1805. In October 1806 he was graduated and commissioned a first lieutenant, which was exceptional. He did not leave West Point but was assigned duty as an instructor of mathematics and engineering. He was promoted to captain in 1810; and when Williams resigned in 1813, Partridge became superintendent by virtue of being the ranking faculty member.

Actually, the administration of the academy was in a state of ambivalence, under two hats. Jonathan Williams had worn both at once, as chief of army engineers and as superintendent of the academy. Partridge, upon succeeding to the superintendency, "embarked upon a campaign to make himself in law, what Jonathan Williams had been in fact: the unquestioned master and accepted guiding force of the Military Academy."[17] Partridge proposed new regulations declaring that a permanent superintendent should be appointed who would have exclusive control of the institution and that the commandant of the Corps of Engineers would merely be the inspector of the institution.

Partridge, unknown to Swift, went to Washington and secured not only the approval of Secretary of War Monroe but appointment by him as superintendent in accordance with the new rule. When word of this reached Swift, he exploded, "The Military Academy shall be under my control or I will have nothing to do with it." Monroe reconsidered the matter but concluded that the chief of engineers could not actually reside at West Point and effective administration required a resident superintendent with authority. Therefore, he confirmed the appointment of Partridge to the post in March 1815, which contributed to Swift's finding his situation "intolerable."[18]

During the next two years Partridge ran the school in detail, putting in long hours of work and taking great personal interest in each cadet. Most of them thought he was "an excellent teacher, a fair and just administrator, and most of all obviously devoted to them." His relationships with the faculty were another matter. President James Monroe, accompanied by General Swift, came to inspect West Point in the spring of 1817. Upon his arrival, a representative of the faculty handed Monroe a sealed envelope containing a deposition signed by the entire Academic Board which criticized Partridge for neglecting the curriculum and overemphasizing military drills. Angered, Monroe told Swift that Partridge should be court-martialed and replaced. Swift told Partridge he could either resign as superintendent and be reassigned to other military duty or go on leave pending the convening of the court-martial. Partridge chose the latter; but as soon as Monroe and Swift had departed, he "refused to go on leave, arrested every professor on the post for participating in a cabal, and proceeded to teach all the courses himself."

In July, Swift informed brevet Major Sylvanus Thayer that he was appointed superintendent and should proceed to West Point to take command. Thayer handed Partridge his letter from Swift, and upon reading it, Partridge "stomped off" without a word and departed West Point the next day. Six weeks later, on 29 August 1817, Partridge returned, was received enthusiastically by most of the cadets, and informed Thayer that he was taking charge again. Thayer left the post, reported Partridge's actions to Swift, and two days later returned, accompanied by Swift's aide-de-camp. The latter placed Partridge under arrest, and his court-martial followed, presided over by General Winfield Scott. During this trial Scott met Crozet and was quite favorably impressed. On some counts Partridge was cleared, but he was found guilty of disobedience of orders and mutiny and ordered to be cashiered. The president remitted the sentence and allowed Partridge to resign.

Although he had been defeated, Partridge did not fade away but kept up a lengthy series of charges against the faculty, Swift, and others. Partridge was then thirty-three, and he said to Swift, "Should I live to be seventy, this subject shall never within that time be abandoned unless justice be done."[19] He died at sixty-eight, carrying his grudge to the grave. Swift reflected in later years that Monroe and Calhoun had ousted Partridge not because of his want of ability but "because his aspect was uncouth, a want of what is called genteel carriage, an awkwardness of manner that gave a repulsive first impression." Actually, wrote Swift, "many of the youthful officers in the Army in the War of 1812 owed much of their success in the field to the patient training which they received from 'Old Pewter.'"[20]

Although Crozet was not one of the principal instigators of the complaints against Partridge, he was identified with those who were, notably philosophy professor Jared Mansfield and mathematics professor Andrew Ellicott. A historian partial to Partridge asserts that Partridge "held Crozet in high esteem" and that Crozet was not "wholly contaminated" by his association with Mansfield and Ellicott. Partridge in fact had nominated Crozet to succeed him as professor of engineering when he relinquished the post in December 1816 to devote his full efforts to being superintendent. Crozet was appointed professor the following July.[21]

A year after Thayer had resumed firm command at West Point, Crozet wrote a long letter to General Swift, unburdening himself of some complaints. First, he wanted a salary increase that would place him "on the same footing as the professor of philosophy." A child, Adele Eugenie Crozet, was born 3 August 1817, which meant increased expenses. He argued in addition, "I felt a certain vexation of feeling, to see the professor of the art of engineering classed as third, in an institution where it seems to me, the acquirement of that branch of science should be the principal, as it is the ultimate study and the complement of the other sciences." Moreover, he had voluntarily added to his teaching program descriptive geometry, principles of artillery, grand tactics, and topography, "because there were no instructors for them." Besides the "disagreeable situation natural to West Point" (its remoteness from any city and its cold climate), he cited "many other causes of vexation, which emanate from the manner [in which] the professors are here treated." Crozet was certain that the federal government, in hiring them, "must have placed confidence in their age, their experience and in a sense of their duties; which are not much attended to here." At West Point, he complained, "I have not even found the common regards of politeness." Only his personal obligation to Swift, he told the general, bound him to "persevere." He chose not to elaborate upon the "vexations" but to propose "remedies." His first choice was "an employment, which would remove me from [this] spot." He was determined after two years at West Point to leave at the earliest opportunity, but it would not appear for another five years. Meanwhile, he coped with the situation as best he could.

Another remedy he urged upon Swift in this same letter, an administrative reform, was to name "a Director of Studies of the Academy, distinct from the Commanding Officer." An officer with expertise in military discipline who could also "perfectly understand a correct direction of the studies" was unlikely to be found, said Crozet. "His command which is purely military, if absolute, will frequently be clogging." Moreover, a separate director of studies would shield the professors from the "abuses of military power."[22] Not only the faculty but the cadets suffered from an excess of zeal in the use of military power. In 1818 Thayer appointed an army officer, Captain John Bliss, to be commandant of cadets. Bliss was a martinet so unnecessarily harsh in his disciplinary actions that Secretary of War John C. Calhoun eventually dismissed him. Afterward, Thayer continued to employ a commandant whose assistants lived in barracks with the cadets, reported infractions of discipline, and assigned demerits and penalties.[23]

In addition, Crozet was disappointed that Thayer was not generous in providing assistants in the classroom. When Thayer took charge in 1817, Crozet asked him for two, "one for Theory and the other Graphic," but Thayer refused the request. A year later Crozet complained that Thayer was asking for "7 assistants for the Professor of Mathematics, 3 for the professor of Ph[ilosophy]: 3 for the French, 1 for drawing: nothing for *Engineering*." Crozet's engineering class then consisted of about forty cadets, which he thought "would require fully as many assistants as that of Ph:."[24]

Crozet's envy of Jared Mansfield's preeminent position on the faculty seemed to be reciprocated by Mansfield's view of any and all French colleagues. So far as he was concerned, they were "anathema." Mansfield continued until his retirement in 1827 to receive a higher salary than any of his colleagues, French or otherwise. In a letter to his son-in-law in Paris, John O'Connor, who was engaged in translating Baron Simon Gay de Vernon's *Treatise on Fortifications*, Mansfield remarked that "Crozet and his wife & child are well. He is a man of Genius, but very singular & all the Frenchmen keep a kind of separate community here. They will not conform to our manners & modes of living; whence they are not liked by our people."[25]

In writing to Swift in October 1818, Crozet studiously avoided any personal criticism of Thayer. During the first six months of 1819, however, Thayer's actions built Crozet's resentment to the flash point. "I have avoided it as long as I could," he wrote, not to Swift this time but directly to Secretary of War Calhoun. "The Superintendent has assumed by degrees an almost unlimited power; without regard either to the character or to the rights of such a respectable body as the Academical staff, he has given such absolute orders and from step to step, he has at last treated them in a manner approaching to scorn. It could not be borne any longer."[26]

The most provocative incident occurred at an oral examination of cadets, with members of the Board of Visitors and professors sitting as a panel of interrogators and the superintendent presiding. Thayer did so "in a most arbitrary manner; ordering the questions, interrupting the professors, submitting them to rules the most absurd and insulting." Crozet elaborated: "To all observations [he] has always imposed silence in a peremptory manner; his usual answer being *the superintendent will have it so* . . . Without consulting any one, he has ordered us to assemble from *Eight* in the morning to *Seven* in the evening. . . . He was not satisfied with that: without asking our consent, against the established rules, he ordered us, all at once, to assemble from *four* in the morning to *seven* in the evening . . . it is moreover impossible for any man to keep for 15 hours his attention bent on such abstract subjects, and therefore the object of the examinations . . . is certainly not accomplished."[27]

A "large majority" of the professors, Crozet continued, asked him to "make some observations" to Thayer. He had hardly begun when Thayer "imperiously ordered" Crozet to be silent and remarked to all present that "*whenever he gave an order he did not choose to hear any discussion.*" Crozet then turned to address his colleagues, stating that "whatever concerned them and related to the studies of the Academy ought to be decided by a majority of the members." Thayer, angered by this defiance, abruptly interrupted Crozet, declared the meeting adjourned, and told Crozet to consider himself under arrest. Crozet "replied that he would not consider himself under arrest; he was not in military service, & had never subjected himself, in this country, to any military authority."[28]

That evening in his quarters Crozet received a letter from Thayer charging him with "neglect of duty, disobedience of orders, &c&c." "None of us ever supposed that our duty admitted of any orders, except the decisions of the majority of the Acad. Staff," Crozet wrote Calhoun. "The *superintendent* calls himself my *commanding officer* although I see no reason actually existing to consider him as such. When I accepted my appointment, I certainly did not understand that I was made a military man by it." Crozet went on to assure Calhoun that he did not "come forward as an accuser" or seek any "public reparation." He simply wanted to "point out the causes of the continual dissatisfaction in the Acad[em]y, that they may be destroyed in their principles." The essential principle, as he took this opportunity to reiterate, was to separate the combination in the same person of military commander and director of studies. "In all military schools there is a military commander for interior discipline and a director of studies who assembles the professors and superintends the execution of their decisions. Here the same person holds both stations." Crozet concluded with the hope that the secretary of war would issue for the academy "some precise regulations, which it will be no more possible to transgress."[29]

Having received no reply from Calhoun after the lapse of two weeks, Crozet sent a second letter. "Your absence from Washington might be the cause of my letter not having reached you; and as I have heard of your return, I take the liberty of addressing you this 2d letter," he ventured. Over three more weeks followed during which Crozet had no reply from Calhoun, so he wrote a third letter. "For the object of my former communications, I refer to them, as I suppose they must be in the war office," he wrote, a bit testily. "It is not difficult for me to prove that nobody except Colonel Mansfield and Cap'n Douglass has done so much for the Acad'y as myself: the late improvements of the Academy are moreover due to the individual exertions of the professors; and the present Superintendent, who seems to forget it, and to take now all the credit of it to himself, has no other claim above his predecessor than to have acted at first according to the ideas of his staff, so long disregarded before: but for reasons too long to be explained here, his conduct is entirely changed." What Crozet requested of Calhoun, he reiterated, was a ruling to clear the air. Thayer's action against Crozet was "only the consequence of my proposition made to the staff in order to prevent further difficulties that: *the staff being directors of the instruction, nothing should be done without having met with their concurrence and decision.* . . . we hope your Excellency will sanction it by an article of regulation."[30]

All the while, Calhoun was indeed keenly aware of Crozet's complaint, but he was reluctant to take any action against Thayer. As historian Edgar Denton asserts, "John C. Calhoun brought order and regularity to the War Department and gave Thayer almost *carte blanche* in regard to the operation of the Academy."[31] Hence, Calhoun said nothing to Crozet and passed the decision on the matter up to President Monroe. "The case of professor Crozet (whose papers I also transmit) is decided by that of the cadets," Calhoun wrote Monroe, "and Major Thayer might be ordered to submit his charges against him to the same court which has been constituted for the trial of the cadets, if you think it advisable to reassemble it."[32]

In the fall of 1818 an incident had occurred involving some cadets in which Crozet's confrontation with Thayer became thoroughly entangled. The whole matter focused upon the basic principle of authority at the academy, and the outcome was unfortunate for the cadets, for Crozet, and for the academy. During a parade in November, Cadet Edward L. Nicholson "constantly and deliberately marched out of step." Enraged, Commandant of Cadets Bliss physically laid hands on Nicholson and cursed him in public. In barracks that evening, 180 cadets signed a petition to Thayer complaining of this and other abuses by Bliss, and a committee of five cadets (which did not include Nicholson) went to see Thayer. He told them they had "no right to form a combination and present a petition."[33] The five cadets wrote another, longer petition and attempted to present it to Thayer the next day. This time Thayer ordered them to leave West Point. They went to the nearby town of Newburgh, where they wrote and published a pamphlet intended to publicize their case and lead to a congressional inquiry.

Thayer attempted to counteract this action by calling on the chief of army engineers for a court of inquiry, which was held and backed Thayer. Meanwhile, the cadets were placed under confinement at West Point pending their court-martial, physically separated from other cadets and not permitted to participate in classes or studies, in a manner as one of them put it, "to corroborate the imputation of mutiny, and make us farcically dangerous."[34] A court-martial met at West Point late in May 1819 to try the first of the five cadets and ended disclaiming jurisdiction on the grounds that the cadets were not under military law. President Monroe refused to accept this ruling, however. Attorney General William Wirt asserted that the corps of cadets were a part of the land forces of the United States and had been "constitutionally subjected by Congress to the rules and articles of war, and to trial by courts martial."[35]

The five cadets had been in confinement for six months at the time of Crozet's dispute with Thayer and subsequent arrest. He was suspended from his teaching duties, and Lieutenant Henry Brewerton was appointed to teach at least one of Crozet's classes. Calhoun suggested to Monroe late in August that the court-martial should be reconvened and should be asked to consider the attorney general's opinion. "It appears to me, with the light which it furnishes," said Calhoun, "the court will see cause to change their original opinion." He then added that Crozet's case would be "decided by that of the cadets" and that Thayer might prefer charges against Crozet in the same court-martial. Monroe agreed. The court was reconvened at West Point on 4 October and assigned the task of trying the five cadets and Crozet. Once again, the court disclaimed jurisdiction over cadets and, by implication, professors as well. And, once again, the president disapproved the court's decision and was "of opinion that the Professors, teachers, and Cadets are governed by the rules and articles of war." The president did, however, remove the cadets from suspension and restored them to regular status at the academy, "in consideration of the long suspension of the Cadets which from their age has operated as a severe penalty."[36] It actually had been a greater penalty than either the president or Calhoun seemed to assume, for not one of the five cadets rejoined the corps. "Having been twelve months under arrest, while my Class have been prosecuting their studies, and having in consequence of my arrest, lost the standing which I will hold in my Class," wrote one, "I am induced from these and other reasons equally cogent to tender you my resignation."[37] Crozet did not resign, much as he looked forward to the opportunity, but resumed his teaching duties.

Congress finally looked into the matter in January 1820, but its investigation turned out to be a mere whitewash. Speaker of the House Henry Clay presented "a Memorial from sundry citizens late Cadets alledging certain improper conduct in the officer commanding the Mil[itary] Academy." Calhoun declared to the chairman of the House Military Committee that the Board of Visitors strongly supported Thayer, as did he. "If Major Thayer be open to the imputation of error in the discharge of his official duties it is in adhering perhaps too rigidly to law and regulation in the administration of the affairs of the Academy," he concluded.[38] Nothing came of the House investigation, the charges against Thayer effectively having been swept under the carpet. Neither does it appear that any substantial changes took place at West Point following these events. The court-martial continued to be used in enforcing cadet discipline, even for such innocuous offenses as playing cards; however, during the late 1820s dismissed cadets were increasingly reinstated. In such a deteriorating system, discipline inevitably became a greater problem.[39]

In December 1819 Jared Mansfield pursued the question of reform at the academy in a letter to Calhoun. He did not think martial law appropriate to the routine enforcement of cadet discipline. No greater punishment could be meted out to a cadet than expulsion from the academy, he asserted, and the "judge of the propriety, or necessity of such expulsion" should be the heads of the academic departments. "If martial law cannot reasonably extend to Cadets, much less can it extend to Teachers, Instructors, & Professors endued with the rights of citizens. . . . Neither the military academies of England, or France, by the Authorities which I have been able to consult, are under martial law. . . . They are under the control, & direction of a *board*, residing on the spot. . . . At the Polytechnic School, the mil[itary] Commander, & the various Professors & Teachers constitute such a Board. . . . Some such system, must be adopted for this Academy."[40]

In 1821 Mansfield addressed another sixteen-page letter to Calhoun complaining of Thayer's inaction. The professors "are precisely in the situation of citizens ruled by an Autocrat," he said, "for all here are supposed to be under Martial Law, tho' none of the Professors or Teachers ever dreamt of such a condition, before they reached West-Point. It is like conducting a blind man to a precipice, when he had been promised a safe and pleasant walk." France, he reiterated, was "more celebrated for her Mil. Academies, & the Mil. Art generally than almost any other country" and administered none of them by martial law. "As mil. academies have been wholly unknown in this country before the attempt to establish one at this place, & as we appear to have originate[d] one *de novo*, it is not surprising that we should have deviated so far from all the others, in the most essential points of its government."[41] Although improvement in discipline at the U.S. Military Academy would eventually come, it was only after Crozet had departed the West Point scene.

Despite the travails that Crozet encountered at the academy, the fact remains that he was well prepared to transmit the superior French technology to the comparatively ill-prepared trainees for commissions in the United States Army. He had been exposed to the best training in military and civil engineering available in Europe in the first decade of the nineteenth century. Appointments to the Ecole Polytechnique were sought by many but went only to the most competent. Both Crozet's training and his experience by the time of Napoleon's final departure from France comprised solid preparation for his subsequent life as teacher and engineer.

The cadets at the academy when Crozet arrived in 1816 were the heirs of a short-lived tradition. The academy had been in existence a mere fourteen years and during that time had suffered from a lack of financial support by Congress, administrative confusion and uncertainty, and academic inadequacy. Crozet arrived at a time when important changes were getting under way. General Swift was promoting a new building construction program, Partridge was being displaced by Thayer, and a new and better academic curriculum was on the verge of being introduced. Crozet was an important part of this transition but, so far as he was concerned, an unappreciated part.

Although Partridge apparently favored him from the time Crozet arrived in September 1816, Crozet did not return the esteem. In his opinion, Partridge ignored the views of the faculty in academic matters, and Crozet welcomed the assumption of control by Thayer as a breath of fresh air, because Thayer acted "at first according to the advice and ideas of the staff, so long disregarded before." Unfortunately, Crozet noted, Thayer's conduct was soon "entirely changed," characterized by "the most absolute command and disrespect of the professors."[42] Had it not been for Thayer's attitude toward him and his work, Crozet probably could have accepted West Point as he found it. He often remarked that the cold climate and remoteness from cities were aspects of West Point that he disliked; yet his later employment in Virginia required spending much time in areas still more remote than West Point, and he complained little about that.[43]

The establishment of the University of Virginia at Charlottesville in 1819 attracted Crozet, and he wrote directly to Thomas Jefferson in 1821 to offer his services. Jefferson replied, saying that although the buildings would be finished "in the course of 2 or 3 years," the funds for hiring professors had not been provided, nor was it yet certain that the legislature would do so."[44] Crozet's opportunity to leave West Point came, at last, in 1823, and he seized it. The Virginia Board of Public Works, established in the same year that Crozet emigrated to the United States, was in need of a new principal engineer to superintend the planning and construction of roads and canals throughout the state.

During his seven years at West Point, Crozet undoubtedly had made a noteworthy and lasting contribution to the engineering curriculum of the academy. He took over the engineering department from Partridge and applied the best professional standards of the day. He pioneered in this country in the use of descriptive geometry, the basic language of engineering. He taught cadets how to construct, accurately and serviceably, bridges, fortifications, buildings, canals, and roads. His successor, David B. Douglass, built on Crozet's work, as did his successor in turn, the renowned Dennis Hart Mahan.[45] In spite of his dissatisfaction with West Point, Crozet is remembered there for having made needed and lasting improvements in the engineering curriculum.

Once Crozet had left for Virginia any ill feelings that may have existed between him and Thayer seemed to disappear, as evidenced in their subsequent correspondence. In 1821 Crozet had published the first volume of a projected two-volume text on descriptive geometry, used as a text at West Point. In 1823 Crozet began work on the second volume "at the request of the Superintendent," but his departure for Richmond in April forced him to shelve the project. Thayer wrote to Crozet in the winter of 1824–25 urging him to complete it so that the academy could adopt it as a textbook. Crozet believed that he would have time during the winter months to do so and that 400 copies at a selling price of $2 each would defray the cost of printing. "In publishing this work," Crozet declared, he "had no other object in view than to be useful to the Academy: My success in this respect will be ample reward for my labour."[46]

He never finished it. The demands upon his time and talents in his newly adopted state of Virginia were too many and too insistent to permit it.

3

Principal Engineer of Virginia
1823–31

Crozet was eager for a career change; moreover, he was probably a better qualified candidate than his new employers had reason to know. His character and personality by the early 1820s had been formed on the anvil of war, imprisonment, disillusion, emigration to a far country, and adaptation to a totally new environment, language, and culture. Highly intelligent and well educated, he proved remarkably adaptable. His English vocabulary was equal to that of the best educated Americans, although his manner of punctuating sentences was a bit odd. Uncompromisingly honest, Crozet placed stringent demands upon himself, as seen in his readiness to teach courses for which there was no instructor, and he expected the same of others. He was aware of the element of personal pride in relationships with people and on occasion seemed willing to acknowledge having the same stumbling block in himself. Therefore, he was not one to hold grudges, as seen in his later dealings with Thayer. Although the written evidence is fragmentary, what little there is depicts a faithful, loyal, and loving husband and father. When he went to Virginia to assume new duties as state engineer, Crozet was thirty-three years old, in the seventh year of his marriage to Agathe, and the father of five-year-old Adele and two-year-old Alfred Saint Armand Crozet. His new work would require him to be away from home much of the time between March and November of each year, which only made him appreciate the winter months the more.

What did Virginia need that this engineer trained in a foreign land could supply? The War of 1812 had demonstrated to the whole country the need for a more adequate system of transportation; and as the eastern seaboard states turned their faces westward in the post-war era, this need presented itself in a new dimension. Early in 1816 Governor Wilson Cary Nicholas called the attention of the Virginia

General Assembly to the active interest of New York and Pennsylvania in securing the western trade. The legislature responded by passing an act (5 February 1816) to create a fund for internal improvements and a Board of Public Works to administer it.[1] The Virginia Board of Public Works included the governor, who presided ex officio, the state treasurer, the attorney general, and ten citizens representing Tidewater, the Piedmont, the Valley, and the Trans-Allegheny. Its function was to recommend to the legislature the incorporation of specified private companies to build turnpikes, canals, or improved waterways and subscription by the state from the fund for internal improvements to two-fifths of the authorized capital stock. Private investors were to put up the other three-fifths, with the state starting its payments as soon as 20 percent of the private money had been paid. This became the basic financial pattern of Virginia's system of mixed enterprise. A major change occurred in 1835 when the state's share was increased to three-fifths.

The fund established in 1816 amounted to about $1.5 million, consisting mainly of shares previously owned by the state in the few internal improvement companies already started by private entrepreneurs: the Dismal Swamp Canal, the James River Canal, the Appomattox Canal, the Potomac Company, and the Little River Turnpike Company. Not much could be done with the small earnings of about $115,000 per year on this capital fund; thus, private investment was indispensable.

The Board of Public Works was not created as a central planning agency with wide authority but rather to advise the legislature on the claims and merits of competing projects. It also provided, through the principal engineer, the necessary technological competence for such judgments, including his superintendence of works in progress, as well as regular inspection of completed works in operation.[2] Unfortunately, the Virginia legislature was willing to delegate to the principal engineer more responsibility than authority, a subject of bitter complaints from Crozet over many years.

The Virginia Board of Public Works was looking for its first principal engineer while Crozet was in his first year of teaching at West Point. Even President James Madison in April 1816 devoted time and attention to implementing the act passed in Richmond in February. "At the receipt of your letter," Madison wrote Governor Nicholas, "I made inquiry of Mr. [Benjamin H.] Latrobe concerning the young

French engineer to whom Commodore Decatur referred (M. Surville), and found that he had returned to France." Latrobe replied with a fourteen-page letter, for whose length he apologized. A good road could be built by a good land surveyor, said Latrobe, but the skills for canal building were scarce in America. "In the question as to the employment of an English or French Engineer, it is very certain that the French Engineers have generally,—I may say *always*,— a better education in the *science* of their profession than the English."[3]

Virginia's first principal engineer was neither an Englishman nor a Frenchman, but Loammi Baldwin of Massachusetts, called by his biographer "the father of civil engineering in America."[4] Induced by the willingness of the Virginia legislature to meet his demand for a $4,000 annual salary, Baldwin arrived in Virginia in January 1817. He spent most of the next two years on river surveys across the entire state before returning to his native New England to assume the post of engineer of improvements for the city of Boston. His successor, Thomas Moore, a Virginian, took up the unfinished work late in 1818, conducting river surveys of the James, the Kanawha, and others until, while surveying the Potomac River in the fall of 1822, he suddenly became ill and died. When Bernard Peyton, secretary of the Board of Public Works, advertised the vacant position in the newspapers, Crozet was one of about twenty applicants, of whom several were as highly qualified as he.

One of these was Ferdinand Hassler, a Swiss mathematician and geodesist who emigrated to America in 1805 and taught mathematics at West Point and at Union College. In 1811 he was sent by the secretary of the treasury to London to obtain instruments needed for surveying the coast, and upon his return in 1816 he was appointed superintendent of the Coast Survey, only to be removed by an 1818 law excluding civilians from the post. When he applied for the position that went to Thomas Moore, Hassler named as references not only General Swift, who supported him strongly, but Jefferson and Madison, men he thought "may remember me from my transactions relative to the survey of the coast." They did not. He also named Secretary of War William H. Crawford as a reference, a poor choice because Crawford wrote to Governor James P. Preston of Virginia that Congress had changed the coast survey law in favor of military personnel only because of dissatisfaction with the slow progress Hassler had been making in the work. As for his knowledge of roads and canals, Crawford declared, any "evidence of it exists on the other side of the Atlantic."⁵

Soon after Moore's untimely death, Crozet wrote a letter of application to Peyton. On the same day General Winfield Scott wrote Peyton, "I have caused Mr. Crozet to be informed of the vacancy. . . . In point of genius, theory & practice, I have no question but that he is the first man in America for the vacancy in question." In his letter to General Swift asking for support, Crozet remarked, "The essential and characteristick quality of an Engineer is a penetrating and inventive Genius, a mind which in Cases of difficulty can leave the beaten path to form new conceptions; those who possess such faculties alone are Engineers, and a trial of their abilities is the only way to discover them. . . . I think myself equal to the task." Aware that the position would take him to all corners of the Commonwealth, Crozet added, "As to the *Activity*, that kind of service requires, it is one of the principal reasons which makes me apply for the office." Swift remarked to Winfield Scott, "Capt. Crozet was introduced to me in 1816 by the Baron Quinet (one of the French Provis. Govt.). I have found him to sustain constantly the talents & character for which he was recommended."⁶ Crozet probably would have considered that faint praise.

At this juncture another strong contender for the position entered the lists, Major Stephen H. Long of the army engineers. Already famous as an explorer of the Colorado mountains, Long had the support of War Secretary John Calhoun. Even Jefferson was persuaded by "a friend in Philadelphia" to take up his pen and write a word for Major Long. Jefferson was aware of Long's recently published two-volume account of his travels but had not yet seen it. "My first wish is that that may be done which is best for our country," wrote Jefferson; "my second is that that which is best may happen to be that also which is the wish of my friend."⁷

By the last week of January the Board of Public Works had made up its collective mind. The choice was not Crozet, nor Long, nor Hassler, but Colonel William McRee, the officer who had accompanied Thayer to Europe in 1816. Scott wrote to Peyton, "If I had not expressly heard that he would not accept . . . I should certainly have recommended him in preference to any man in America." Should McRee refuse the offer, Scott added, "I still hope that Crozet may get the vacant place."⁸ McRee, then in Wheeling, took three weeks to consider the offer before declining. With McRee out of the running, the board had to decide between Crozet and Long, which took all of March. Late in that month banker Langdon Cheves wrote in support of Long, "Should he not receive this appointment, he will under the orders of the Government, proceed immediately on another expedition similar to that which he formerly commanded." The Board of Public Works was publicly committed to announce its decision on April 7 and may have been persuaded by a last-minute letter from Scott once again recommending Crozet.[9] In the end, Crozet was selected, and Long went to explore northern Minnesota and the Great Lakes. Crozet finished the spring semester at West Point and then journeyed to Richmond early in July 1823 to commence his new duties as principal engineer.

Antebellum Virginia, extending from the Atlantic to the Ohio River, was the largest state east of the Mississippi River. The James River was the central waterway, but Virginia's vast area was laced with many more or less navigable rivers, though many required herculean effort to make them so. Virginians were long accustomed to using these waterways as highways. Thomas Moore's instructions had directed him to survey various rivers and designated tributaries from the Nansemond and Blackwater rivers in southeastern Virginia to the Cheat and Tygart's Valley rivers in remote northwestern Virginia.[10] Late in the summer of 1822 Moore had joined a party of commissioners surveying the Potomac River, where, as Governor James Pleasants reported to the General Assembly, he died "a victim to his public duties." Crozet began where Moore had left off.

Starting late in the season, Crozet surveyed the Slate River, a tributary of the James midway between Lynchburg and Richmond, then went to the Potomac, where he surveyed the South Branch and two of its tributaries. The remainder of the season was spent surveying for the location of a road between Staunton and Parkersburg and another between Romney and Winchester.[11]

In northern Virginia the Chesapeake and Ohio Canal, begun before Crozet arrived in Virginia, was of more interest to residents of Alexandria, Georgetown, Washington, and the state of Maryland than to legislators in Richmond, and in the end Virginia appropriated only a fraction of the total actually spent on it.[12] But this artery was very important to residents of northern and western Virginia, and the legislature could not afford to ignore them. Above Cumberland, the Potomac split into the North Branch and South Branch, the latter the more promising at least for a sluice system. Crozet was not enthusiastic about this possibility, however, and wrote, "Of all systems of improvements, that which offers the least chance of success, is a sluice navigation." An alternative was a system of locks and dams, which was more expensive, but not nearly so expensive as a canal built alongside the river and across bends.[13] The Chesapeake and Ohio Canal would eventually reach Cumberland, but no farther, as the Baltimore and Ohio Railroad superseded it.

Between the line of the Chesapeake and Ohio Canal and that of the James and Kanawha rivers lay a band of territory approximately 150 miles wide stretching from the Shenandoah Valley northwestward to the Ohio River. West of the Allegheny range the land was rugged, a sea of mountains and valleys with little level land until one approached the Ohio Valley. In the vicinity of Cheat Mountain near the center of this region, rivers originated flowing in every direction of the compass. The Virginia legislature resolved in January 1823 to survey the route for a road straight through this difficult terrain from Staunton to the "mouth of the Little Kanawha River" at Parkersburg.

The assignment drew heavily on Crozet's experience and mathematical skills. The topography of the country forced him to navigate as though on the ocean. "The survey was made partly by triangulation, from mountain to mountain, with a large theodolite, partly with the chain and compass, when the nature of the country forced me to resort to this inaccurate method," he reported.[14] For one thing, magnetic variation ranged from "1 deg. 37 min. east" in the area just west of Staunton to "3 deg. 35 min. at Parkersburg." For another, the earth's curvature had to be taken into account in locating such a long road, altering compass headings to remain on the direct line, a great circle route. Unlike the sea, however, the line could not stay even approximately level. As the crow flew, the line between Staunton and Parkersburg was 156 miles long; as the road wound, it was 215 miles, a 38 percent increase. One advantage to the route, Crozet noted, was that it would "head all the principal streams"; that is, it would cross them near their headwaters, where they were still small, thus avoiding the necessity for large bridges. Crozet urged construction of the road at an initial width of 12 feet, for, he explained, "with this width, eight or nine miles of it would not cost more than one mile of a road 30 feet wide." It could always be widened when the traffic increased; the important thing was to locate it well in the first place. This road would eventually become the Staunton and Parkersburg Turnpike, built by state funds, but it would take years for the legislature to realize that private funds could never provide the necessary amount of capital.

About 75 miles southwest of the Staunton and Parkersburg line lay the Kanawha River, formed by the confluence of the New and the Gauley at Gauley Bridge about 50 miles upstream from Charleston. Of these rivers, only the Kanawha was navigable in its natural state. Before Crozet came to Virginia, the James River Company built the Kanawha Turnpike, a road from Covington to the head of navigation below the Kanawha Falls near Gauley Bridge. Crozet would not have the opportunity to examine this road until 1825. Meanwhile, it was in the hands of the commissioner of the Kanawha Road and Navigation, Colonel William N. Anderson, who decided on the north side of the river for the planned extension of the road west of the falls because it had "more of the winter sun." Anderson also contracted with James Moore of Pennsylvania to build bridges over Greenbrier and Gauley rivers.[15]

Although the Kanawha Turnpike provided a usable substitute during the antebellum years, many Virginians entertained a vision of an all-water route connecting the navigable waters of the Kanawha with those of the James. This dream persisted for an incredible number of years; the U.S. Army Corps of Engineers made still another survey for it as late as the 1870s. The all-water route from Richmond as far as Covington was of great interest to the Board of Public Works and to the legislature when Crozet arrived in Virginia, and his report on the James River Canal, a vital segment of the route, was the centerpiece of his work for 1824.

The principal originator of the idea of an all-water route to the west was George Washington, who traversed much of the Trans-Allegheny on horseback and on foot before the American Revolution. After journeying to the Ohio Valley region in 1784, he recommended to Governor Benjamin Harrison of Virginia that the state should promote the extension of both the Potomac and the James as channels to the west. In response the Virginia assembly enacted bills incorporating the Potomac Company and the James River Company. Out of the first grew the Chesapeake and Ohio Canal, and out of the second came the James River and Kanawha Company. Neither of these projects ever became an all-water route, but both became the lines of railroads in later years.[16]

The original James River Company, chartered in 1785, was a private enterprise. Washington was elected president by the stockholders, but his primary interest was in the Potomac Company, of which he became the active president, so Edmund Randolph became the acting president of the James River Company. The charter required that the navigation be opened to tidewater, which necessitated digging a canal around the falls just above Richmond to Westham, about 7 miles, later extended to Maiden's Adventure Falls, 30 miles above Richmond. The rest of the work was simply a river improvement project, keeping the bed clear of obstacles and opening and enlarging sluices where necessary. The company began charging half tolls in 1794 and full tolls in 1806. Profits to the stockholders flowed in, along with complaints from users that the river was often impossible to navigate. The stockholders, earning as much as 16 percent on their investment, were content to let matters drift. Petitions eventually prompted the legislature to act, and on 17 February 1820 the state purchased the charter of the company.[17] The James River Company, without changing its name, changed its status from a private company to a state enterprise. What would be accomplished now depended upon the legislature, a weak reed as events proved.

At its February meeting in 1824, the Board of Public Works laid out Crozet's tasks for the year, including scattered river and road surveys, mainly in the Trans-Allegheny section: roads from Kanawha Falls to Point Pleasant, Clarksburg to Point Pleasant, Staunton to Callahan's (west of Covington), and the navigation of Cheat River.[18] In what soon became a disturbing pattern, however, the legislature passed an act authorizing the Board of Public Works to borrow $400,000 at 6 percent for the purpose of building a canal on the James River "between the Irish falls and the mouth of the North river," and on 20 March it revised Crozet's instructions, giving this work priority status. In this instance the reasons for the assembly's change of the board's directions were valid, but all too often the changes appeared to be the result of legislative manipulation more in the interest of some locality or individual than of the public. The canal was to be located where the James flows through the Blue Ridge creating the James River gorge. The status of the river between Maiden's Adventure and Lynchburg and beyond that to the Blue Ridge could be overlooked for a time, because any all-water route to the west first demanded a canal through the gorge.

Crozet was on the scene within days after the order, and by late April he and William Anderson, commissioner of the Kanawha Road and Navigation, had staked out the canal through the Blue Ridge.

Crozet then departed for other surveys, leaving Anderson to negotiate contracts for constructing locks and a dam at the upstream end of the canal. Much to Crozet's chagrin, Anderson altered several of Crozet's specifications for the work. First, he moved the dam site from three-fourths of a mile below the confluence of the North River with the James to a point immediately below it; second, he switched from single to double locks; and third, he reduced the canal depth from 4 feet to 3. When Crozet learned of these changes he was indignant, and the Board of Public Works, unable to quiet his protests, passed the decision to the office of the attorney general, one of its members. Crozet's plan for single locks prevailed, and a compromise depth of 3½ feet was determined, but the dam stayed where Anderson had relocated it.[19] The attorney general noted that the law said the canal was to extend all the way to the mouth of the North Branch and declared that a 3/4-mile stretch of slack water at the western end would not answer this specification. Crozet did not easily reconcile himself to this ruling and resented Anderson for some time afterward.

Returning to the James River survey, Crozet was required in November to consult with Benjamin Wright, of Erie Canal fame, who was called in by the legislature as a special consultant. He immediately took issue with Wright on the matter of feeders into the canal, which Crozet thought could be spaced at much greater intervals than 16 miles. He explained that the famous Languedoc Canal of France was fed for over 40 miles from a single reservoir, and that closer spacing was unnecessarily expensive. He also found Wright's plans for masonry too elaborate. "Though prudence recommends to rather over-rate the pressure than fall short of it, yet economy fixes a limit to the dictates of prudence," he protested.[20]

Two of Crozet's surveyors in the summer of 1824 were Wilson Fairfax, who may have been one of the five West Point cadets who were court-martialed with Crozet, and John Hartwell Cocke, Jr.[21] The latter wrote to his father, General John Hartwell Cocke of Bremo, overlooking the James in Fluvanna County, some of his impressions of Crozet. Fairfax had been having some trouble with his surveyor's level, and when Crozet arrived, the three of them went out to test it. Crozet insisted that "it was good and only our want of management that produced error. . . . Fairfax was very much mortified, and Crozet not a little pleased, I believe to shift thus much of the blame from himself to Fairfax." Incidentally, added the younger

Cocke, Crozet "is quite incensed against the commissioner for changing his plans." Two months later, Cocke reported that "Crozet seems to be quite dissatisfied with the manner in which matters have been settled between himself and Col Anderson in regard to the canal through the blue ridge.... As far as I can judge, Crozet's plan is much the best, and it seems that Col Anderson has involved himself by his contracts in such a manner as not to be able to change now, however much he might wish.... Crozet shows too much feeling on the occasion to convince men's judgments. He will do the cause of public improvements no good by his foolish peevishness."[22]

During the year 1825 the Board of Public Works again planned more jobs for Crozet than he could possibly accomplish. Crozet left Richmond for the field about mid-April to survey the Appomattox and Willis's rivers for connection by a canal and several similar surveys in Southside Virginia. Late in June he began to crisscross the state in compliance with the board's instructions. First, he headed west to survey roads from Romney to Clarksburg, from Clarksburg to the Ohio, and from Morgantown to Smithfield, Pennsylvania. While in the area he examined Tygart's Valley River and the Monongahela. In late August he returned briefly to Staunton to locate the road between there and Callahan's, and then leaving this to Fairfax, who as assistant engineer had earned Crozet's ungrudging praise for his work, he went on to examine the Blue Ridge Canal. Next, accompanied by Anderson, Crozet went to the Kanawha, examining the 94-mile turnpike from Covington to Gauley Bridge and also the navigation of the Kanawha River for the first time. In his report on this work he pointedly did not mention Anderson's presence. Crozet had words of praise, with which he was never lavish, for the builders of this road traversing "a very broken and rugged country" west of Lewisburg. The bridge across Greenbrier, just east of Lewisburg, he called "one of the most splendid wooden bridges ever built," with two spans of 211 feet each and a stone pier in midstream. Its builder, James Moore, had also constructed Gauley bridge, which "in the midst of a remarkably wild scenery, looks exceedingly beautiful," with three spans of 160 feet each. Before the road reached the Gauley River, it descended from Hawk's Nest along the New River cliffs, "where it certainly required the most indefatigable zeal and activity to find out the path for a road." With winter approaching, Crozet returned to Richmond in late October, ready for work on reports and maps. However, a severe attack of pleurisy delayed his reports until mid-March 1826.[23]

A significant portion of the report on his work in 1825 dealt with the link between the navigable headwaters of the James River system and those of the Kanawha River system. The principal tributary of the James above Covington is Jackson's River, which Crozet surveyed for 24 miles from its confluence with the Cowpasture River to a point north of Covington. From there a 15- or 20-mile-long canal westward across the Allegheny Mountain could reach the upper Greenbrier River, a tributary of New River and the Kanawha. Crozet found the 24 miles of Jackson's River formidable, requiring for navigation forty dams and locks at a cost of at least $600,000, even without the canal across the mountain. Years would pass, and neither of these works would ever be attempted. Indeed, the difficulty and expense of this segment of the contemplated all-water route caused many of its erstwhile supporters to welcome the railroad as a viable alternative in the early 1830s.

Such topographic problems did not confront the canal below Lynchburg, but there were others. On one of his return trips to Richmond in 1825, Crozet found that a leak in the Dover aqueduct, part of the James River Canal, was being repaired by lining it with clay. Hydraulic lime, for making concrete that would harden under water, was an expensive import from New York State at the time. "It is a matter of regret, that hydraulick lime has not been yet discovered in the vast limestone district, above the Blue Ridge," he remarked. "Locks and aqueducts are too important, and also too difficult to repair without considerable injury to the trade, to admit of parsimonious views in their erection."

In the Richmond area, Crozet surveyed for a canal from the coal pits near Midlothian to the Richmond area south of the James, then called Manchester—about 8.5 miles. This project involved constructing an unloading basin at Manchester as well as a canal with eleven locks, at an estimated cost of over $300,000.[24] A survey for a canal connecting the James and the Appomattox rivers involved deep cuttings and a tunnel at a cost of over $250,000. The coal and tobacco interests were powerful lobbyists, and Crozet soon learned that the legislature was very generous to internal improvement projects close to Richmond. However, legislators also knew that they would be wise to keep sweeping crumbs off the table for their western constituents;

western surveys took much of Crozet's time, if not so much of the state's money.

Crozet's most important work in 1825 was his survey for the James River Canal. He reported on everything else in March 1826 but did not submit the James River report, a separate document of nearly 150 pages, until July. The opening section dealt with various technological aspects of canal building as they applied to the James. He warned that a lateral canal, constructed independently along the margin of the river, would encounter "numerous bluffs which extend quite to the river, and leave no other alternative than to encroach upon its bed by raising the canal on an artificial bank, protected outside by stone work." Keeping the canal supplied with water was properly done by feeders. Streams should never be allowed to flow directly into the canal but should be carried under it by culverts, with feeder water being brought down from a higher point by a lateral cut. The canal was directed by law to be 30 feet wide and no less than 3 feet deep; Crozet recommended 3½ feet, deep enough for boats but shallow enough for stone-paved fording places, saving the expense of much bridge building. The locks were to be the same as at the Blue Ridge: 10½ feet wide and 76 feet long. Between the canal and the river would be an earthen embankment, for which he recommended paved slopes rather than stone walls at places subject to abrasion on the river side. Problems for farmers were created where the canal intersected fences, so he suggested "floating gates or fences, composed of two buoyant frames supporting a paling," which "might also be made to answer the purpose of a foot-bridge across the canal."

The total expense of building an independent canal between Maiden's and Covington, 212 miles, he estimated at $4.7 million, not including the Blue Ridge Canal already built for $400,000. Add the cost of the section between Maiden's and Richmond, 30 miles, at about $600,000, and the total was $5.75 million. Should it be done? This was a hard question, and Crozet counseled caution.

Crozet was not ready to scrap plans for the all-water route to the Ohio River. He pointed out that the federal government had sent surveying parties totaling twenty-two engineers over a two-year period to explore the ground between Cumberland and the Ohio River for the Chesapeake and Ohio Canal. They had concluded that 3,837 feet of lockage would be required, plus over 7,000 feet of tunneling, including a proposed 227-foot tunnel under the highest ridge. The state of Virginia had sent but two engineers and four assistants for only one season, and they had located a 94-mile road, surveyed the James, the New, the Greenbrier, and the Kanawha, plus several tributaries, and concluded that 3,913 feet of lockage would be required, plus over 17,000 feet of tunneling. Imagine that both canals were in operation, he suggested. Would the goods being transported up the Ohio from Kentucky, Tennessee, and southern Ohio pass by the Kanawha River and go on to Pittsburgh to enter the Chesapeake and Ohio Canal? He thought not. He ended by recommending more thorough examination of the summits between the James and Kanawha rivers.

His report for 1825 was not complete without two important addenda. The first was a nine-page, two-column comparison of the advantages and disadvantages of canals as opposed to lock-and-dam river improvement. He concluded that the use of steamboats on the river would "remove the principal objections to lock and dam navigation." Cost was also a factor. The canal between Maiden's and Lynchburg he estimated at $2.1 million; the lock and dam improvement at $800,000.

The second addendum was on the subject of railroads. It was late in June 1826 when Crozet was putting the finishing touches on this report, and he was aware of the great debate on canals versus railroads that had been raging in Pennsylvania since the spring of 1825.[25] Among his six pages of comments were these:

> The resistance opposed by friction varies according to the nature of the substances placed in contact; it is proportional to the weight moved, *and remains the same whatever may be the velocity given*; in this last peculiarity consists the advantage of rail-ways.
> On a canal . . . the resistance increases as the square of the velocity of the boat. . . .
> But recently a new propelling power has been introduced . . . the locomotive engine. . . . Prudence alone fixes a limit to the velocity. . . . some of the sanguine advocates of rail-ways extend this limit to 9 miles an hour. . . .
> At slow rates, however, the same power will transport more on a canal than on a rail-way. . . . the superiority of rail-ways increases rapidly with the speed. . . .
> A rail-road has been spoken of as a substitute for the navigation of James river. . . . but it would actually cost more than a canal. . . . it must be graduated with mathematical precision . . . it must not form abrupt curves; hence numerous deep cuts and expensive embankments. . . .
> It must be carried over *every creek* by *stone* or *iron* bridges. . . .

there can be no doubt that, upon every consideration of expense, a railway along James river is not advisable.[26]

It was difficult for Crozet, as it was for most of his contemporaries, to regard water transport as having been outmoded by the railroad, for, in fact, at that date it was not, and it would never be completely. The Virginia legislature did not make a decision in 1826 in favor of a canal along the James, a lock-and-dam improvement, or a railroad. A kind of legislative paralysis set in which was not relieved until the crisis year of 1831 when the pressure of public opinion at last forced a decision.

During Crozet's first year as state engineer, he made a preliminary survey of a road from Staunton to Parkersburg. In March 1824 the legislature agreed to match any county funds raised for the road, which produced some local money, and Crozet was directed in 1826 to locate it from Staunton to Riffle's Run in Randolph County, just south of Beverly on Tygart's River. In performing this survey, Crozet noted a phenomenon "unconnected with the object of this report" which he could not fail to mention. Cheat River flows northeastward, literally along a mountaintop. About 6 miles to the west of it and parallel runs Tygart's Valley River, 1,647 feet below the level of Cheat River. The Cheat is also 787 feet higher than Greenbrier River, flowing southwestward from the south slope of Greenbrier Mountain, only 5 miles distant. At a distance of 16 miles lie both the South Branch of the Potomac and a tributary of the James River. "A feeder taken out of Cheat River through Greenbrier mountain, would retain its supply on this damp mountain, and might very likely be made to reach with great facility the point of the Alleghany, where the waters of Greenbrier, the Potomac, and James river part. . . . From this point the water might be distributed in any proposed direction."[27] Although no such project was ever built, the potential of this physiographic phenomenon undoubtedly played an important role in keeping alive for so many years the concept of an all-water route.

In 1826 another inspection of the Blue Ridge Canal was in order. Anderson had been replaced as commissioner by David Garland, who remained unnamed but not uncriticized in Crozet's report, for he too had made several changes that Crozet did not like. For one, Garland built a dam at Cushaw Falls, where boats crossed to the south bank and where Anderson had agreed with Crozet that none was necessary. Garland's reason for it was "that the current in the river is too strong for boats to cross in safety in high water." Crozet wrote, "The dam, for the purpose of safety, is useless at low water, since there was a natural and deep pond of perfectly still water at this crossing place, and I can scarcely suppose that the commissioner intended that a dam of three feet lift should stop the current in such a rise, say from 10 to 15 feet, as would render the crossing dangerous." Garland had also dispensed with several culverts, to be regretted, Crozet predicted, when "heavy rains descend in torrents from these mountains."[28]

Governor John Tyler, who was intensely interested in internal improvements, made a trip to the Kanawha Valley in the summer of 1826 with Crozet. In his subsequent message to the legislature early in December, Tyler reviewed Crozet's estimates and urged the legislators to decide between the canal and the lock-and-dam system on the James River. Furthermore, Tyler added, "the work should be performed under the direction and controul of the Principal Engineer," for good and compelling reasons. If "subordinate agents are to be permitted at pleasure to controul the views of the Engineer; if his opinions are to be respected by them, or disregarded at pleasure . . . his office . . . becomes almost useless. . . . I regard Virginia as having in the person of her Principal Engineer a gentleman of the most unquestionable talents; one, who unites to diligence in the discharge of the duties of his station, an ardent devotion to the public interests, and to an extensive theoretical knowledge, sound practical views."[29]

By this time Crozet had been principal engineer of Virginia for three and a half years. He had learned much about the geography, economics, and politics of the state, and he had clearly defined ideas about the possibilities for transportation development. It was the dawn of the railroad age, so early that the Baltimore and Ohio line had not yet been proposed. The next year would witness this event, which worked so rapidly to change nearly everyone's perspective, and notably Crozet's.

Meanwhile, during the years 1827–30 tensions were building in Virginia due to the lack of any vigorous action by the legislature to fund internal improvements. On all sides were heard increasingly loud complaints about Virginia's retrogressive economy and unfavorable comparisons with neighboring states, especially New York, Pennsylvania, and Maryland. Not surprisingly, as the critical year 1831 drew closer, tensions and frustrations built up in Crozet also.

Early in 1827 Crozet's schedule appeared to be a return to the treadmill. He was directed by the Board of Public Works to survey the James and Jackson rivers once again, this time "with a view to their improvement by dams and sluices." Dutifully, he took close soundings of the low-water channel all the way to Covington, noting every eligible site for a dam; the results filled six field books plus many maps. Once again he objected to sluice navigation, insisting that the river could be better improved "almost the whole way" by locks and dams. At only three places would canals be necessary: one at the Blue Ridge, already built; a second at the Seven Islands below Scottsville; the third at the gap of Richpatch Mountain, upstream from Buchanan.

One factor convincing Crozet that locks and dams were the answer was the discovery of hydraulic lime in Virginia. John Hartwell Cocke, Jr., had spent much of the summer of 1827 searching for deposits and had found them on farms along the North River, 7 miles above its confluence with the James. Crozet had satisfactory results in testing Cocke's samples and even better results with a stone found in Montgomery County.[30] Before planning the construction of all dams with hydraulic lime, however, Crozet advised an energetic search for a sufficient quantity. The issue was of great economic importance. The discovery of hydraulic lime in Virginia allowed Crozet to lower his estimate of the cost of a lock-and-dam system up the James to Lynchburg from $800,000 to $664,140, which included $120,000 for the Seven Islands Canal.

His revised estimate translated to $5,490 per mile, or $1,850 per foot of lift. He went on in his 1827 report to calculate the volume of traffic, the prospective revenue from tolls, and other investment factors. Extensive ironworks were now sending their pig iron and some wrought iron down the James, and the products of Valley farms were being carried on the Staunton and James River Turnpike to the James at Scottsville. Carrying goods on the river from Lynchburg to Richmond then cost $7.42 per ton. Crozet calculated that the cost could be reduced to $4 with locks and dams, assuming the vehicles were steamboats. D. I. Burr of Richmond assured Crozet he could build steam engines of 10 horsepower for "a price which would not raise the cost of the whole steam-boat to $3,000." Burr's boats would be 60 feet long and 12 feet wide and would be capable of towing two barges each loaded with 30 tons at 3 to 4 miles per hour.[31] Changes in technology, available resources, and markets all seemed to bolster the prospects for locks, dams, and steam-powered boats on the James River.

Although Crozet was forced again in 1827 to spend much time on small scattered projects, many of them a waste of time and money, one in particular evoked his enthusiasm: a survey for the connection of the Roanoke and the New rivers by a canal. The point selected for crossing the Blue Ridge was about 5 miles south of Christiansburg, a place where hydraulic lime deposits were found. He made a tabular comparison in his report of both the James River and Kanawha and the Chesapeake and Ohio canal routes with the Roanoke and New River route. The C&O would require deep cuts of ¾ of a mile and a tunnel of 3¼ miles; the Roanoke and New River would require deep cuts of ⅔ of a mile and no tunnel. The difficult section of New River was the 17-mile stretch between Bowyer's Ferry and Kanawha Falls, where the river dropped nearly 300 feet. Thomas Moore, and before him John Marshall and his party in 1812, had navigated this formidable cascade of white water, and they agreed that a lateral canal was out of the question. By 1827 a railroad could provide the answer for this portion of the line, unquestionably a preferable alternative to 3 miles of canal tunnels.[32]

Governor William B. Giles delivered his annual message to the legislature on 3 December 1827, reporting "several instructive conversations with Captain Crozet, our able, frank and indefatigable State Engineer." Giles had asked Crozet "to suggest the points of improvement most wanted, and the difficulties which have heretofore prevented their completion." Crozet listed as his priority items: first, a road from Covington to the James River at the Blue Ridge; second, extending the Kanawha Turnpike to the Ohio River at Guyandotte (later Huntington); third, the road from Winchester to Parkersburg. His list revealed a concern for the market isolation of the people in the Trans-Allegheny. "There is no difficulty in assigning the true cause of the incompletion of these roads," said Giles. "It is the inability of the inhabitants of that section of country, through which they will pass, to furnish three-fifths of the funds required by law. . . . It should be done by the State; and out of State funds."[33]

Giles also referred favorably to the "grand and splendid project" of connecting the Roanoke and New rivers and linking them with the James. Crozet, however, was by no means prepared to abandon the James River and Kanawha as Virginia's main line; the Roanoke-New line was to be an additional route west. As for the main line, Giles reminded the legislature that four parts of it had been constructed: (1) 30 miles of canal from Richmond to Maiden's Adventure; (2) 7 miles of canal in the Blue Ridge; (3) 100 miles of turnpike from Covington to just beyond Kanawha Falls; and (4) the improvement by sluices of the Kanawha River. "To render this long line of communication productive, the improvement of James river is indispensable," the governor urged, certainly from Richmond to the Blue Ridge Canal. From there to Covington, it would be advisable to build a road immediately pending eventual completion of the water route. So also should the Staunton-Parkersburg road and the road from Winchester to Parkersburg be built, both, he recommended, entirely at state expense.[34]

When the Board of Public Works laid out Crozet's itinerary for 1828, the legislature accorded first priority to eastern river surveys left over from the previous year: the Nottoway, the Rappahannock, and the Piankitank. To his relief, when Crozet finished those futile ventures he was directed to survey the Roanoke River, "with a view to connecting it with the New by canal or railroad, as the legislature shall decide." In his report on this survey, Crozet said that a railway connecting the Roanoke and the New did not "present any difficulty," but he was not convinced of its superiority over a canal on this route. "The great experiment in progress in Maryland," he said, meaning the Baltimore and Ohio Railroad, "will soon furnish the solution of this important problem."[35] For the portion connecting the Roanoke with the James, however, his choice of a railroad was unequivocal, because he estimated a canal at $1.2 million and a railroad at $400,000 for the 25-mile distance between Big Lick (later Roanoke) and Buchanan.

At the annual meeting of the Board of Public Works in January 1829, the members outlined the tasks for the overworked principal engineer. River improvement still figured prominently: the Meherrin, the Nottoway, Roanoke River into North Carolina at Weldon, Acquia Creek, Sleepy Creek, the Kanawha. Roads, too, were scheduled: Covington to Richmond, Harpers Ferry to Tennessee, Warrenton to Staunton, Charleston to Point Pleasant, Charleston to Guyandotte, Beverly to Clarksburg. All of this, the board admitted, was "more than can, in all probability, be executed within the year."[36]

Crozet spent much of the summer of 1829 in Charleston, locating the roads to Guyandotte, to Point Pleasant, and to Gauley Bridge, as well as examining the Kanawha Turnpike east of that point. During this sojourn Crozet wrote a letter which survived by happenstance and offers one of the rare glimpses into his personal life. Colonel William Couper, author of the 1936 biography of Crozet, quoted the letter which had been discovered "in the secret drawer of Crozet's personal desk." Written in July by Crozet to his eleven-year-old daughter Adele at home in Richmond, it is a warm, fatherly missive, encouraging her in her reading, writing, drawing, and gardening. "Do not forget to keep some seeds of the best vegetables," he advised. "It is not too late to sow a little crop of peas." He was also concerned about her health. "Your mamma says that your health is better, this is the most agreeable news I could receive—take care of it. Be very prudent, do not presume on your strength, an accident might throw you back a good deal yet."[37] Adele's health was indeed a matter for serious concern; the young girl died the next spring, in March 1830, a sad loss for Crozet, his wife Agathe, and their two younger children, Alfred Armand and Claudia Natalia.

Tiring of the legislature's interference with the tasks it specified for the principal engineer each year, the Board of Public Works in January 1830 presented its list in stated order of priority: (1) a free road from Staunton to Warm Spring Mountain; (2) locating the Lexington-Covington Turnpike; (3) the Kanawha Turnpike extension; (4) the Kanawha River navigation; (5) the Meherrin, Nottoway, and Blackwater rivers (note the downgrading); (6) a road from Danville to Wythe Courthouse. Then, speaking to the legislature over the head of the engineer, the board added: "RESOLVED, That if, after the adjournment of this Board, the General Assembly shall pass any laws or resolutions, requiring the services of the Principal Engineer, they be referred to the ex-officio members of this Board, and made subject to their order." Clearly the Board of Public Works had some questions about the extent of its authority, just as there were questions in Crozet's mind about his own. The legislature, true to form, prescribed additional duties after the adjournment of the board, but this time it tactfully added to each one, "so soon as his previous engagements will permit."[38]

The year 1830 saw an action of the federal government that resulted in greater pressure on state governments to take responsibility for financing their own internal improvements. The eastern seaboard states, north and south, generally approved. Governor John Floyd in his address to the Virginia legislature of 6 December 1830 complimented President Andrew Jackson on his Maysville veto, which earlier in the year took the federal government out of most subsidy programs for roads and canals for decades to come. Against such federal power "Virginia has uniformly protested, and wisely," said Floyd. "The States are competent to the improvement of their own domestic condition, and the obligation which rests upon them to do so is high and imperious." It had been ten years since the state had taken over the James River Company, so let the legislature get busy and complete the river improvement, urged Floyd. He pointed to the good condition of the fund for internal improvements and the state's credit, insisting that there was no financial impediment. The people were not wealthy and could not be expected to finance improvements from their own private resources. "The Board perceives no other alternative than a resort to a loan, to complete the improvement," Floyd continued. "Assuming that 1,500,000 dollars will be sufficient to defray all the cost of completing the James river improvement, it will require an expenditure annually of 300,000 dollars for five years . . . it is believed that a loan can be obtained at an interest ranging from four to five per centum. Taking the maximum rate, each installment would create an interest debt of 15,000 dollars, chargeable upon the income of the Fund for Internal Improvement."[39]

Floyd went on to stress the potential benefits of a railroad from New River in Montgomery County to the James in Botetourt, the need for roads from both Winchester and Staunton to Parkersburg, from Richmond to Fredericksburg, from Danville to Wythe Courthouse, and from Lexington to Covington, and the importance of a new long road from the Potomac via the Shenandoah Valley to the Tennessee line. He praised Crozet for his work in the Kanawha Valley, and praised the "enterprising citizens of Petersburg" for their railroad. As for the James River problem, he urged the legislature to place it "directly under the control of the Board of Public Works." Crozet joined Governor Floyd in a vigorous argument in favor of more authority for the board, saying that for "some years past" his work had been of an exploring character, but now a knowledge of Virginia topography had been obtained, and it was time for decisive measures. A middle course of mixed enterprise had been adopted, aimed at realizing the advantages of both private and public investment but unfortunately reaping the benefits of neither. The board, Crozet pointed out, had been required often by the legislature "to contribute to improvements, wherein it had no agency." In many instances the legislature directed "that improvements should be made according to the directions of your Engineer," which "has in no instance been completely adhered to: wide departures on the contrary have often taken place, which, generally, after the execution of the work, have proved to its detriment. Thus the intention of the law is defeated."[40]

Crozet would resign within the same year, and it is likely that his lack of authority was a greater motivation than the more apparent reason, the railroad issue. The Lexington and Covington Turnpike, built by a private company to connect the eastern terminus of the Kanawha Turnpike with the Shenandoah Valley, is one example of Crozet's complaint. In February 1829 the legislature authorized a Lexington company to build a turnpike from Lexington to Covington and required the principal engineer to locate it. Starting from Covington, the location along Jackson's River, then across country to the foot of North Mountain, was not difficult. Between there and Lexington, Crozet had to decide between two passes, Black's Gap or Collier's Gap. The latter route was shorter by half a mile, but Crozet preferred Black's Gap because of the necessity at Collier's Gap "on the east side, of making a sharp turn on the rocky face of the mountain, which there slopes 30 degrees, and on the verge of perpendicular rocks."[41] Crozet made his detailed survey and submitted it to the company, which then decided in favor of the Collier's Gap route. Crozet had no veto power and could only express regret upon hearing of the decision. The Collier's Gap route still exists as VA 770, built in 1831 with a high stone wall set without mortar supporting a hairpin turn near the top of the east slope. Cars must come to a full stop and gauge the turn before making it. Downhill wagons pulled by four-horse teams had to stop, unhitch, and have two men negotiate the turn, one on the tongue and one on the brake. This bottleneck sharply reduced the usefulness of the road as a connecting link to the Kanawha Turnpike. The Black's Gap route later became U.S. 60 in the twentieth century and is still in use.

In connection with the Lexington and Covington survey, Crozet also directed surveys across the Blue Ridge east of Lexington for a road from Covington to Richmond. There were four possible gaps: Irish, White's, Indian, and Robertson's. White's in the twentieth century became the location for U.S. 60, but Crozet in 1829 found none of them usable, the descent on the east slope from each one being too long and steep. "It would be better, in every respect," he concluded, "to intersect the Staunton and James River Turnpike at Waynesborough."[42] This is the route of Interstate 64 today, U.S. 60 being comparatively little used. Clearly, the accuracy of Crozet's evaluation of the lay of the land has been repeatedly confirmed by twentieth-century highway engineers.

In the winter of 1830–31 the internal improvement program in Virginia had nearly come to a halt. The Board of Public Works, with the governor as its president and Crozet as its engineer, was frustrated by a legislature that conferred upon it the responsibility for linking the state internally with a system of canals and roads, and lately a few pioneer railroads, but gave it no real authority to plan or build an integrated system. The legislature appropriated a great deal of money, but too much went to logrolled schemes scattered across the state. The companies that looked for private investors for three-fifths of their authorized capital usually looked in vain. The legislature did next to nothing with the James River Company while it was under state ownership. In retrospect, the reasons appear to have been essentially political in nature.

When Crozet arrived in Virginia in 1823 the political leadership of the planter society of Virginia east of the Blue Ridge was in control, from their stronghold in the Virginia legislature. They were suspicious of and hostile to any perceived threat to their privileged position, which included not only the federal government but the governor and administrative branch at home, whose power was severely limited by the state constitution of 1776 and only slightly less so by those of 1830 and 1850. The conservative leaders had no intention of allowing a free hand to the governor or his agency, the Board of Public Works, nor its agent, the principal engineer, in the important matter of internal improvements. Improved waterways and roads reaching westward involved not only the expenditure of tax revenues if not borrowed funds but also disseminated economic power and hence potential political power westward, out of their hands. Crozet quite naturally assumed the role of advocate of the economic interests of the sections of Virginia west of the Blue Ridge, where he spent much of his time at the behest of the Board of Public Works and the governor, and thereby became an adversary of the dominant faction in the legislature by their definition, not his.

The legislature could not avoid granting some concessions to the pressures of interstate rivalry for the western trade, but it could do so in such a manner as to postpone any concentrated effort toward a thrust westward; hence the protracted delays in the James River project, the clinging to eastern river improvements, and the logrolling of support for scattered and disconnected turnpike companies. By the ninth year of his work as principal engineer, Crozet realized that the relief of his frustration was nowhere in sight. When the crisis of 1831 over the James River Canal project built to a climax, his decision to leave Virginia was not the result of any sudden or whimsical turn of mind but of his totally clarified view of the political realities of the situation.

4

Year of Crisis in Virginia, 1831

Events in Virginia, or rather the absence of them from 1827 through 1830 because of legislative paralysis, led to a year in which public attention became so concerned with the Old Dominion's failure to compete with neighboring states for the western trade, or even to develop its own internal economy, that the legislature was finally forced to act.

Discontent with the apathetic attitude of the legislature toward internal improvements was voiced in the Valley as Crozet left West Point. Valentine Mason began printing a weekly newspaper, the Lexington *Intelligencer*, in May 1823 and in the second issue introduced a series of essays by "The True Virginian," probably a Washington College professor. The writer complained that Virginia, the oldest and once the most populous of the states, had slipped badly. In 1800, he said, Virginia had 300,000 more people than New York, but while Virginia had grown by 175,000 by 1820, New York had gained 788,000, and both Pennsylvania and Maryland had gained more persons per square mile than Virginia. Virginians were as prolific as any other people, but their children were growing up and leaving the state. "It will require skilful perseverance, and a more general reformation," he concluded, "to make the artificial deserts of Old Virginia 'blossom as the rose.'"[1] The series of thirteen essays urged the state government to lead in developing roads and canals and encouraged readers to be willing to pay taxes.

The "True Virginian" and his counterparts writing in other Virginia newspapers were voices in the wilderness, unheard or unheeded. In 1828 several of the leading men of Virginia, including Madison, Marshall, and Monroe, organized at Charlottesville an internal improvement convention with delegates from thirty-nine counties. They drafted a memorial asking the legislature to complete the canal along the James, to improve the Kanawha River from the falls to the Ohio, and to extend the Kanawha Turnpike to the Ohio.[2] The legislature gave some attention to the Kanawha improvements but remained unable to make a firm decision about the James.

The Virginia Constitutional Convention of 1829–30 also was composed of a distinguished group of Virginians. Dominated by the eastern slaveholding aristocracy, it accorded the western counties only a small increase in representation in the state legislature and a somewhat expanded franchise. The convention was "thoroughly undemocratic in its outlook and actions and gave a body-blow to the aspirations, both political and commercial, of the rich and growing counties of western Virginia."[3] From that time talk of splitting the western counties off into a separate state became common.[4] In all the remaining years before the Civil War, western Virginians could recognize very few acts of the legislature designed to cement their allegiance firmly to the powers that ruled in Richmond. The Trans-Allegheny received appropriations for turnpikes but not for a mile of railroad before the Civil War. A gesture toward a more generous policy would be made in the constitutional revision of 1850, but it was no more than a token. On the eve of the war, Governor Henry Wise urged vehemently but belatedly that a program of railroad building should be extended to the Ohio Valley in order to prevent the division of the state. The events of 1830–32 were a "cloud no bigger than a man's hand," whose ominous nature was apparent to some but not to enough of those leaders who could have done what was needed.

President Andrew Jackson's veto in 1830 of the Maysville Road bill played a role in the sequence of events in Virginia. Another proposed road was the "National Turnpike to New Orleans," to be built by the federal government from Washington through Virginia and beyond to its destination. It was to pass through the Shenandoah Valley. The Lexington *Intelligencer* praised Valley communities for their petitions urging the legislature to support it, but editor Mason had no great expectations. "The hackneyed cant of 'State Rights' will be sufficient to array every member of the Assembly against the measure," he wrote. "In this Valley, the great mass of us have never doubted the power of Congress, to 'provide for the general welfare,' in making roads, canals, or adopting any measure that did not infringe the positive rights of states."[5] Mason was right; the few voices in the Virginia legislature that supported the National Turnpike to New Orleans were silenced when the Maysville veto occurred. The Richmond *Enquirer* exulted, "He [Jackson] has arrested that little, local, grasping, debasing, log-rolling system of appropriations."[6] Jackson also vetoed the Washington-to-New Orleans turnpike bill.

Citizens of Petersburg had hoped for federal aid in building a railroad from there to Weldon, N.C. On 29 June, a few days after the Maysville veto, the local citizens convened at the courthouse and "authorized" the city government to subscribe for 2,000 shares of Petersburg Railroad Company stock. Within a week $300,000 was raised from stock sales. "Money, as if by enchantment, has become plenty," wrote a delighted editor, "and thousands are now spoken of with the familiarity of hundreds a few days ago."[7] This positive attitude was badly needed in the legislature; it would appear in other Virginia towns and counties, but it would prove too slow in percolating upward to Richmond.

At Lynchburg early in September 1830, a public meeting of its citizens was "numerously attended" and was characterized by "a spirit friendly to *immediate* and *decisive* action."[8] Local merchants needed to get their commodities—mainly tobacco—down the James to Richmond and Norfolk. At that time, they were sending their goods downstream in common bateaux, which could carry only five to seven hogsheads. They hoped instead to use steam-powered boats 90 feet long and 18 feet wide, capable of carrying 37 tons of goods plus sixty-four passengers. The Lynchburg merchants were convinced that the lock-and-dam plan advocated by Crozet would be the best possible answer to their needs. Worried about the potential competition from tobacco growers in the lower Roanoke River valley in North Carolina should Petersburg complete its railroad to Weldon, the Lynchburg committee did not adjourn until it had established a local committee "whose duty it shall be to correspond with such Committees as may be appointed in other towns and counties." Some were there who recalled how public opinion was activated in the Revolutionary days by committees of correspondence and believed that striking fires around the state could force changes in Richmond.

The town of Fincastle in Botetourt County was too small to do much organizing, but it was not too small to speak an eloquent word. "It is a fact of general notoriety, that our State is on the retrograde," wrote the local editor. "Those who have yet a spirit of enterprise . . . disgusted with the narrow prospect of success, shrink from the task, and fall back into some western retreat, where they soon become luminaries to the country of their adoption. . . . the dull and unenterprising are left here."[9]

The Lynchburg committee of correspondence made a point of holding personal consultations with Crozet. "The plan of locks and dams, from Maiden's Adventure to Lynchburg, as recommended by Mr. Crozet in his able and satisfactory reports to the Board of Public Works, in 1826 and 1828," it concluded, "is the only plan that promises a result." Crozet had estimated that the cost would amount to $664,140 and that tolls should produce $64,000 annually. The Lynchburg committee made its own estimates to verify this by studying warehouse books and talking with flour inspectors, millers, merchants, boatmen, and others. The members found that an average of 18,000 tons of goods a year was then being carried on the river between Lynchburg and Richmond, three-fourths of it down and one-fourth of it upstream. Current charges for tolls were $5 per ton via the bateaux, but a mere $3.50 per ton would return $63,000 on 18,000 tons. The $1.50 per ton saved would net Lynchburg an annual saving to the trade of $27,000. In Lynchburg wheat and flour were always worth 25 or 30 cents less than in Richmond, the difference to be "ascribed in part to the cost of transportation; but mainly to its uncertainty." Improve the James, the committee said, and a bushel of flour from Lynchburg could be delivered in Richmond at a cost of not over 9 or 10 cents. In addition to the financial reward, the Lynchburg committee believed that better transportation would "divert a portion of the labor of this section of the country from the cultivation of tobacco, to that of grain," a healthy change in its opinion. "Some inadequate idea may be formed of it by those who have had an opportunity of comparing the well-cultivated and highly-improved farms, the fat and thriving stocks, and the plentiful living of the grain-grower, with the worn-out plantations and starved cattle of the tobacco planter."[10]

The Lynchburg committee had high hopes, but it was also realistic. It closed the report by saying that so much money had been spent already for so little improvement that it would be difficult to "convince the public mind, that any given work, requiring the expenditure of a large amount of money, ought to be undertaken." It continued, "The only work ever undertaken by the State, that promised any benefit to her [Lynchburg], was the James River Canal, and that has been abandoned at a point, which instead of making it useful, makes it positively injurious to her. She pays in tolls, upon this Canal, an annual amount of little short of $30,000—while neither the cost of transportation, nor the delay, uncertainty, or danger of the navigation, has been at all diminished by it." Lynchburg had the vigorous support of Governor John Floyd, who identified himself with the growing chorus demanding action by the legislature and urged upon the General Assembly the improvement of the James River by locks and dams.

Other Virginia communities emulated the actions of Lynchburg. In October 1830 the citizens of Wythe Courthouse held a "numerous" meeting of citizens, urged the "uniting of the Eastern and Western waters of Virginia," and appointed a committee of correspondence to "impart such information as they possess" on routes for railways, canals, and roads. They noted with regret that even "*Ohio*, which forty years ago had scarce a single white inhabitant," had been advancing in wealth and population faster than Virginia. The editor of the Richmond *Enquirer* admitted there there were grounds for concern and even confusion. "We undertake a work; spend a great deal of money upon it—and then we come to find that the work is not half so good as one that might have cost a great deal less. . . . While we are digging the canal, the rail road system is opened, and would have superseded the Canal."[11]

Early in 1831 readers of the Richmond *Enquirer* were presented with Crozet's entire report to James Garland, chairman of the House of Delegates' subcommittee on roads and internal navigation.[12] Garland had asked for a carefully considered opinion of the James River and Kanawha route, and Crozet had put much effort into his answer. First, as regards the James River improvement, he could add but little to his extensive reports of 1826 and 1828, which advocated locks and dams in preference to a canal, "chiefly on account of its greater economy, and of its extending benefits alike to both sides of the river." The Garland committee specifically asked, "*Whether a rail-road should be a successful and valuable substitute for the navigation of the river, on its whole line, or in part?*" Crozet's answer revealed that he was not yet thoroughly convinced of the superiority of the railroad in every location and that water transportation still seemed to him to be the logical and economical choice. "In part, a rail-road might be expedient only in the upper section, in connexion with the crossing of the Alleghany, but not otherwise, nor elsewhere, because frequent translation [transshipment] of goods should be avoided," Crozet began. "A rail-way on the superior scale required along James river, would cost at least as much as a canal . . . [moreover] it can accommodate only one side of the river. . . . articles to be transported on the lower part of James river are miscellaneous, bulky, and scattered along the line. They do not require speed of transportation."

Crozet favored water transportation between Richmond and Lynchburg, but not west of Lynchburg. For the route from Lynchburg by way of Salem, Montgomery County, and the New River, he preferred a railroad connection to the Kanawha Valley. "From Salem to New River, it is 47⅝ miles: rise, 1,047 feet; fall, 309; in all, lockage 1,356. The cost of the canal would probably be about $2,000,000. That of the rail-way, double-track, $950,000. Difference in favor of the latter, $1,050,000. . . . As to speed, the canal could not be passed in less than four days. The transit on the rail-way would be effected at a moderate rate in eight hours. These considerations are so decisive in favor of the railroad, that it would be useless to mention its advantages as regards it easier ultimate connexion with the heads of Holston, &c."

The Garland committee to which Crozet addressed his report was hard pressed to find answers to difficult questions. "Why is it that Virginia, abounding as she does with natural advantages," asked Garland, "is not rivaling her sisters, in wealth, prosperity, and happiness? The answer is obvious: she has not been as enterprizing. . . . there are more local and discordant interests in Virginia, arising from natural obstacles to a community of interest, than in any other State in the Union." Summarizing, the committee saw two basic difficulties blocking internal improvements in Virginia: first, the failure of the James River Canal project and, second, the jealousies arising from widespread local interests.[13]

Of all the proposed improvements brought before the Garland committee, the most important in its view was the James River. For the stretch from Maiden's to Lynchburg, it was "inclined to the opinion, that the improvement by locks and dams, both as regards economy and durability," was preferable. The improvement of the James River from the Blue Ridge to Covington posed admittedly difficult problems; it had "not been able to come to any satisfactory conclusion" but was "satisfied that a rail-way from some point on the James river to the Kanawha, is preferable to any other," even though it reaffirmed its belief "that railroads never can successfully compete with or supplant good safe water navigation." The Garland committee recommended to the legislature that the state should borrow the sum of $1,236,500, somewhat less than the $1.5 million recommended by Governor Floyd, for (1) the lock-and-dam improvement from Maiden's to Lynchburg at $650,000, (2) an improvement "to be determined by the legislature" from the Blue Ridge Canal to Covington at $200,000, and (3) the remaining $386,500 for various roads, all the debt to be amortized "in four annual instalments."[14]

All these efforts were wasted, however, when two months later the legislature defeated the Garland committee's loan bill. "The proposed system is rejected," lamented the *Enquirer*, which then recited a well-known Jefferson story. "When the Grand Canal of New York was announced, Mr. Jefferson thus wrote to DeWitt Clinton: 'Tis a noble project, but you are a century too soon.' When, a few years after, a second letter of Mr. Clinton announced its completion, with a query: 'What do you think of it now?,' the old Philosopher's frank reply was:—'I now perceive that in regard to your resources and energies, I committed an error of one century in my calculations.'" The editor closed by asking, "How many years are we 'too late'?"

The same legislature that defeated the loan bill nevertheless passed the Petersburg Railroad bill, subscribing to two-fifths of the capital stock of $400,000. The editor of the *Enquirer* was fascinated with reports of new railroads and their achievements. "Astonishing operations" of the Manchester and Liverpool were reported from England, one trip hauling "between 80 and 90 tons of goods!" On the Baltimore and Ohio Railroad, then operating to Frederick, 60 miles west of Baltimore, "the regular load of a single horse ... has been 100 barrels of flour, which is easily drawn at the rate of upwards of six miles an hour." Massachusetts was building the Lowell Railroad; North Carolina, the Fayetteville Railroad. Virginia was not exactly asleep, the editor noted: the Chesterfield Railroad from the coal pits to the James River was being completed; the Petersburg Railroad was advancing rapidly; and Winchester was promoting one to intersect the Baltimore and Ohio at Harpers Ferry.[15]

The Winchester project actually caused Richmond concern as it threatened to draw Valley wheat off to Baltimore. The legislature now agreed that it was time to do something for Winchester, and at long last it passed a bill "to provide for the construction of a turnpike road from Winchester to some point on the Ohio River." This would be known as the Northwestern Turnpike, constructed entirely by state funds. In addition, a bill was passed by the legislature "Directing a Survey of the Shenandoah river and country adjacent thereto, and the South Branch of the Potomac ... with a view of ascertaining the relative advantages of the improvement of said river, by locks and dams, or by a canal, or of a rail-road through the valley, and make a report to the next General Assembly."

The enticing possibility of a railroad in the Shenandoah Valley led George W. Summers of Kanawha County to introduce a bill in the Senate to incorporate the Staunton and Potomac Railroad. Summers had a provision in his bill authorizing the company to extend the railroad to Charleston "or to some point on the Ohio river in the State of Virginia." The direction of the proposed line caused the Senate to explode in debate. Opponents of the bill argued that the scheme of extending the railroad from Staunton to the Kanawha was intended to carry the western trade to Baltimore, which would "injure the works which the State had already established for connecting the James River with the Kanawha." Supporters of the Summers bill argued that it was a violation of the rights of the Valley people to sacrifice their interest to the James River interest.[16]

Lines were being drawn in the crisis year of 1831. The Valley fought for its railroad, but the James River interest prevailed. In 1831 the legislature came very near to abolishing the Board of Public Works but merely reorganized it instead. The governor, lieutenant governor, treasurer, and second auditor constituted the new Board of Public Works, and the ten citizens representing the four sections of the state were dropped. The legislature also cut the salary of the principal engineer from $3,500 to $2,500 annually.[17] That was a clear message to Crozet: his supporters in the legislature were a minority, mostly members from the Trans-Allegheny, and their voice on the board was silenced. The eastern delegates were lining up with the James River interest to fight him.

Senator Charles Cocke of Albemarle County, a spokesman for the James River interest, expostulated on the floor of the Senate against allowing the Staunton and Potomac Railroad to extend its road to the Ohio River. In reviewing the history of the relationship between Virginia and the Baltimore and Ohio Railroad, Cocke recalled that in March 1827 three commissioners from Annapolis had asked permission to extend their road through Virginia to the Ohio River; the permission was granted with a proviso "restricting the company to the mouth of the Little Kanawha, as the lowest point at which they should touch the Ohio." As a member of the House of Delegates at the time, Cocke had voted "with great cheerfulness, for granting the privilege." Then the B&O Railroad applied in 1829 for permission "to sweep through the valley of the Shenandoah, and to continue their road thence to the Ohio." A bill to this effect passed the House of Delegates "without notice or comment"; in the Senate, however, the bill was rejected. Cocke concluded, "I have gone into this brief history, Mr. Speaker, to show to the Senate the zeal and pertinacity with which the Baltimore Rail Road Company has pursued their favorite object of coaxing or teazing you out of the superior social and commercial facilities which the geography of your State presents. . . . While they are so lynx-eyed as to all that concerns their interests, let us not be utterly regardless of our own—let us not, like Esau of old, 'sell our birth-right for a mess of pottage.'" Singling out Senator William McComas of the Trans-Allegheny's Logan County, Cocke upbraided him for daring to say that Virginia would "never make this great western improvement; and that, therefore, we ought to surrender the means of making it into the hands of others."[18]

The legislature ended by ordering a new survey of James River, but it complicated matters by authorizing the "Governor and Council to employ *another engineer* to assist the Civil Engineer of this State, to survey the River in the course of the year, and to report to the next Legislature the various plans for improvement and estimates of expence." This was another sharp message for Crozet; in addition to cutting his salary, the legislature would now invite a consulting engineer from outside to call his plans into question. The legislature adjourned during the first week of April 1831, and the *Enquirer* looked upon its work with wry approval. "Say what you will of the rejection of the *loan bill*," wrote the editor, the legislators had at least done "more than any of their predecessors for years past."[19]

The more things change, the more they remain the same, readers of this editorial may well have reflected. The generosity of the legislature had consisted mostly of granting the people permission to spend their own money on internal improvements. The most significant accomplishment was the Northwestern Turnpike, which would be built by the state from Winchester to Parkersburg; but the James River project received merely an order for a new survey. This was not much progress, and the *Enquirer* soon admitted it.

> When we see the citizens of Baltimore holding out the extension of their Rail-Road to Staunton, and to the Ohio. . . . When we see the Citizens of the Valley looking to this outlet, for their legitimate route to market—When we see even the good people of Botetourt and of Rockbridge, turning their eyes from the James to the Potomac. . . . When we see even some of the citizens of Lynchburg, "bone, as it were, of

our bone, and flesh of our flesh," turning their eyes wistfully to the same point, from an utter despair of the exertions of the citizens of the lower James River country, or of the Legislature of the State.... It really *begins* to be time for us to be up and a-doing.[20]

The *Enquirer* announced to readers in its next issue that "Internal Improvement" would henceforth be a "standing head" in the newspaper; the column featured the motto, "Now's the day, and now's the hour."

One of the acts passed by the legislature in April was one to incorporate the Lynchburg and New River Railroad Company, a mere charter without any appropriation to support it. In May a group of eighty merchants and citizens of Richmond called for a public meeting on the last day of the month to consider what to do about the Baltimore threat. Out of this movement developed Richmond's "Committee of Thirteen," headed by Chief Justice John Marshall, charged with determining wherein lay the city's best interest in the matter of internal improvements.[21] Both Marshall's committee and the commissioners for the city of Richmond named in the act incorporating the Lynchburg and New River Railroad agreed that such a railroad would be "one of the great links in the chain of public improvements for leading the trade of the south-western portion of the United States to the centre of Virginia." One of the commissioners was Nicholas Mills, principal owner of the Midlothian coal mines, whose son in time would marry Crozet's daughter Claudia.[22] Mills and others called for an immediate survey of the route, by Crozet if possible but by another engineer if necessary. Crozet did take charge of the New River Railroad survey, and he was provided a staff of assistants to pursue it while he went to examine other works such as the Northwestern Turnpike under the direction of Charles B. Shaw.

The Richmond *Enquirer* was strong for the New River Railroad and the Committee of Thirteen, but all concerned were acutely aware that the railroad would do Richmond little good without the vital link between Richmond and Lynchburg. John Marshall convened the committee at the second auditor's office on 6 June with every member present. After three hours of discussion it voted a resolution to raise in Richmond by subscription a sum of money "in aid of the appropriation made by the Legislature, for procuring the services of an Engineer."[23] In Charleston, the Kanawha *Banner* expressed delight to hear of these things happening in Richmond and admitted it had been inclined to charge both the *Enquirer* and the *Whig* with indifference toward internal improvements in Virginia. "Between them, they have it in their power to awaken the whole Commonwealth," said the *Banner* editor. "With all the natural advantages of this place, what have the people of Richmond ever done to improve their condition, or to invite to their market, the rich products of the upper country?—In what company have they ever subscribed one cent to construct a road or open a canal? . . . Have not the representatives of Henrico invariably opposed every measure, having for its object the improvement of the State, and to be carried into execution by the public fund?" The Charleston editor commended the "spirited movements by the citizens of Richmond and Lynchburg" in promoting the New River Railroad, and he expressed satisfaction that Crozet would "proceed to superintend in person" the route.[24]

At the state Capitol on the evening of Tuesday, 14 June, Mayor Joseph Tate chaired a meeting of Richmond area citizens to hear the report of the Committee of Thirteen from John Marshall. The Chief Justice began by pointing out that the James River "is and ought to be the first object of solicitude." It had become the "absolute property of the State," so it could not be improved by any agency but the legislature. Much money had already been spent on it, "for which the Treasury cannot be reimbursed in tolls, nor the people benefitted, unless the plan, or some other, be carried into execution." The governor had been trying to obtain the services of an engineer to assist Crozet in a new survey of the river, according to instructions from the legislature, but had been unsuccessful, presumably because the money provided was not enough. There was no time to wait for the next session to increase the amount, so Marshall urged the raising of private funds in Richmond to match the appropriation and double the amount available to the governor.[25] A number of Richmond businessmen responded to Marshall's appeal with contributions.

Governor Floyd at last succeeded in obtaining the services of a consulting engineer in July in the person of Judge Benjamin Wright, the same man who had examined the James River in company with Crozet in the fall of 1824. Twenty years older than Crozet, a self-educated engineer of much practical and successful experience, Wright could have been expected to arrive with his opinions already more than half formed. When he appeared in Richmond on 23 July, Crozet was in the field, so Wright studied "all the reports, plans, profiles and estimates, &c. which have been made from time to time in the valley of James river and New river, and the intermediate country." Crozet returned to Richmond on 3 August and conferred with Wright the next day. Their minds did not meet.

"If we were members of a board or committee, the opinions of the majority must of course decide the report," said Crozet, "but between only two persons, if full and free conference and enquiries fail to produce a concurrence of opinion, the separate and conscientious views of each, are of course all that can be expected."[26] Crozet told Wright that in his opinion all the surveys necessary had been performed, and Wright fully agreed. All that was needed was for the government of Virginia to decide what it wanted to do and get on with it. Wright reviewed the alternatives as he saw them: (1) dams and locks on the James; (2) a continuous canal alongside the James; (3) a railroad from Richmond to Lynchburg and westward.

As for the lock-and-dam system favored by Crozet, Wright said, "I cannot make such an improvement for double the money estimated" by Crozet; it would take well over $1 million, not $664,140. Crozet's support of this method was based largely upon its comparatively low cost of construction, so Wright's judgment was a body blow. As for a railroad, if it should be adopted, said Wright, "it ought to start from Richmond instead of Maiden's Adventure: this would destroy all the use of the present canal." Furthermore, he thought that a railroad would cost more to build than a canal, that locomotive engines required "great mechanical skill," and finally that "property cannot be as safe from storms and depredations as in a good canal boat under lock and key." The canal was Wright's choice, along the north shore of the James "with such connections with the river as can make it accommodate the south side." It should be 50 feet wide on the surface, 30 feet wide at the bottom, and 5 feet deep throughout. He thought it could be built from Maiden's to Lynchburg, "*under good management,*" for $18,000 to $20,000 per mile, "provided water cement can be obtained at or near the Blue Ridge." Such a canal would accommodate boats 75 feet long, 14 feet wide, drawing 4 feet of water, and carrying 70 to 75 tons.[27]

Wright definitely favored the canal from Richmond to Lynchburg, was uncertain about its extension from Lynchburg to Buchanan, but clearly advocated a railroad from Buchanan to the New River. He was uncertain whether a canal or a railroad should be built down the New River to the Kanawha, but he believed that a railroad should be built from the New River to Tennessee. Having made these partly definite and partly equivocal suggestions, Benjamin Wright departed Virginia for other jobs waiting for him in the North, having visited for barely three weeks and not having traveled west of Lynchburg. He said, "The public mind is now so unsettled in their opinions, on the comparative advantages and disadvantages between railroads and canals, and considering that it will take some little time to have the good people of Virginia satisfied, I have had doubts in my mind, whether it would be useful for me to return here again."[28] The editor of the *Enquirer* was uncertain as well about the value of Wright's judgment. "Though we are not yet prepared to coincide with his opinion, of which we have not heard all the developments," he wrote, "yet this we can confidently vouch, that we have scarcely seen a man of more unpretending manners, and of less mystification and reserve in matters of his own profession, than this distinguished Civil Engineer."[29] Apparently Wright exuded charm, if not good advice. Even Crozet was more than civil to his opponent, and he said to Wright before he left Virginia, "Our concurrence or difference of opinion will naturally result from a comparison of your report to mine. And whatever this may be, if it shall have the effect of putting to an end the irresolution and inactivity which threaten to be ruinous to the interior of a state to which I am devoted, I shall be satisfied."[30]

Having retired from the state Senate in 1829, Joseph Carrington Cabell of Nelson County was persuaded to reenter politics in the critical year 1831 in order to champion the cause of the canal from Richmond to Lynchburg and possibly beyond, thus succeeding Benjamin Wright as Crozet's chief antagonist. As president of the James River and Kanawha Company, successor to the James River Company, he was unrelenting in his determination to thwart Crozet's every move, even though his opposition to Crozet was never expressed publicly. Cabell began his campaign for a seat in the House of Delegates in August, and he wrote to his friend John Hartwell Cocke about his first major speech to the voters of Nelson County in defense of the "James River Interest." He said, "It was a dry & perplexed & difficult subject. . . . when I finished my speech I saw that I had succeeded in conveying my views to the people and that it is only necessary to explain the subject to the people & they will go with us."[31] Cocke encouraged Cabell in his effort but warned, "You have many & formidable obstacles to overcome. . . . the greatest difficulty of all will be to obtain so general a cooperation among the various detached interests you will meet with in the House of Delegates—as to get a majority to vote the funds. I have always thought the cause of our failure of late years—was to be ascribed mainly to the want of some *leader* who was really qualified to command the public confidence in devising operations of such magnitude."³²

Cabell also heard from William M. Rives of Lynchburg, who actively supported both the canal from Richmond to Lynchburg and the railroad from Lynchburg to New River. Rives saw the railroad as enhancing the political chances of the canal and urged, "Unless we identify the South West with the James river interests, both politically and commercially, I apprehend we shall find it difficult to obtain any appropriation whatever for the latter." Rives was also convinced that the state should build both the canal to Lynchburg and the railroad from Lynchburg to New River and on to Tennessee. "I deprecate the idea of that great interest being again subjected to the control of a joint stock company, or submit to an imperfect & defective mode of improvement. No tinkering or piddling with this main artery of the State, is my motto. Have an adequate improvement, or none at all."³³

Cabell had misgivings about the proposed New River Railroad from Lynchburg, and he reproached Wright for having left Virginia too abruptly. "I am very desirous that Judge Wright should be apprized of the very great importance of not giving up or disparaging the connection of our river with the Kanawha," said Cabell. "I fear Governor Floyd, and Col: J[ames] P. Preston may have made upon Wright too strong an impression in favour of the Southern Route. If we lose the Central West we are undone. . . . I regret exceedingly that he did not remain longer in the state. If he had spent the fall in traversing our mountain vallies his opinions would have commanded more weight."³⁴

John Coalter, formerly a high-ranking official in the James River Company, tried to persuade Cabell to abandon the canal in favor of a railroad from Richmond to Lynchburg, warning him of a storm building in the Valley. "If you took the *Enquirer* you would see the movements to the west, which you may not in the papers you take," wrote Coalter. "They propose a convention at Staunton, to consist *entirely* of the western people, & the western papers, *not those of the state*, are requested to publish the call. The object is a rail road from Kanhawa to Parkersburg . . . & one from Tennessee to Lynchburg. . . . They will blind your eyes by affecting to promote the James River improvement, but they value it as nothing, if they can push the Baltimore Road to intersect with a Rail Road to the west." The people of the Shenandoah Valley and the Trans-Allegheny had been "soured by the hostility shown to the improvement of the Shenandoah." Coalter's last words in this missive were prophetic: "The next Legislature will either destroy Virginia & produce its separation ultimately . . . or they will preserve the State."[35]

In August 1831 a convention was held at Abingdon in Southwest Virginia promoting the Lynchburg-to-Tennessee railroad. Colonel James P. Preston of Richmond, who was governor when the Board of Public works was established in 1816 and its first president, was elected president of the convention, and William Rives represented Lynchburg. Most of the Virginia delegates were from southwestern counties, but all were outnumbered by delegates from eastern Tennessee. Crozet at the time was surveying the route of the proposed railroad, somewhere between Wythe Courthouse and Abingdon, and he visited Abingdon while the convention was in progress to inform the delegates that a double-track road "laid upon stone in the most durable manner" could be built for $14,000 a mile, totaling $4,503,000 for the 322 miles from Lynchburg to Knoxville. The potential traffic, he estimated, would easily amortize the cost.[36]

Crozet's survey of the route for this railroad from Lynchburg to the New River examined four possible routes from Lynchburg: (1) up the James to Buchanan and "across the country" to Salem; (2) via Liberty (later Bedford) to Buford's Gap and to Salem; (3) a route which "passes directly over the ridge between James river and Roanoke, descends Otter river, and thence follows the Roanoke up to Salem"; (4) up the James beyond Buchanan to its confluence with Catawba Creek, thence southward up the Catawba Valley and the North Fork of the Roanoke to the New River. Crozet preferred the Buford's Gap route, which in the twentieth century became the route for both U.S. 460 and the Norfolk and Western Railroad. He estimated that the distance of 111 miles could be built for $1,226,750 and that the traffic could earn more than 10 percent on the investment. "I consider, however, the extension of the rail-road to Tennessee a highly desirable component part of this scheme." He explained, "What adds most to the recommendation of this extension is the fact, not generally known, that it would traverse a most beautiful and fertile country. Instead of deriving its revenue, as I had formerly supposed, chiefly from the trade of Tennessee, the improvement would, in fact, be supported on its way thither by the vast resources of this remarkably fine valley."[37]

Having surveyed the ground of Southwest Virginia between the

New River and the Tennessee border for the first time, and thereby becoming convinced of the potential value of a railroad traversing it, Crozet reluctantly concluded that he could make no further useful contribution to the Virginia internal improvement program. On 18 November the *Enquirer* commented on the impending resignation of Crozet as principal engineer. "We had lately more than once heard it suggested in other quarters that Col. Crozet had it in contemplation to resign his appointment," wrote the editor, "but believing him to be eminently qualified for the office we were loth to credit it; and although we are no longer permitted to doubt that such is his intention at present, we still hope that he may be induced to abandon it. . . . it will not be an easy matter if it [the state] loses the services of Col. Crozet to supply his place by an engineer of equal merit."[38]

Crozet and Governor Floyd had exchanged letters on the subject just a few days earlier. On 28 October, Crozet wrote to the governor that he did not "wish to be a candidate at the next election." Resigning from an office he had held for nine years called forth "most lively feelings," he admitted. "I cannot easily forget, that a stranger in the state, I was received and uniformly treated with the most kind and liberal hospitality. Never reminded that I was not a native Virginian, I naturally forgot it myself, and Virginia became another home to me . . . It has been my whole ambition to re-pay public kindness, as far as lay in my power, by useful and faithful services."[39]

Floyd had no alternative but to accept Crozet's resignation, because the legislature controlled his salary and had cut it drastically. This and other hostile moves, in particular bringing in Wright for the clear purpose of contradicting Crozet's view of the James River route to Lynchburg, caused Crozet to resign. Underlying the immediate conflicts was the accumulated frustration resulting from the legislature's persistent refusal to accord the principal engineer or the Board of Public Works any real authority. Couper, referring to Joseph C. Cabell, says that Crozet "found a lion in his path." For all of Cabell's hostility to Crozet, neither he nor Crozet ever mentioned the other's name in any public records. Both men dealt with issues and avoided personalities, at least in their published writings.

As Crozet reported on his final year of service as principal engineer and prepared to leave the state, he had a word for the Board of Public Works on his possible successors. The survey of the Lynchburg-to-Tennessee railroad route had been begun by James Herron and Thomas H. DeWitt, who completed the project under Crozet's supervision. On the Northwestern Turnpike, the location was begun early in the spring by Charles B. Shaw, assisted by James D. Brown. Crozet had divided his time in 1831 mainly between these two operations, and he praised Shaw in particular for "industry and intelligence." Crozet then summarized his own position in his message to the board.

> For nine years, gentlemen, I have used my best exertions in promoting the cause of internal improvement in the state. While collecting a great mass of local information, I have often regretted that Virginia did not avail herself immediately of advantages, which . . . it may be said will at some future day make her the first state in the Union. . . .
>
> To the regret I frequently felt at the delays and procrastination to which the system of internal improvement was subjected, has succeeded the conviction that these will rather prove, on the contrary, to have been productive of good. . . . Had her works been completed sooner, she might not as readily avail herself of the new advantages of the rail-road system. . . . But farther delay might be injurious. . . . Self-defence requires immediate action.[40]

The wisdom of Virginia's mixed enterprise system, he asserted, "is every day made more apparent"; that is to say, provided the state "exercise an efficient superintendence over the works, through a board of public works, or other body, and their engineer." Without some authority to compel adherence to his plans, "the office of state engineer is quite inefficient." Long turnpike roads, such as the Northwestern or the Staunton and Parkersburg, should be exclusively state enterprises because only in this way would they be well located, kept in good repair, or built at all through undeveloped country. "I would go farther and add, that all turnpikes built by the state should be free," for the toll system was neither equitable nor efficient.[41]

In the portion of his final report dealing with the James River improvement, Crozet's pent-up resentment toward the interference of Judge Wright came to the surface. "For a long time a system of navigation was the only kind of improvement thought of, and the competition was between a lock and dam navigation and a canal. For two years past, rail-roads have acquired many additional advantages," he began. "Between these three modes we must now make a choice: the decision is important, it involves the best interests of Virginia, and I feel the weight of the responsibility I have to encounter, in giving an opinion at this decisive moment."

On the lock-and-dam improvement, Crozet defended his own

estimate against Judge Wright's. Crozet's estimate in 1828 was $664,140, predicated upon the availability of sufficient hydraulic lime at the Blue Ridge. There was now some doubt about this, so he allowed it would be safer to return to the $800,000 estimate. Wright had said he could not do it for double the lower estimate, or $1,328,280. Crozet examined the historic cost of existing dams on James River, starting with Bosher's dam, the most expensive at $1,600 per foot lift. The average of all existing dams on the river to Lynchburg was $1,175 per foot lift. This rate, multiplied by the whole lift of 328 feet for the distance between Maiden's and Lynchburg, came to $385,400 for the required fifty-seven dams. Add to this 328 feet of lockage, at the "high rate of $1,000 per foot lift," plus a canal at Seven Islands costing $124,370, and the total sum would be $837,770. Two dams had been built on the Potomac on Wright's plan, with an overall average of $1,241 per foot lift. Apply that rate to James River, and his estimate would come to $859,418, making the figure of "double the money estimated" inexplicable, even by Wright's own experience. Wright had not ended his criticism of the lock-and-dam proposal there, however, but had gone on to object to steam as a moving power, on grounds that it would require too much mechanical skill. "Is this a general principle," asked Crozet, with a touch of sarcasm, "or merely applicable to Virginia?" Moreover, Crozet added, "this gentleman objects on account of the *great mechanical skill* required; and we shall find all along, that steam power will not do in any shape in Virginia, but that we must, now and forever, confine ourselves to negro power, and let the other states retain and enjoy the superiority which attends every where the application of mechanical skill."

Enough of the lock-and-dam plan; Crozet was more interested in railroads, to which he now turned his attention. Judge Wright had said that "if a railroad should be adopted, it ought to start from Richmond instead of Maiden's Adventure: this would destroy the use of the present canal." Therefore, Wright concluded, the canal plan should be preferred. Such a rationale puzzled Crozet. "Would it be sound to persevere in that which has ceased to be best, and reject that which new inventions have rendered most desirable, because what has been done before, might lose part of its usefulness? This might be the course of an individual with limited means, but never can be that of a state." Wright had also said he did not "believe" a railroad with two tracks could be constructed for less than a good canal. "This is not a matter of belief," responded Crozet, "but of actual fact and experience." The 54½ miles of the Baltimore railroad, from Ellicott's Mill to Point of Rocks, had cost $20,168 per mile. Most canals had already cost more than that, "and the Ohio and Chesapeake canal, so far, about double." Wright's comment on the comparative safety of property "in a good canal boat under lock and key" Crozet dismissed as puerile. "I do not suppose it would require a great deal of mechanical skill," he said, to lock up a freight car.

Crozet then turned his attention to the type of improvement recommended by Wright for the James River: a continuous canal. Wright had favored one 50 feet wide and 5 feet deep, which he thought could be built "*under good management* for 18 or $20,000 per mile." Experience on both the Pennsylvania canals and the Chesapeake and Ohio Canal did not justify "so low an estimate for so large a canal," said Crozet. The C&O Canal, 60 feet wide and 6 feet deep, had been estimated in 1828 at $23,760 per mile; by 1831, with two-thirds of the work completed, it had cost $40,962 per mile. The reasons for this cost overrun were "occasional enlargement of the intended dimensions; unforeseen quality of ground for excavation; rise of the price of labour, &c.&c." If the Virginia legislature should determine to build a canal, Crozet added, he would recommend a width of 40 feet and a depth of 3½ feet, which could "pass boats as large as desirable" and would allow fording instead of bridging.

Having left Judge Benjamin Wright's recommendations in tatters, Crozet then offered his own conclusion as to what should be done with the James River. If economy was to be the basic guideline, he would urge the lock-and-dam system; however, if the state decided in favor of a substantial investment in a truly competitive system, the railroad was the obvious choice. Advances in railroad technology between 1826 and 1831 had changed Crozet's mind.

> If Virginia is prepared to expend three millions of dollars upon an improvement up to the mountains, it is certainly not to a canal I should wish to see them applied. . . . Canals have done their best; rail-roads, now at least equal to them, are still advancing toward perfection. The rail-road system is the triumph of the age; the ultimate effects of its introduction are incalculable, and, with the certainty that it will produce important changes in the commercial and even political world, its early adoption is safer than its rejection in favor of another system, from which no farther developments are to be expected. Such are my opinions and such their motives.[42]

Despite Crozet's arguments, the Virginia General Assembly, pressed by Joseph C. Cabell, proceeded, haltingly as usual, to follow the advice of Judge Wright to build a continuous canal from Maiden's Adventure to Lynchburg.

For a few months Crozet was uncertain about his next employment opportunity. In November 1831 he had joined General Swift, George W. Whistler, and W. G. McNeill in New Jersey to examine "the Trap Ridge near Hoboken for a tunnel."[43] When no employment developed from this, he returned to Richmond to complete his reports to the Board of Public Works in his accustomed meticulous detail and await opportunities. At the end of March 1832 the Louisiana legislature created the position of state engineer, and Crozet was a willing and highly available candidate. In the fall he was offered the position, and before the end of the year he and his family were residents of New Orleans.

In his nine years as principal engineer of Virginia, Crozet had accomplished much, but by no means as much as he was capable of doing with the cooperation of the legislature. He had traversed the state near and far, learning its poorly mapped topography, giving the benefit of his expertise to the officials of projects both deserving and undeserving, writing clear and specifically detailed reports on his work each winter for the benefit of the Board of Public Works and the legislature, and receiving thanks for his efforts only from the board and its governor-chairmen and a number of newspaper editors. The legislature supported him grudgingly, fearing the effects upon its political power of any real success of his program for a transportation network.

During the latter months of 1830 and throughout 1831 a groundswell of public opinion arose in Lynchburg, Abingdon, Staunton, Petersburg, Winchester, and even Richmond, in the form of public meetings or conventions demanding legislative action in support of railroads and/or canals.[44] The Richmond *Enquirer* added its voice as did also the Garland subcommittee on roads and internal navigation in the House of Delegates. Under such pressure the legislature could no longer avoid the issue; it thus adopted a strategy designed to force Crozet out. There can be little doubt that the majority of legislators who called in Judge Wright to question Crozet's plans expected the outcome to be exactly as it was.

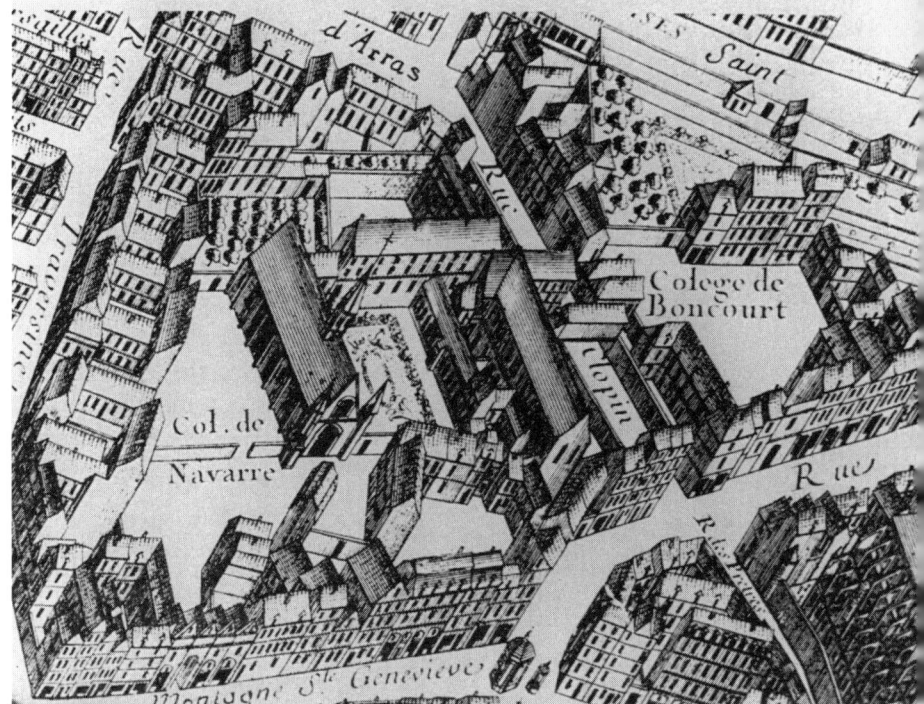

College of Navarre in 1734, site of Ecole Polytechnique, Paris, France.
(*Courtesy of Ecole Polytechnique, Paliseau, France*)

Quarters No. 3, at U.S. Military Academy, West Point, N.Y. Artist's adaptation of photograph in A. B. Berard, *Reminiscences of West Point in the Olden Times*, 1886.

House at 100 E. Main St., Richmond, owned by Crozet, 1828–32. (*Courtesy of Valentine Museum, Richmond*)

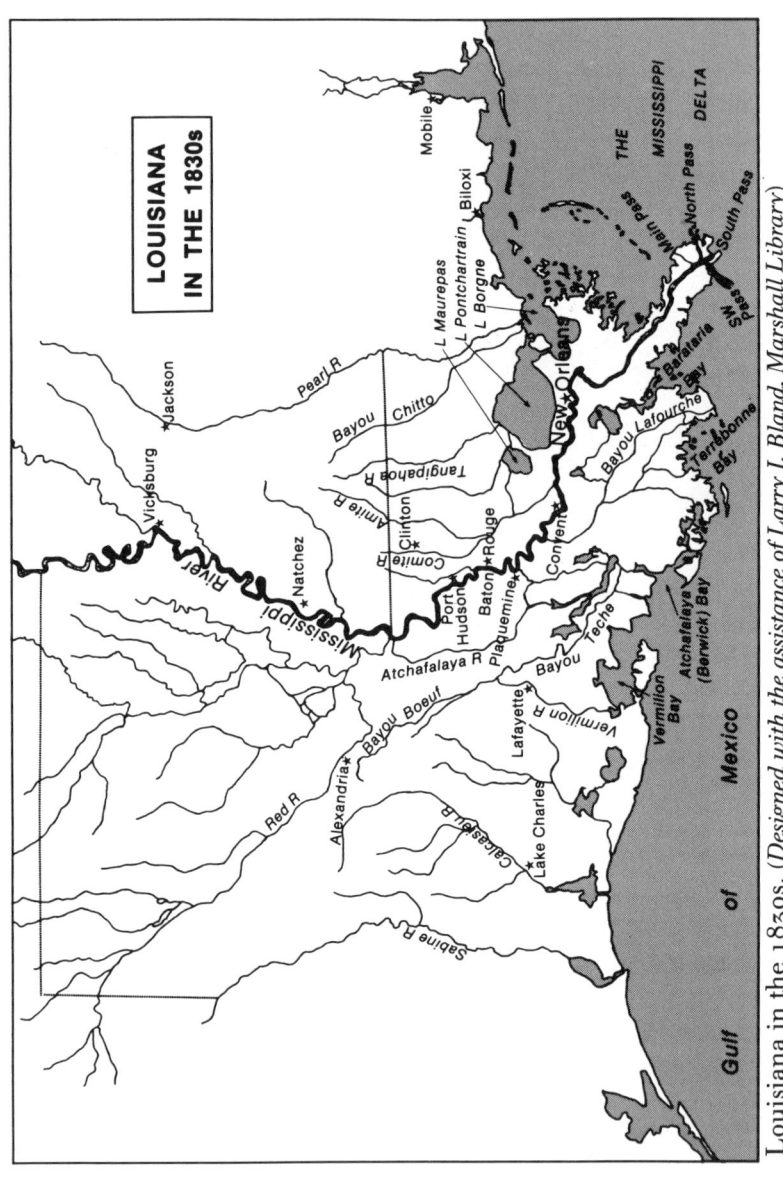

Louisiana in the 1830s. (Designed with the assistance of Larry I. Bland, Marshall Library)

Manresa House of Retreats, formerly Jefferson College, Convent, La.

Painting of the North River Canal at its junction with the James River and the Blue Ridge Canal, by Edward Beyer. (*Courtesy of Virginia State Library and Archives*)

Drawing of VMI in 1842 by Cadet C. P. Deyerle. (*Courtesy of Virginia Military Institute*)

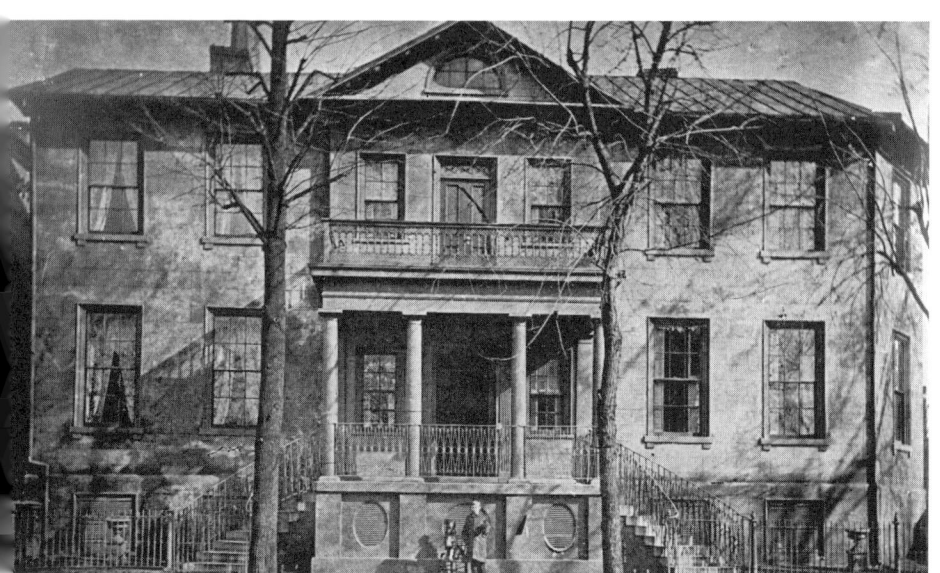

Edmund Randolph house, site of Crozet's office in the 1850s. (*Courtesy of Valentine Museum, Richmond*)

Crozet, from a daguerreotype taken in the 1850s. (*Courtesy of Virginia Military Institute*)

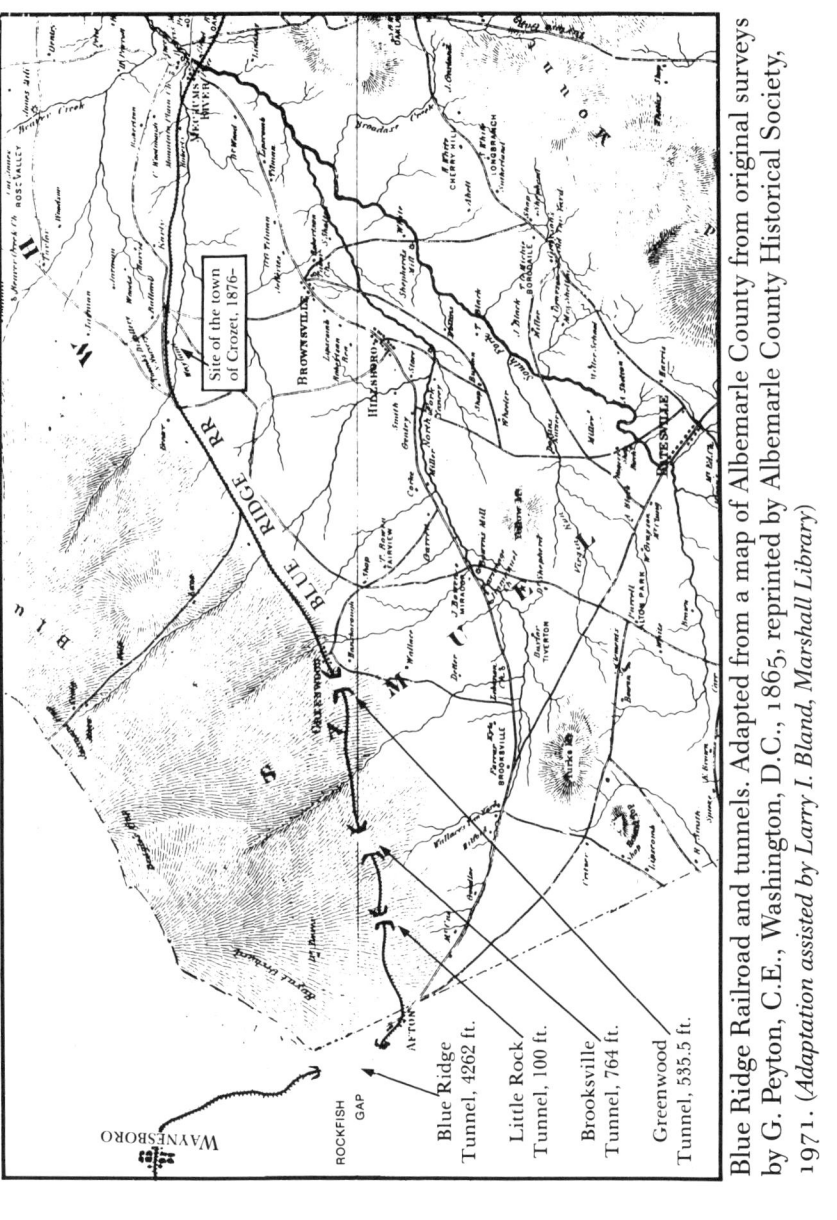

Blue Ridge Railroad and tunnels. Adapted from a map of Albemarle County from original surveys by G. Peyton, C.E., Washington, D.C., 1865, reprinted by Albemarle County Historical Society, 1971. (*Adaptation assisted by Larry I. Bland, Marshall Library*)

West portal, main tunnel, Blue Ridge Railroad. (*Courtesy of Library of Congress*)

East portal, main tunnel, Blue Ridge Railroad. *Left*: east portal of new C&O Railroad tunnel, 1944; *Right*: original east portal, Crozet tunnel. (*Courtesy of Library of Congress*)

Interior, main tunnel, Blue Ridge Railroad. (*Courtesy of Library of Congress*)

5

Louisiana
1832–37

Crozet found his opportunity to be state engineer of Louisiana attractive. For one reason, French was in common use in the schools, in the newspapers, and among a substantial element of the population. He could feel at home using his native tongue, although his command of English was by now complete. More important to him, Louisiana was building the first railroad west of the Appalachians, the Pontchartrain Railroad, chartered in 1830 and in operation by 1832.[1] It was a short line connecting New Orleans with the lake traffic, but it indicated that Louisiana was a promising state for railroad development, and Crozet could hardly wait to press it forward.

The most convenient means for traveling to Louisiana from Virginia in 1832 was by coastal packet from Norfolk or Portsmouth around Florida and across the Gulf, then through the passes at the mouth of the Mississippi River and upstream to New Orleans. The Crozets and their two young children, Alfred Armand, ten, and Claudia Natalia, about eight, probably traveled to New Orleans by sea; and when they disembarked, they were in a different world from either Virginia or France.

Louisiana became the eighteenth state in the Union in 1812, much reduced in size from the Louisiana Purchase territory. New Orleans, with a colonial history nearly as old as that of Charleston, South Carolina, dominated the state. In 1830 one out of five Louisianians lived there; by 1840 the city's population had more than doubled to over 100,000, and one out of three Louisianians lived there. New Orleans lived on exports of cotton, sugar, tobacco, and other farm products that flowed into its docksides from farms and plantations along the Mississippi and its tributaries. The Mississippi River dominated the economy as New Orleans dominated the political and social scene in Louisiana. But water transportation had several major problems: clearing the snags, sandbars, alluvial deposits, and abandoned rafts from the rivers and bayous and extending the range of water transport farther into the hinterland. The railroad offered the possibility of solving the latter problem.

There was a cloud on the northern and eastern horizon of New Orleans clearly visible to Crozet as he arrived in Louisiana but not recognized by its agribusiness and political leaders. With the completion of the Erie Canal in 1825 and the vigorous efforts of Pennsylvania and Maryland to extend transportation lines westward in competition with New York, the axis of the main lines of trade in the interior of the nation was beginning a gigantic wheeling motion—from north-south along the Mississippi and its tributaries to east-west by means of the developing railroad network.

Americans in any of the states could be excused for their inability to discern this emerging trend in 1830 or even 1840, for only in that decade did railroad technology become reliable. Even the avant-garde Crozet had his doubts about it from time to time during the 1830s. In New Orleans complacence remained undisturbed during those years, for the railroad was seen as no more than another way to bring the cotton and sugar out of the hinterland to the mighty Mississippi. The governor and the legislature certainly had no intention of abandoning the traditional waterways with which Louisiana abounded.

Governor André Bienvenu Roman (1795–1866), who not only chose Crozet to be the state engineer for Louisiana but soon became his good friend, and in time connected by a marriage between their families, grew up on his father's sugar plantation in Saint James Parish, which straddles the Mississippi between Baton Rouge and New Orleans. André was the eldest of six sons born at the rate of one each year between 1795 and 1800.[2] Graduating from Saint Mary's College in Baltimore in 1815, he married Aimée Parent in 1816 and established his own plantation in Saint James, where they raised five children. Roman was elected to the House of Representatives in 1818 and served almost continuously until 1831, several of those years as speaker. He became governor in 1831 for four years, sat out the interim period mandated by the state constitution, and was reelected governor in 1839. He has been regarded by historians as "one of Louisiana's ablest governors" and during his first term became a leader of the new Whig party.[3] Crozet's residence in Louisiana began during Roman's first term and terminated during that of his Whig successor, Edward Douglass White.

In his inaugural address to the legislature at the end of January 1831, Roman expounded his views on internal improvements. The problem was not so much that the legislature had refused to appropriate money for transportation, for it had done so, but rather that the appropriations had been partial in both senses of the word. They had been casual, "without there having been any surveys, draughts, or estimates of costs, prepared before hand," and they had been awarded to favored persons. He urged the members to pass a law "providing for the appointment of a board composed of two engineers" to make such surveys and estimates. This would be an additional governmental expense, he admitted, "but the saving would soon demonstrate that such an expense is economy."[4]

The legislature did not respond, and Roman repeated the message early in 1832. Louisiana was merely watching other states becoming "covered with canals and railroads," he warned, and was neglecting "even works of the first necessity."[5] The public debt of the state had been reduced by nearly half during 1831, and receipts during the current year "will exceed our expenditures," so the time could hardly be more favorable for making the investment. This time the legislators acted, passing on 31 March 1832 "an act for the appointment of a civil engineer and appropriating monies for internal improvements."[6] The Louisiana legislature was more generous than Virginia's, setting the engineer's salary at $5,000 per year. At the same time, it had no intention of relinquishing control over the work of the state engineer.

Crozet arrived in Louisiana late in October 1832 when the legislature was not in session. Governor Roman sent him in December to examine the bayou Plaquemine as his first undertaking, on which Crozet reported to the legislature when it convened in January 1833.[7] Entrance to the bayou Plaquemine was at the village of the same name on the west bank of the Mississippi just below Baton Rouge. The bayou provided access to the river for the parishes of Iberville, Saint Martin, and Saint Landry. The term *bayou*, probably derived from the Choctaw word *bayuk*, meaning a small stream, was applied to waterways tangential to the Mississippi or other main rivers supplied by overflows from the main stream—something like tributaries in reverse. Crozet reported that the river was high during his visit, which "proved rather an advantage, as it gave me an opportunity of estimating more accurately the difficulties existing at that place." He continued:

> Plaquemines is situated in the concave part of a large bend of the river, all round which the main current impinges carrying along with it, the immense body of drift timber which descends the Mississippi ... it precipitates itself ... into the Bayou Plaquemines ... and produces serious and increasing impediments. ...
>
> In order to prevent the introduction of the floating timber through this Canal, there was built, a short time since, across it, a barricade of framed piles, some distance below its entrance. I saw this work standing, and witnessed also its destruction. The accumulation of drift timber against it, urged forward by the immense pressure of the current, as the stream rose, could not be resisted: the whole structure was swept away, and the mass of drift floated with the wreck into the interior.
>
> Another and more serious damage was done; the current, impeded in the middle by the large body of accumulated timber, escaped at the sides, with increased power, undermining both banks in its progress, and more particularly that on the side of Plaquemines, where a part of the levee itself crumbled down; thus exposing the village and adjacent country to a vast inundation. ...
>
> The danger to which Plaquemines is exposed admits of no other remedy than the closing of the Canal by a substantial levee. ... the work to be done would consist of enlarging and, in places, straightening the bayou, so as to allow at all times of the free passage of the description of steam boats that navigate the interior, and protecting the mouth of the bayou against the introduction of drift timber.
>
> This may be done in two different ways; either by closing altogether the entrance of the bayou with a solid and substantial levee, up to which the bayou Plaquemines should be enlarged, so as to leave between the two navigable lines only a narrow space, over which the steamboats, being brought within sight of each other, could easily exchange their loads.
>
> Or by constructing at the mouth a framed work to turn off the drift timber, and provided with suitable openings by which the water of the Mississippi, and also steam boats, might be admitted.[8]

The first plan, Crozet allowed, would be cheaper, but it would block egress of Mississippi waters into the bayou, considered important by many, and it would impose an inconvenient transshipment. The second plan would obviate both objections but would be more expensive. "Unfortunately," Crozet added, "we have here but weak banks for abutments, and a loose soil for support." Expense of maintenance could prove a continuing drain. The first plan he estimated at $100,000; the second he refused to estimate until lower water made more accurate measurements possible.

In his address to the legislature in January 1833, Roman formally and officially announced that he had "appointed during the recess a civil Engineer for the State, whom I have every reason to believe will fulfil . . . expectations." Then, as an afterthought which Roman probably regretted later—certainly Crozet regretted his having said it—the governor declared, "The Legislature have created an office of Civil Engineer, and that officer is now ready to execute any survey that they may order." He should have suspected what advantage the legislators would take of it. The House on 18 January specifically directed the civil engineer: (1) to survey a public road from Baton Rouge eastward to the Tickfaw River; (2) to survey the Tickfaw for obstructions to navigation into Lake Maurepas; (3) to explore the bayou Bartholomew and "point out the means for rendering its navigation safe in going up to the residence of George Amberson"; (4) "to reconnoitre the point of the Cut-off in the Parish of Pointe Coupee, and to ascertain whether it would be advantageous to cut said point [a bend of the Mississippi above Baton Rouge] and what would be the probable result"; (5) to survey the bayou Grosse Tête in Iberville Parish; (6) to ascertain if the bayou Vermillion in Lafayette Parish could be made navigable for steamboats. The assignment was staggering—and not yet complete.

When the Senate added its own list of projects on 25 January, it directed Crozet: (1) to survey a public road from Baton Rouge through East Feliciana Parish; (2) to clear Ward's Creek bayou; (3) to examine the routes of the Barataria and Lafourche Canal and the Lafourche and Terrebonne Navigation Company. He was to give these private companies "all the aid in his power."[9]

The resolutions of the two houses were adopted on 28 January, and yet the list was not complete; on the same day, still more tasks were imposed on Crozet—such as examining several more rivers and bayous and a number of public roads, estimating the cost of improvements, and reporting on them "to the next session of the Legislature."[10] If any member of the House or Senate had a pet project for his constituents, his friends, or himself, he did not miss the chance to add it to the list of tasks for the civil engineer. One can imagine Crozet's dismay upon reading his assignments. It was clear that legislative interference with the efficient conduct of his office would threaten Crozet even more in Louisiana than it had in Virginia.

Recognizing the problem, Governor Roman advocated establishing a duly constituted board of public works with the task of evaluating needs and assigning priorities. Providing for an engineer was one step, Roman told the legislature, but the essential second step was providing for a board of public works, "whose duty it would be to direct the works of the Engineer, to provide him with the assistants he may require, and to superintend the disbursement of the funds appropriated for public works." The legislature at first balked at this, fearing loss of control. The House committee on internal improvements asserted its opinion "that it would be expedient that the General Assembly should, at each session, specify the order in which the operations of the Engineer are to be executed; what parts of the State are to be explored, and to what points he is to attend successively, in order that, at the following meeting, the General Assembly may be provided with full and entire reports."[11] The legislature nevertheless agreed to take the governor's "second step," and on 4 March 1833 Governor Roman signed an act to incorporate a Board of Public Works and to create a fund for internal improvement. In a pattern similar to Virginia's, the board was headed by the governor, and the other members were the treasurer, the attorney general, and nine annually appointed citizens representing each of the three congressional districts; the latter were not required to be present for conducting business. The board met twice a year, in December and April. The board had the power to enact regulations for the office of the civil engineer, but the legislature did not yield an iota of its authority to direct his every move.

As for the fund for internal improvement, it was the paltry sum of $20,000, "to be annually drawn out of the duties collected on sales at auction." This was no more than a toe in the door of state finances, but at least the door was opening, and within eight years the Board of Public Works had spent close to $600,000 in the deepening of natural waterways such as the bayou Plaquemine.[12] The act creating the board said nothing about railroads but specifically stated that the fund was "to be applied exclusively to the purpose of rendering navigable, and uniting by canals, the principal water courses, and of more intimately connecting by public highways, the different parts of this state."[13]

However, many planters saw railroads as an answer to their problems and, in their enthusiasm, flooded the legislature with petitions for railroad charters. In several cases, they were successful. For example, the river town of Port Hudson, on the east bank a few miles above Baton Rouge, was the outlet for a rich farm region around Clinton, about 20 miles northeast. Oxcarts hauled the cotton from Clinton to Port Hudson at the rate of about one bale per ox. In February 1833 the legislature chartered the Clinton and Port Hudson Railroad Company, with the state agreeing to invest in two-fifths of the capital stock whenever private subscribers had purchased three-fifths. The C&PH Railroad was required to raise half of the $500,000 by selling stock for cash; the other half could be exchanged for mortgages on real estate and slaves. With these properties as security, the railroad could then issue up to $250,000 in bonds to acquire construction funds. The planter-dominated legislature "coerced the prosperous New Orleans Gas Light and Banking Company into buying all the railroad bonds" and forced the company to lend the railroad $100,000 at 6 percent.[14]

Crozet's initial survey for the Clinton and Port Hudson Railroad was completed in the summer of 1833 amid the hazards of an epidemic of cholera. The Board of Public Works outlined his duties in May 1833, at which time there was a "devastating epidemic on the western waters," which, reported Crozet, "left me . . . only the Floridas [the counties north of Lake Pontchartrain and east of the Mississippi] for a safe field of operation." He proceeded to examine the Falaya and Tangipahoa rivers, and then the route for the Clinton and Port Hudson Railroad. But even the Floridas were not safe, for the sickness expanded into that area in August. "Nearly all of my company fell sick at the same time," he reported, "and I had to regret the loss of one of my assistants, L.B. Davis, a very promising young man."[15] Nor was Crozet himself immune. Governor Roman in his message to the legislature on 10 December wrote, "The ill-health of the Civil Engineer, not having permitted [him] to make all the surveys ordered by the Board of Public Works, the report to be submitted to you by that body, will be much less complete than it would have been." He went on to observe that the epidemic had "caused, as might have been expected, considerable delay in the construction of our public works." At the height of the plague, he added, "everything was neglected for the preservation of health, which became the only subject of attention."[16]

Crozet and his assistant engineer, D. N. Welch, estimated the cost of the Clinton and Port Hudson line at $176,000 for the 22 miles, or $8,000 per mile.[17] With prompt construction, the new line could have been an immediate success; but a conspiracy evolved at Baton Rouge, Port Hudson's rival, to take the railroad away. In 1836 the Baton Rouge group pushed through the legislature the incorporation of the Baton Rouge and Clinton Railroad Company, with a capitalization of $600,000 and state aid. The company sold some stock and graded some roadbed, but it failed in the panic of 1837. Instead of a railroad, the route became a plank road in the 1840s.[18] Crozet had seen politics act as a stumbling block to the development of a sensible and practical system of transportation in Virginia. In Louisiana the wielding of political influence for personal or local gain was even more blatant than in Virginia.

Crozet's report to the legislature on the results of his first full year as state engineer occupied the entire front page of the New Orleans *Bee* for Saturday, 11 January 1834.[19] The supplementary report of William A. Dawson, secretary of the Board of Public Works, required most of the second page. Crozet first established the point that Louisiana planters had to have economical transportation to New Orleans. "We possess the mart of a most extensive country," he wrote, where "every kind of produce, whether of the soil or of industry, is cheap, and can be brought down the Mississippi at a low rate of freight. The sea introduces likewise competitors from far distant ports. How can the planter withstand such odds against him, unless favored with an easy access to New Orleans?" Hauling cotton by oxcart simply would not do. Crozet recognized that the Mississippi was "capricious and uncontrollable, [and] its power must be submitted to." Moreover, it "must ever be the main artery" of Louisiana's trade.

Crozet tentatively suggested cutting off some of the great bends of the Mississippi. On most rivers, cutoffs were objectionable, he asserted, "on account of the reduction of depth, increase of the current and new bars, by which they ultimately rather injure than benefit the navigation." The Mississippi was so deep that these objections did not apply, but even so, there were hazards. "A cut-off," said Crozet, "will, of course, produce an acceleration of the current, and consequently the destruction of marginal property on the side against which it will infringe, below the new channel. As a result, in the end, a new bend, nearly equivalent to the former, will be made by abrasion on one side and a corresponding *batture* on the other, the higher and better ground of the two having been carried away and consequently higher levees becoming necessary."

As for lateral routes bringing goods from the interior parishes to the Mississippi, it deceptively appeared to be common sense to build canals linking the river with the lakes and bayous. "Between the navigable waters of the interior, no doubt can exist as to the preference to be given to canals," he asserted. But where the Mississippi rose as much as 30 feet in times of high water and man-made levees lined both banks to contain the river, a canal link with the river was virtually impossible. "The descent of the country, being from the banks of the Mississippi towards the interior, contrary to what occurs elsewhere; the stupendous works that canals would require, would have to resist the whole pressure of the stream." Railroads would be preferred to canals in this situation. "I say rail roads, because, for the general purposes of trade, common roads are too often impassable in this low and level country, and turnpikes require materials too far removed to be obtained at a cost less than that of rail roads."

While he was on the subject, he brought to the legislature's attention the railroad he had had in mind for Louisiana from the time he had left Virginia. "Among the rail roads of vital interest, I do not hesitate to place one; towards which I consider my operations of the season as having made a beginning; I mean a great line from the Mississippi towards Washington City, which, leaving the river at a suitable point, should take its direction through Mississippi and Alabama, towards the southernmost bend of the Tennessee river, and thence along the great valley of the Tennessee through the state of that name, and then through Virginia." The "operations" that he considered a beginning were those on the Clinton and Port Hudson Railroad, which he "would consider of little value if not extended to the Mississippi line," to become a link in his proposed New Orleans-to-Washington railroad.

The remainder of Crozet's report dealt with his survey of the Falaya and the Tangipahoa rivers. The Falaya flows into Lake Pontchartrain on the north side through Covington. Steamboat travel would require only a few hundred dollars worth of snag and branch clearing, in his opinion. The Tangipahoa, a few miles to the west, he regarded as essentially hopeless. "It is swift, much obstructed by timber, and very crooked. . . . Its crookedness will ever render [it] unfit for the navigation of large crafts, and straightening the bends is liable to the objections I have already mentioned."

Attached to Crozet's report of 16 December was a supplement, an update of the report on the bayou Plaquemine he made to the subboard on 19 October 1833. Crozet had found an opportunity to take measurements at lower water levels and was now prepared to make more specific recommendations and estimates. "Three distinct works appeared to me necessary," he reported.

> 1st. Deepening the channel for a six feet navigation as far as the point where the pond is sufficiently deep and thence cleaning out the bayou to the Indian village.
> 2d. Closing the canal by a levee and reopening the old bayou.
> 3d. Protecting the mouth of the bayou by a substantial jetty against the introduction of timber as far as consistent with a free and safe entrance for steamboats.

The total estimated cost he gave as $196,800, which he admitted "greatly exceeds what I had supposed before I had an opportunity of estimating the difficulties." He thought it would be worthwhile, however, "considering the increasing prosperity of the large district of which this is the key." A direct canal to the Indian village from the river would not exceed 6 miles, but considering the hazards of the rising of the Mississippi, sometimes recorded at Plaquemine at 60 feet, the canal would be much more expensive.[20]

Following Crozet's reports came that of William A. Dawson, secretary of the Board of Public Works. Dawson reviewed the long list of tasks assigned to Crozet by the legislature, then wrote, "To the extraordinary unhealthiness of the season may be attributed the reason why these works are not so far advanced as anticipated by the Board." He complimented Crozet as "the talented Engineer now at the head of affairs" and expressed the hope that a more healthful season would produce more permanent results. Dawson added, "The Board is resolved as far as it is concerned, to prosecute with vigour, all, and none but such improvements as may be deemed most important, without regard to sectional feelings or interests." Despite his firm stand, Dawson probably had little confidence in the prospect of the legislature's adhering to such a principle.

The idea of a railroad from New Orleans to Washington appealed to the editor of the *Bee*. "Washington might be brought within six days distance of our city by a rail-road," he wrote, "if our citizens would shake off their fatal apathy." If the entire road cost ten million dollars, Louisiana could emulate New York, borrowing for her part of it on state bonds and counting it an investment.[21] A reader who signed himself "Z" had his long letter printed, urging the state to set up a commission, send members to the governments of the intervening states, and get the project moving. But the legislature had other, more local interests to serve; it sent Crozet out to survey the bayous Lafourche, L'Embleme, and Vermillion, the Tickfaw river, and so on, because the planters who ran the legislature were interested only in water connections with the Mississippi River and New Orleans.

The patience of Governor Roman sometimes snapped. "I cannot understand how the Civil Engineer is called upon for his opinion of the practicability of those improvements with the sums appropriated," he wrote in a message vetoing one of these bills. In the case of the Tangipahoa River, Crozet had already surveyed it and estimated the cost of improving 30 miles above the mouth at $6,000. The legislature responded by appropriating $4,000 with instructions to improve the entire length. In the case of the Falaya, Crozet had estimated that "between 3 and 4 hundred dollars" could do all the clearing necessary, but the legislature had appropriated $3,000 for the job, which would arouse anyone's suspicions.[22]

Crozet dutifully performed the work prescribed by the legislators, although his patience dwindled with the passing months and their apparent disinclination to pay close attention to his reports. In surveying the Atchafalaya, for example, Crozet found that the discarded rafts and other debris obstructing navigation could be removed for comparatively little expense, but the money appropriated was not being spent intelligently. Contractors, with few exceptions, were notoriously unreliable, usually taking the money without performing the work properly. Crozet recommended bypassing them, doing the work with the state's own labor force. Governor Roman agreed and urged the legislature to consider the purchase of slaves for the Board of Public Works. Free labor was scarce and expensive, being paid "as high as two dollars a day for the work now under execution at Plaquemine." Hiring slaves would cost even more than free workers during times of cultivation or harvest. "One hundred slaves could probably be purchased for $70,000," Roman urged.[23] The legislature agreed, and in April 1834 it authorized the Board of Public Works to purchase up to 150 slaves out of the fund for internal improvement. The board would have complete control over their employment and could hire them out to planters during appropriate seasons, with all profits reverting to the fund for internal improvement.[24]

In the final section of this act, the legislature added as if by afterthought, "the present commission of the civil engineer of this state, shall expire on the third Monday of January next, and . . . hereafter the term of office of said civil engineer shall be limited to the term of two years." But when the appointed Monday in January 1835 arrived, the rule would apply to someone other than Crozet.

In the meanwhile, the legislature required still another project of Crozet, to "report on the means of preserving the city of New Orleans and its vicinity from the inundations occasioned by lakes Borgne and Pontchartrain." The two lakes were brackish—a mix of salt and fresh waters—and rose and fell with the tides. The greatest elevation, Crozet reported, was about 4¼ feet; therefore levees 5½ feet above the low level should be "amply sufficient to exclude the water of the lakes at all times." A system for protecting the city could be built for about $70,000, he estimated. More than that was needed, he added, for the governing bodies had to consider "the complete draining and reclaiming of all the swamps which surround New Orleans, now unproductive and to the deleterious emanations from which, the destructive autumnal epidemics are attributable. But for these, this city would soon be the most populous in the Union." Governor Roman strongly supported this objective in his message to the legislature in January 1835. "A plan for draining these swamps has been prepared under the direction of the Board of Public Works," he said; "the expenses have been calculated; they will amply be repaid by the increased value of the land reclaimed."[25] The governor maintained his interest in the problem, and after his retirement from office, Roman would head the New Orleans Drainage Company which effectively carried out the swamp-clearing project.

The summer of 1834 saw prosperous times in the nation. In New Orleans the cholera was gone, the weather was hot, and the mood was indifferent to the efforts of eastern merchants to reach the western markets. The writer of a letter to the editor of the New Orleans *Bee*, however, caught a glimpse of the cloud on the horizon. "One of our most intelligent and active commission merchants," he informed the editor, "stated that the house to which he belonged had shipped for Louisville ten tons of merchandize, which had been agreed to be delivered at that place in fourteen days from Philadelphia—freight, $1.33 per cwt." Goods were being sent to Pittsburgh by a combination of railroad, waterway, and turnpike and from Pittsburgh westward via the Ohio River. Moreover, they had "shipped 95 packages of merchandize for St. Louis, which were to be delivered at St. Louis in twenty one days from Philadelphia,—freight, two dollars per hundred." New Orleans, he concluded, "has seen her most prosperous day ... necessity does not compel western men to buy of us." His letter was typical of many published by the *Bee*, to which the editor frequently added his own exhortations to alert New Orleans businessmen to the dangers of increasing competition. Eventually, he met with some success. At Bishop's Hotel on the evening of Thursday, 20 November 1834, a group of New Orleans businessmen led by George Eustis met to organize the New Orleans and Nashville Railroad Association.[26]

The legislature had refused for over a year even to order a survey for the New Orleans-to-Washington railroad which had been urged by Crozet. In South Carolina, plans were under way for a railroad from Charleston to Louisville, and even to Memphis. The New Orleans businessmen, becoming conscious of the threat of commercial isolation, agreed upon an alliance with Nashville; a railroad to Nashville would bypass Memphis and head off Charleston. A historian of Louisiana railroads writes, "Proponents of the great national railroad were still active and remained skeptical of arguments that the shortest route to Washington was through Nashville."[27] Crozet was one of the skeptics and said that those who advocated the Nashville terminal missed the point of the whole enterprise. Once the valley of the Tennessee River was reached in northern Alabama, he insisted, the way through eastern Tennessee into Virginia was provided by nature. Eventually, the New Orleans and Nashville Railroad ended in failure when the state of Mississippi, influenced by Natchez and Vicksburg, jealous rivals of New Orleans, refused to cooperate.

At a meeting of the Board of Public Works in April 1834, the members were informed that Crozet was "about to resign." As the year 1834 drew to a close, Crozet concluded that he could accomplish little or nothing more as civil engineer of Louisiana, so he submitted his resignation. Governor Roman informed the legislature officially when they met on 5 January 1835 that Crozet had resigned during the recess. Roman was not at all certain that another state engineer should be appointed to succeed Crozet. "To give the first impulse to our internal improvements, to determine on some difficult questions, such as the clearing out of the Atchafalaya, the reclaiming of the swamps of New-Orleans and in some other matters, it was indispensable to have at the head of our public works a man of experience," he said. "This object having been attained, I believe that what remains to be done can be accomplished by giving the board of public works the power to employ such engineers as the nature of the works under their charge may require."[28] Both Virginia and Louisiana experimented with such a system for a time, found it wanting, and returned to employing a state engineer.

Governor Roman was more clearly in the forefront of his peers in another area of public concern—public education, an interest which Crozet shared. Crozet left his job as state engineer to assume the presidency of a state-supported college of which Roman was the acknowledged founder, Jefferson College at Convent, Louisiana. In his first inaugural as governor in January 1831, Roman urged the establishment of a state-supported college in Saint James Parish. "Four hundred young Louisianians are now receiving their education either in colleges of the other states of the union, or of Europe," he asserted, and spending at least $100,000 annually outside of Louisiana in doing so.[29] Louisiana contributors had already given $50,000 in seed money and had adopted the name and constitution of Jefferson College in September 1830. Robert Carter Nicholas, representative from Saint James Parish, introduced the bill of incorporation which was passed and signed by Governor Roman in February 1831. Vavasseur plantation, about 60 miles upstream from New Orleans at Convent, on the east bank, sold the college promoters 65 acres for $3,500.[30] Steamboat captains called the site "College Point."[31] The main building, 300 feet long and 44 feet in depth, with Greek columns on all four sides, faced the river. Construction was finished late in 1833, and classes began in February 1834.

In December 1833 Jefferson College was running newspaper advertisements notifying the public of its opening on the first Monday of February 1834. The designation "college" is misleading; interested readers were informed, "To be admitted, pupils must be at least ten years old, read and write, have been vaccinated, and furnish proof of their good conduct, if they have been in any other school." Pupils who took the "classical course" paid $300, all others $250. As of 21 December 1833, the president of the college was still looking for teachers of Latin and Greek, French, drawing, music, a dancing master and a fencing master.[32] For Crozet, the environment and program of this school would be very different from teaching engineering to West Point cadets.

In keeping with the views of Thomas Jefferson, no religious qualifications were required of either students or faculty. In an effort to protect French culture from American encroachments, French was spoken one day and English the next, on campus and in classrooms.

The mother tongue of all faculty members had to be French.³³ The first president of the college was Bernard Granet, age forty, doctor of laws, author of books on education, and an experienced teacher in Louisiana. Mme. Granet ran a French-English boarding school for young ladies on Royal Street in New Orleans. Granet was appointed to head Jefferson College in February 1833, months before it was ready to open, but within a month after classes began, Granet had resigned and was in Baton Rouge heading a boys' school in conjunction with his wife's relocated establishment.

William Couper in his biography of Crozet said that other members of Crozet's family lived in Saint James Parish but gave no documentation. The United States Census Report for the parish in 1860 contains confirming data and more. Couper mentioned Anna Crozet as a niece, and Crozet referred to a brother, although not by name, in his will, written in 1863 after Agathe's death.³⁴ The census report lists a William Crozet, age sixty-two, born in New York State, presumably in 1798. It also lists as his children Anna Crozet, age thirty-one, born in Pennsylvania; Marie Crozet (probably the "Mary Crozet" mentioned by Couper), age twenty-six, born in Philadelphia; and Adolphus Crozet, age twenty, born in Saint James Parish.

Crozet's father, François, was in Paris in 1814 when Crozet returned from Russia, but we have no knowledge of his whereabouts during the late 1790s, so his sojourning in New York—and thus William's birth there—is a possibility. If Claudius was in fact a resident of New York as a young boy, it could have been a factor in his decision to emigrate there in 1816. It may be that sometime after 1816 William followed him to America, married, and was living in Philadelphia when two children were born: Anna (1829) and Marie (1834). Perhaps William was drawn to move to Louisiana because Claudius was there. A third child, Adolphus, was born to the William Crozets in 1840, after Claudius had returned to Virginia. Anna married Felix Roman in 1846, when she was seventeen. Felix may have been one of the five sons of Governor Roman or the son of one of the governor's five brothers.³⁵ The census report of 1860 lists Felix Roman as a farmer in Saint James Parish. A sister of Crozet's, Eliza Crozet Magne, also lived in Saint James Parish, according to Couper. Neither she nor her two children, Marie and Paul Magne, are listed in the 1860 census report. Couper said that by then they had returned to France for a visit, which was more than likely extended by political events in America.

The sudden departure of Granet left the directors of the college with the problem of finding a new president. Their attention was drawn to Crozet for reasons that are not difficult to surmise. He was dissatisfied with his job as civil engineer, was possessed of impressive educational as well as engineering credentials, was a native of France, and had close personal contacts with Governor Roman, as well as Attorney General Etienne Mazureau and railroad president D. L. Burthe, directors who along with Roman were principal leaders in founding Jefferson College. Mazureau and Burthe were also native Frenchmen and had emigrated to Louisiana during the reign of Napoleon I.[36] "What some supporters of the College must have thought of the appointment of an ex-Napoleonic soldier as president of their school can only be imagined," remarked one historian.[37] But Crozet had no love for warfare, even though he had many soldierly qualities such as unrelenting self-discipline. In fact, he had come to detest Napoleon and regarded him as "finally a traitor to his country and to mankind," according to a friend of later years in Staunton, Virginia, John D. Imboden.[38]

Crozet notified the Board of Public Works in April 1834 of his intention to resign as civil engineer, and he probably completed the formalities of the transition in late summer 1834, in time for the fall session of the college. *Proviseur*, or president, of Jefferson College, Crozet also served as professor of mathematics. An "A. Crozet," perhaps Agathe, was professor of Latin and Greek.[39] While Crozet was there the student body numbered around 100, and it would rise within a decade to between 200 and 300. In 1835 the legislature voted $15,000 in state aid to the college for each of the next ten years, which was cut to $10,000 after eight years due to the economic downturn.[40]

Some insights into Crozet's work as president of Jefferson College may be gleaned from his correspondence with Huguer Jules de La Vergne, treasurer of the college, beginning in July 1835. The letters, in French, deal mostly with the problems of student financial accounts, yet occasionally there is a revealing remark. For one thing, it appears that from the beginning La Vergne and Crozet did not get along well. Some of the payments from parents were sent to La Vergne, some to Crozet, and La Vergne was distressed that Crozet did not turn over promptly to the treasurer the payments he had received. After reviewing his complaint and setting his terms, La Vergne wrote, "Si les conditions qui précèdent convenir, je continuerai à remplir les fonctions de Trésorer du Collège." Otherwise, he implied, he would resign.[41] The situation apparently did not change during Crozet's tenure of office, for La Vergne continued to append to his own accounts a separate "Comte de M. C. Crozet, Proviseur," listing students, amounts, and the balance due to the treasurer.

Crozet's dedication to Jefferson College was short-lived, perhaps because he became bored with the work. He stayed there only until the end of the second trimester in February 1836, a year and a half after his arrival, and was succeeded by Dr. Thomas R. Ingalls.[42] Crozet moved back to the house he owned in New Orleans, having accepted an offer from the city government to conduct a survey of street drainage problems. This choice alone indicates the depth of his dissatisfaction with Jefferson College. As civil engineer for the city of New Orleans, Crozet's task was to report to the council "on the intersections of those streets which are not graduated in a proper manner, and also to report if it is not preferable to have stone bridgelets built," that is, foot bridges across the gutters. Crozet found that at a number of locations pumping was necessary to keep sidewalks clear in heavy rains. As for pedestrian "bridgelets" across the gutters, "salubrity demands" that they should be of stone, said Crozet, even though they presented a hazard to turning vehicles at narrow corners, "by which frequent and serious accidents might result." Building storm drains under the streets was not practicable, with the water table barely under ground, so wide gutters along the sides of New Orleans streets were essential.[43]

When New Orleans was admitted to the Union in 1812, the state population was barely over 40,000, and that of the city of New Orleans, 18,000. By 1836 New Orleans alone had 80,000, a remarkable growth "notwithstanding we have been visited by pestilence that has swept off our inhabitants, and retarded others from settling here." The New Orleans *Bee* editor further exulted, "We think that a new era is about to commence. . . . and where does a wider field open itself than in the accomplishment of schemes for Internal Improvement. The days of planning must be converted into days of *action*."[44] Unfortunately, the delaying of action had extended through a period of prosperity and economic growth, and a new depression and decline were just around the corner.

The Whig party remained in power in spite of the panic of 1837, and in 1839 A. B. Roman was elected to a second term. In his inaugural address delivered on 7 January 1840, Roman told the legislature, "The greater part of the public works are languishing in our state for want of funds sufficient to complete them." He urged a $2 million bond issue for the purpose, by means of which the legislature could "contribute by liberal subscriptions to the success of those that are considered the most useful to the country, and thus establish the great line of communication which ought to be opened to procure to the products of the interior parishes an easy access to the Mississippi."[45]

The priorities had not changed: access to the Mississippi was still the first order of business in Louisiana's concept of internal improvements, while interstate railroad lines languished in distant second place. But Louisiana's problem was far behind Crozet when Roman delivered his second inaugural; by then he had returned to Virginia and was dealing with the effects of the economic downturn there upon that state's internal improvements program.

6

Return to Virginia as Principal Engineer, 1837–43

Crozet's experience in Louisiana was a bitter disappointment. As state engineer, he had been forced to waste time in clearing bayous for sugar and cotton planters to have access to the Mississippi River. The legislature paid little heed to the important project of building a railroad to Washington via the Tennessee River valley and Virginia. His brief time at Jefferson College was no real improvement; although he enjoyed classroom teaching, school administration was not to his liking. On top of all this, his health had been impaired by the miasmic climate. On the point of returning to France, he received a letter from Governor David Campbell of Virginia inviting him to return to his old job as principal engineer, and he accepted gladly.[1]

One may only speculate upon the reasons why the legislature did not protest when the governor, a native of Botetourt County in western Virginia, recalled Crozet. During 1832–35 the James River Company had been reorganized as the James River and Kanawha Canal Company, refinanced with two-fifths of its capital from private sources and three-fifths from the state government, and established in political ascendancy with Joseph C. Cabell at its head. In 1837 Crozet was no longer perceived as a threat to the company, so it could risk his reappointment as state engineer and allow the state to benefit from his unquestioned talents. Railroads were proliferating as never before, and several lines of long, state-constructed turnpikes were under way. The company and its advocates in the legislature probably believed that Crozet could attend to these projects and leave the James River and Kanawha Canal alone.

"It is with heartfelt satisfaction that, after an interruption of six years, I address you again in the same official capacity as formerly, and especially under circumstances so much more promising," Crozet wrote Governor Campbell. Virginia, he said, "has been awakened to her true and great interests, and an active spirit of improvement has now taken the place of her former indifference."[2] His enthusiasm was justified in as much as the James River Canal was under construction and the state had chartered a number of railroads and invested state money in their stock during his absence. Moreover, Crozet added, "I feel happy at the prospect offered me of carrying to a successful completion some of the important projects at the birth of which I have assisted."

One thing had not changed: the legislature still had no intention of allowing control of Crozet's work to slip from its hands. Virtually every report on a public work that he wrote from 1837 on began with the statement, "This survey [or location, or examination] was made in obedience to an act of [date]." Consequently, he felt little compunction about lecturing the legislature on what he perceived as its misguided priorities in the cover letter preceding every annual report to the board.

Having failed to interest Louisiana in initiating a New Orleans-to-Washington railroad, Crozet resumed efforts to promote the project from the Virginia end and received some encouragement from Tennessee. In 1836 Tennessee had ordered a railroad survey "from the most eligible point on the Mississippi river, to run through the centre of the state, as near as practicable, to the Tennessee river; from thence ... to terminate on the Virginia line."[3] Crozet warned the legislature in 1837 that if Virginia "suffers the great rail-roads, branching off at or near Knoxville, to draw the share of trade to which she is justly entitled, towards Charleston, Savannah and New Orleans, it may not be an easy matter afterwards to turn back the current from the channel it will have formed for itself."[4] Lest the James River Canal people regard him as their adversary, he acknowledged that "the Kanawha route will exercise its influence on the central states, Kentucky, Ohio, &c," while the Virginia and Tennessee railroad would draw "nearly all the land travelling from Georgia, Florida, Alabama, Mississippi, Louisiana, Texas, Arkansas and Tennessee." Crozet saw the Virginia and Tennessee railroad as potentially more valuable to the Old Dominion, but he wisely urged the development of both systems.

Unfortunately, the renewed spirit of enterprise that Crozet saw in Virginia was suddenly dampened by an economic depression that followed the panic of 1837. The business cycle oscillated at first, but after 1839 its trend was downward, and the Virginia government became increasingly deficit conscious. As of 1 January 1839, the state owed over $5 million for internal improvements, with annual interest of $285,000, more than the income from all improvements combined.[5] In December 1839 Governor Campbell reported that against an income of $178,000, charges of $367,000 left a deficit of $189,000. "No rational expectation can be entertained" that "the internal improvements in which the state has embarked will for a long time, if ever," produce enough revenue to be self-sustaining, he lamented. He urged the legislature to provide at least for the punctual payment of interest on the debt, and he deplored the "utter impracticability" of getting loans abroad. Crozet feared that, as Governor Campbell said, "the pecuniary embarrassments of the country may, by paralyzing the resources of our wealthy citizens, check the spirit of enterprise." Crozet added, "Virginia possesses probably the best harbour in the Union; to this estuary let all her commerce be made to converge." The Virginia government also should focus its attention on transportation lines that reached other states, Crozet urged. Extend the James River line by some means to the Ohio River and the railroad to Tennessee. "It is not a general and extensive system which is objectionable; the small unconnected works alone are unproductive, and become ruinous if too multiplied."[6]

Campbell's successor in 1840 was Governor Thomas W. Gilmer, a native of Albemarle County who "began his administration by inspecting the state's roads, schools, canals, railways and other facilities at his own expense." Gilmer also complained that the state had put too much money into a plethora of small and unconnected works which produced little revenue. "Although many of them have undoubtedly contributed much to the improvement of the secluded regions of the west," wrote Gilmer, "it is beyond a doubt that a wasteful and unnecessary expenditure has frequently been incurred in their construction." Moreover, the state proxies on the companies' boards of directors, who were local residents responsible for attending to the interest of the state government, usually neglected their duties, "the whole business of the improvements being in the mean time under the control and management of a president, treasurer, or some other officer originally appointed in a regular manner, but after a while acting without accountability."[7]

Control by the Board of Public Works had diminished during Crozet's absence in Louisiana. Crozet's field operations during the year 1840 comprised merely "duties prescribed by the legislature." It sent him to survey the Shenandoah River, a project he abandoned as soon as possible as a waste of time. He spent more time than he wished on the Staunton and Parkersburg road and the Northwestern Turnpike, especially on a bridge at Romney. He wanted more time to examine railroads in neighboring states "in order to settle the question of the intrinsic merits of the system in general, about which public opinion is as yet so uncertain and diversified." Continuing to urge a decision by the legislature on the route to Tennessee, he suggested that if the state could not build a railroad at this time, let it build at least a macadamized turnpike as had been done in the Valley. It was 1846 before the legislature finally appropriated $300,000 to build the Southwestern Turnpike from Salem to Tennessee.[8] Still later, in 1849, the legislature at long last incorporated the Lynchburg and Tennessee Railroad, later renamed the Virginia and Tennessee.

In 1840 retrenchment was the main concern of the legislators. In his next annual report, dated 29 November 1841, Crozet lectured the legislators for eight pages in small print on the basic economics of transportation. His main concern was that they would overdo retrenchment in the face of the worsening depression and thereby allow works in progress to deteriorate. "It appears to me that there never was a greater necessity for consolidating the system heretofore pursued, and perfecting the work already commenced," Crozet wrote. "I am aware of the difficulty under existing circumstances, of raising the necessary means, but I am equally impressed with the importance of saving, by new investments, the system from the losses inherent to short and inefficient lines of public works." As for his current view of railroads versus canals, Crozet elaborated:

> In speaking of the superior modes of improvement, I have placed railroads and canals upon an equality . . . because . . . it is my full conviction that *under the same circumstances of location*, there is in the two systems a parity of necessary expenses. . . . In 1831, shortly after the invention of the locomotive engine, I . . . expressed without hesitation a preference for railroads. . . . My faith was subsequently shaken, when the many errors and consequent losses which attended the first steps of the system, discouraged a great number of its friends; but more recently, such have been the improvements introduced in the road bed, the motive power, cars and management that railroads are rapidly regaining the public favour.[9]

The public, said Crozet, "judged from the material fact alone of success and profits," which was "eventually safe, for it will ultimately correct itself." Crozet's ambivalence on the subject of railroads versus waterways undoubtedly was conditioned by political expediency, for the James River and Kanawha Company was powerful, and Crozet dared not challenge its leaders too openly. It is appropriate at this point to examine briefly and evaluate each of the three systems that had been developed in Virginia by the early 1840s: waterways, railways, and finally roads and turnpikes.

Waterways were an important part of the state's transportation system. Some still believed them the most important part, with the James River and Kanawha Company playing the role of centerpiece, or matrix, of the whole. Branches that fed into the James and that received state support during this period included the North River Navigation (Lexington to Balcony Falls), and the Rivanna Navigation (Charlottesville to Columbia). Other waterways that received state support included such widely spaced projects as the Monongahela River Navigation (Weston-Morgantown-Pittsburgh), the Princess Anne Canal (Norfolk to Currituck Sound), the Lower Appomattox Navigation (Petersburg to James River), and the Upper Appomattox Company (Farmville to Petersburg).

When Crozet left Virginia for Louisiana in 1832, the legislature had just decided to go ahead with the James River Canal rather than the railroad from Richmond to the Ohio advocated by Crozet. When the state agreed to subscribe to three-fifths of the reorganized James River and Kanawha Company's stock, instead of two-fifths, in 1835, the enterprise was under way.[10] By the time Crozet returned to Virginia in 1837 the canal was progressing westward from Richmond, but he was not asked to examine it until 1840. He then examined "the whole line from the North River down to Richmond," in company part of the way with principal assistant engineer E. H. Gill and on the remainder with other engineers.[11]

In his seventeen-page report Crozet noted that at the west slope of the Blue Ridge, where the North (now Maury) River flows into the James, the old Blue Ridge Canal thence carried boats through the James River gorge. "The old canal is to be enlarged from 30 to 40 feet," Crozet noted, "and deepened from 3½ feet to 5 feet." At the east end, the canal was to be extended another mile and a half, a move he had "judged proper" in 1824. "Along this pond a tow-path is in progress, protected outside by a stone paving or rip-rap, some of which being round river stones, I fear will not stand." He found the same construction along the next pond. Short canals circumvented the six dams between North River and Lynchburg. "This section I always conceived to be the most difficult of the whole line," he recalled. "Here is a great fall, hardly any suitable soil for a canal, much rock, and frequently bad foundations for permanent works. A continuous canal of the dimensions adopted by the company would have cost enormously, in all probability not less than $60,000 per mile, or about $1,200,000 for the whole distance between Lynchburg and Irish falls, instead of an expenditure of about $450,000, at which I estimate the present plan."

The James River Canal had been just completed from Richmond to Lynchburg, and the water was about to be turned into it. The canal was on the south side of the James from Lynchburg to Joshua's Falls, 10 miles downstream, where it crossed to the north side for the remainder of the distance to Richmond. It was not a continuous canal the entire way but made use of ponds backed by dams at several locations, especially where there were cliffs along the north bank. Crozet noted errors in location, but "few in comparison with the length of the line." In the 146 miles between Lynchburg and Richmond there were fifty-one lift locks, six guard locks, and one accommodation lock for access to the Southside. Some of the locks, he noted, had been cheaply built with dry walls faced with planks, and they bulged into the lift chamber. Some were built entirely of stone, but even these were faulty, with stone batters inside the chamber, "which increases unnecessarily the draft of water in filling the lock. A straight perpendicular wall is the correct plan." There were 202 aqueducts and culverts, of varied quality. The 133 bridges over the canal, necessitated by the 5-foot depth, were all built on the same plan except for a stone bridge at Lynchburg. "The superstructure of wood is simple and has a neat appearance," said Crozet, but he found the substructure hazardous to passengers and crew on canalboat decks, with its minimal allowance for clearance.

The cost of building the canal to Lynchburg had been $4.8 million, or nearly $33,000 per mile, considerably in excess of Wright's estimated cost of less than $20,000 per mile. It was not so much the fault of management, Crozet believed, as that the cost had been underestimated in the first place. He reminded the board that his own estimate in 1831 was $28,000 per mile, and prices had increased since then. He did not think the company was charging enough for tolls, with only about 100,000 tons of traffic between Richmond and Lynchburg. "It is only when it shall have penetrated to the farther extremity of the state, and secured to Virginia the vast business which belongs to her from her geographical position, that its benefits will be truly realized. A partial improvement amounts to a positive sacrifice of wealth and power." A year later, in October 1841, the tolls still had not been increased.[12]

If Crozet advocated a position, Joseph Cabell could be assumed to oppose it. Although Cabell never publicly criticized Crozet, he spoke his mind freely in letters to his friend General Cocke. In March 1841 Cabell wrote from his home at Warminster to Cocke, then sojourning in Alabama, about Crozet's report on the canal. "Crozet's objections to various points on our line of works covers only 17 pages of letter paper manuscript," he began, tongue in cheek, and continued:

> He has, however, said a good deal in our favor, and has mixed up his censure and commendation so artfully as to leave the impression on the public mind that his report upon the whole is rather complimentary than otherwise. His aim has been to divest himself of the character of an enemy to the company, and at the same time to destroy public confidence in the skill of our engineers.... By his personal attention to the members, & the support of the Board of Public Works, he may retain his place for a year or two. But there are many members disposed to put down the office, and an effort was making when I left Richmond, but it will probably fail. He ought certainly not to be the Reporter on our line. We shall find him the eternal enemy of our Company. If you should read his report, you will discover how pointedly he flatters the Valley, northwest, southwest & Roanoke interest; that is, all the interests distinguished by hostility to our line.[13]

If Cabell himself viewed the Shenandoah Valley and Southwest Virginia as areas hostile to the James River and Kanawha line, he must have had a severe case of tunnel vision concerning the importance of the line. Evidence of hostility of either the Valley or the Southwest to the James River and Kanawha line is lacking in the records. Many regional and county internal improvement conventions in these areas during the 1840s urged its completion as well as that of other works perceived to be in their interest.

A major obstacle to completing the work above Lynchburg was the Blue Ridge Canal, which Crozet viewed again in October 1841. One-third of the new extension had been done, but the remainder was delayed for want of funds. "The work, unprotected and unattended to, may be swept by the stream in one of its high swells," he warned. "The present boatmen are no longer skilled in the navigation of this dangerous section of the river . . . and lives as well as property are exposed to even greater risks than in 1824." Let the company raise its tolls on the whole line by 50 percent, he suggested, and the additional $70,000 revenue per year would finance completion of all the work above Lynchburg to the North River in five or six years.[14]

In March 1842 Cabell reported his own concern about the work above Lynchburg and urged legislative support. "We have it in our power to form the most splendid combination of inland navigation on the face of the globe," he wrote Cocke. "Crozet is slily doing his best to defeat me. [Nicholas] Mills does the outdoor work of crying down the company in the streets." In another letter to Cocke he called Crozet "the Cato for the opposition."[15] He said nothing in his official report about Crozet, nor about the idea of increasing tolls. Cabell during the next several months prepared a report on his canal that was published on 1 October 1842, requiring forty-four pages in the annual reports of the board of public works. His elaborate argument contended that regardless of the damaging flood that year, canals were superior to railroads, and he urged a return to the all-water route between Richmond and the Ohio River.[16] Cabell disliked in particular the state's owning a railroad and engaging in the transport business. "A canal would find great embarrassment and difficulty in the management of a long line of railroad, with its vast train of equipments, agents, depots, shops and artificers, all of them foreign to the principal objects of the company's attention, and located, necessarily, at a considerable distance from the principal seat of its ordinary administration."

Cabell also reviewed the history of the James River Company, referring to a number of surveys made in the past, such as that by Moore and Briggs in 1819 and that by U.S. engineers in 1827, but never once did he mention Crozet or any of his several surveys and reports. Nor did he mention Benjamin Wright, who also had recommended a railroad west of Lynchburg.[17] Cabell's position led to a conflict with the company stockholders, who in December 1845 reaffirmed their prior vote in favor of a railroad for the western section. Although Cabell was reelected president, he declined and resigned in February 1846.[18]

West of Balcony Falls, the main line of the James River Canal went to Buchanan, while the North River Navigation line went to Lexington. The several milldams on the 20-mile route to Lexington should be circumvented by short canals, Crozet thought. A continuous canal would cost too much, so he recommended a combination involving three dams and five locks to negotiate the fall of 193 feet between Lexington and the James River. Twenty years later the company had spent over $350,000 in building this line, and it was beginning to collect a little revenue in tolls; to be exact, $643 for the year ending 30 September 1857.[19] The line was not completed to Lexington until 1860. The North River Navigation was a financial dead loss, from beginning to end, but it was useful; in 1859–60 more freight was carried on it than on the main line between Glasgow and Buchanan.

The Rivanna Navigation was old when Crozet first arrived in Virginia. The Rivanna flows by Charlottesville and southward through Fluvanna County into the James at Columbia. As late as 1838 Crozet was ready to recommend investing $20,000 in repairing locks and dams, but not until the company had decided whether its connection at Columbia with the James River Canal should be a feeder or a simple level canal. When the company decided on the latter in 1839, Crozet studied it more closely and found that the cost of over $60,000 "will be beyond the means of the company."[20] The North River Navigation had the backing of the James River and Kanawha Company, but the Rivanna did not, so the latter was allowed to deteriorate.

Virginia's waterways during Crozet's second tour of duty as principal engineer, in sum, were showing evidence of having reached the limit of their potential. The same could not be said of railroads, although for a time during the 1830s Crozet had some doubts about them. Crozet found some railroads already under construction when he returned from Louisiana. One was the Richmond and Fredericksburg, later renamed Richmond, Fredericksburg and Potomac. When he rode on it in 1837, he remarked that "excessive rocking of the cars indicated a derangement in the level of the rails, in consequence of the settling."[21] Two years later he decided there was more involved than the "settling."

> Experience has fully demonstrated the inadequacy of flat rails fastened upon wooden sleepers, especially of oak, to bear the action of heavy engines moving with great velocities: under such a weight the narrow and thin bar yields and sinks into the wood; the sills themselves resting in the present instance upon the natural ground, sink and rise alternately, and ultimately settle very irregularly. . . . In passing over so uneven a surface the train rocks and undulates to the reciprocal injury

both of superstructure and vehicles. . . . The H rail resting on cross sills of good timber, laid from 2½ to 3 feet apart, is the only plan to be depended upon. . . . I think it would be true and sound economy to substitute a heavy iron track to the light plate rail superstructure, which has unfortunately been chosen for all the railroads in Virginia, and is the chief cause of the difficulties under which the companies labour at present.[22]

The line still ran only between Richmond and Fredericksburg in 1840, and Crozet reported it "a well ascertained fact" that the railroad lacked patrons because of the hiatus between Fredericksburg and the Potomac. Moreover, the roadbed continued to be "repaired with flat rails, though edge rails obtain now a general preference."[23] By 1842 the line had been extended north of Fredericksburg 14 miles to Acquia Creek, on the Potomac, still 30 miles downstream from Washington. Water transport completed the route to the District of Columbia, so the name Richmond, Fredericksburg and Potomac was justified even though the remaining 30 miles from Acquia Creek to the District were not traversed by rails until after the Civil War.

Running south from Richmond was the Richmond and Petersburg Railroad, built to connect the capital with Virginia's pioneer railroad, the Petersburg Railroad.[24] The R&P Railroad had the same "thin, brittle" iron, which Crozet thought inadequate. The Petersburg Railroad, which ran to Weldon, N.C., on the Roanoke River, was begun before Crozet left for Louisiana. The high cost of carrying freight on these early railroads inclined them to favor passenger traffic and to secure government contracts for carrying the mail. The Petersburg Railroad made a contract with the Post Office Department to carry "both the great and express mails, by one and the same train, at $300 per mile." Its eight English locomotives and 120 cars carried cotton, tobacco, grain, and flour, bringing in about $60,000 from shippers. Passengers paid around $33,000 in fares, and the Post Office nearly $12,000 for mail service. Against costs of operation of around $60,000, it was a profitable business. Crozet was impressed with the competence of the managers of the Petersburg Railroad.[25]

Petersburg, Portsmouth, and Weldon form a triangle of about 80 miles on each side. Portsmouth also extended a railroad line to Weldon, the Seaboard and Roanoke Railroad, which Crozet examined in 1840. He took issue with the tendency of railroads to favor passenger over freight traffic, urged expansion of freight transport, and offered some analysis. The road was 79 miles long; during the year the engines traveled 104,240 miles on it, making 1,320 trips. The total weight carried was about 10,000 tons, including travelers, which was an average load of only 7½ tons per trip. Cost per ton-mile came to 7.8 cents. Had the engines, with the capacity to pull 60 tons, pulled an average load of 40 tons per trip, cost per ton-mile would have been reduced to 1.7 cents.[26] Historian Peter C. Stewart asserts that Petersburg, Norfolk, and Portsmouth lost ground to rival Richmond because of their inferior railroad development.[27]

Running westward from Taylorsville, a point just north of Richmond on the RF&P, was the Louisa Railroad, incorporated in 1832. By the time Crozet returned from Louisiana in 1837, it was operating from Taylorsville to Frederick's Hall Depot, 22½ miles west, and was being extended to Gordonsville. Just before Crozet's return, the Virginia legislature on 30 March 1837 passed an act requiring a survey of the route for a railroad from Gordonsville across the Blue Ridge at Simmons Gap, a few miles south of Swift Run Gap, to Harrisonburg. Crozet made the survey in the summer of 1838 but offered no encouragement. "Although I know but few mountains that cannot be graded for the use of locomotives," he reported, "I must rank this pass among the number. It is so broken and irregular that even inclined planes for stationary engines are hardly practicable."[28]

Crozet, assisted by William B. Thompson, made another survey in 1839 for extending the Louisa Railroad across the Blue Ridge. This time he reported that the "most favorable pass is at Rockfish gap. A tunnel of about one mile will save the grading of an elevation of upwards of 400 feet on both sides, that is about 14 miles of distance which would be much more expensive and otherwise objectionable than the tunnel." The ridge could be overcome by resorting to a plan "which I am surprised has not yet been used in passing ridges. It consists in successive tacks made where curves would be too abrupt by stopping the whole train on a level landing of sufficient length and then reversing the motion and entering the retrograde track by means of a switch as practised at turnouts. An engine at each end of the train will render these successive tackings a very simple operation, and the double power will authorize steeper grades.... By the application of this plan we can cross the Blue Ridge." During the winter months Crozet refined and elaborated his report on this project, presenting some estimated cost figures: tunnel, 4,475 feet long, $297,000; railroad per mile on the mountain, $53,020; railroad east of Staunton, $20,600 per miles; east of Mechum's River, $15,400 per mile. "Of the propriety of extending the Louisa Railroad to Charlottesville, there cannot be the least doubt," he concluded. "As regards the passage of the Blue Ridge, it is sufficent for the present that its feasibility has been ascertained. . . . And it is very evident that the present business of the road would not pay a reasonable return on so large an expenditure. . . . It is only as an object of state policy that it could be undertaken."[29] In exactly ten more years, Crozet would be invited by the state to direct the construction of this daring project as a publicly financed enterprise.

Crozet had his opportunity to examine the Baltimore and Ohio Railroad in 1841. "This great work has been in the United States the pioneer of the new system of improvement," he told the Board of Public Works. "To the energy and enterprise of Baltimore, the whole country is greatly indebted." The section between Baltimore and Harpers Ferry had been open for several years, and the new section between Harpers Ferry and Cumberland was expected to be open in 1842, beginning with the curved bridge crossing the Potomac into Virginia at Harpers Ferry. Crozet complimented Benjamin H. Latrobe, who had headed the work from its beginning, on his "readiness in adopting improvements." Crozet added, "Besides viewing the road, I went through the various shops, and never felt more gratified. . . . Almost everything is done there by machinery: even the planing, tenons and mortises of timber, and the whole is under [the] excellent management [of] James Murray."

The B&O was then using twenty-eight locomotives, four of them on the Washington branch, weighing from 10 to 14 tons. The company was switching to 20-ton engines with eight driving wheels capable of pulling 150 tons on the 82.5-foot-per-mile grades at 6 miles per hour. The average speed of freight trains was 10 mph, of passenger trains 18 mph. The average charge for freight was 5½ cents per ton-mile and for passengers 5 cents per mile, except on the Washington branch where it was 6¼ cents. Crozet presented tabulated figures showing the cost of 3.507 cents per ton-mile for the year ending 30 September 1840 and 3.934 cents for the year ending 30 September 1841, the increase "evidently due to the diminution of travelling this year." Crozet apologized to the board for the length of his report on the B&O Railroad, but, he said, "I had to oppose what I conceived to be a prevalent error," that railroads could not carry freight economically, "and it could not be done without affording the means of verification . . . and no work affords safer and more ample and carefully registered data than the Baltimore and Ohio rail-road, where alone I have found distinct accounts for burden and passengers."[30] The B&O Railroad was opened to Cumberland in 1842, 178½ miles from Baltimore.

Connecting with the B&O Railroad at Harpers Ferry was the Winchester and Potomac Railroad, already in operation when Crozet returned from Louisiana. In March 1837 the new B&O viaduct across the Potomac at Harpers Ferry completed the connection to Winchester. When Crozet examined the Winchester and Potomac four years later, in October 1841, he found it competently managed but underused, a mere 18,000 tons of freight for the year costing the road 8.5 cents per ton-mile against income of only 7 cents. There had been crop failures in the Shenandoah Valley and lead from the mines of southwestern Virginia was now diverted to the James River Canal, but that was not all. "Had the railroad been extended up the valley instead of the turnpike, the situation of this work would now be much better," Crozet asserted. "The want of sufficient tonnage alone is the necessary cause of high charges here, as elsewhere."[31] But a railroad up the Valley from Winchester was just what the James River and Kanawha Company did not want, and the company prevented its construction for many years.

By the end of Crozet's second tour as principal engineer in 1843, no real network of railroads was materializing in Virginia to bind the several sections of the Old Dominion together. Railroads emanated from Richmond northward, southward, eastward, and westward; but other than the Winchester and Potomac, not one mile of railroad was built west of the Blue Ridge, let alone in the Trans-Allegheny. Moreover, the Winchester and Potomac was blocked in its development by the jealousy of the James River and Kanawha Company. The Lynchburg-to-Tennessee line, which Crozet envisioned as the most vital railroad in the state, was shelved for the duration of the lengthening depression. Fortunately, times would change, and in the late 1840s a new surge of support for railroads would appear, even in the legislature. Crozet would find a place in this renewal, but not as principal engineer of the state.

Meanwhile, a third form of transportation line, the turnpike, requires at least brief attention for the period 1837–43. Crozet was a firm advocate of good roads, although he questioned the efficiency of collecting tolls for maintenance, let alone for construction. He urged the building of long roads to the western borders of Virginia as a preliminary move until a waterway or railroad could be built. Three important ones that crossed the Trans-Allegheny were the Northwestern Turnpike, the Staunton and Parkersburg Turnpike, and the Kanawha Turnpike. Crozet was familiar with every foot of the first two of these roads from their inception, and the third from an early date.

The Northwestern Turnpike, built at state expense, had been urged by Crozet in the 1820s and was finally supported by the legislature in 1831. The road went from Winchester 235 miles west to Parkersburg, essentially the present-day U.S. 50. When Crozet returned to the area in 1837, he traversed the work as far as Clarksburg before illness turned him back, and for the most part he liked what he saw. The legislature had directed him to report "what portion of the road ought, in his opinion, to be M'Adamized, and what additional width ought to be given to said road, &c." He found only 7 miles in detached portions that required capping with stone and judged the Northwestern Turnpike generally wide enough for a road through a new country. However, several bridges were not high enough over the streams. "It appeared to me that . . . these sites were purposely fixed at narrow places: I question whether real economy attends such a selection any where. At a narrow point, the stream must rise higher." Overall, he declared the Northwestern Turnpike "the best as yet made in the state" and predicted it would encourage inhabitants to remain in Virginia and farm.

In general, Crozet thought the practice of condemning one acre of ground for a tollhouse was a mistake, because the percentage of tolls allowed could not support a family. It would be better to buy several acres, let the tollkeeper provide room and board for a few travelers, and incidentally control enough land to "prevent the turning of gates." Toll collection had problems enough under the best circumstances, he added, noting that some of the heaviest users paid nothing. "Free roads, under a general road law, would be the only way to obviate the loss resulting from this unfair practice."[32]

After the Northwestern Turnpike was opened all the way to Parkersburg in 1839, the price of land along it rose from four to ten times its original value. Not only did rising land values check emigration, but the road attracted "a great number of enterprising Pennsylvanians" who moved in and settled. "The Northwestern turnpike," reported Crozet, "begins to be known to travellers as probably the most convenient route to the west." Construction had cost $196,000 ($835 per mile), for a roadbed from 20 to 22 feet in width. A road 15 feet wide, said Crozet, "is, when well shaped, quite sufficient for two wagons; a greater width affords no corresponding advantage, until 22 feet is attained, this being the width requisite for 3 wagons, so that a wagon occupying the centre may then not prevent a lighter vehicle from passing on either side."[33] A stage line was established on it in 1838 and was scheduled to become a double daily line in 1839 if the recommended portions that needed stone capping were finished, so that the road would be "passable in all seasons."

Keeping the road in good repair was a perennial problem. Some believed the most economical way was by contracts with residents along the line, but Crozet disagreed. "I have ascertained," he said, that with state road agents "we can keep it in order for even less than $50 per mile, or very nearly $12,000 for the whole distance, whereas at the rate of even the lowest bid, we should have to pay $18,000, and it is permitted to doubt whether the road would be as well kept." Crozet examined the road again in 1840 and was pleased that the "active and intelligent" superintendent, Josiah D. Wilson, had been given charge of the entire line. Wilson hired maintenance agents at the cost of $29 per mile, while the average offer of private contractors was $105 per mile, thus saving $17,860.

The Staunton and Parkersburg Turnpike, which Crozet had surveyed in the early 1820s, finally received serious attention from the legislature in 1837. This road never became one of the major federal highways in the twentieth century as did the Northwestern Turnpike and the third side of the triangle, the Valley Turnpike linking Staunton and Winchester, which became U.S. 11. Probably the main reason was the difficulty of the ground it traversed. Crozet conferred with Joseph Reid Anderson, Staunton and Parkersburg Turnpike superintendent in 1837–38, about the location and decided on "pretty nearly the same track as in 1826" as far as Tygart's Valley. Beyond that point, Crozet hired D. B. Gretter to "explore the country as far as Parkersburg," the total distance being between 220 and 230 miles from Staunton.

In Crozet's opinion the 92-mile gap between the eastern terminals of the Northwestern and the Staunton and Parkersburg turnpikes was "too far, and the valley in which Franklin and Moorefield are situated wants the facilities of improved communication," as did Warm Springs and Huntersville. In southwestern Virginia, he pointed to the Price's Turnpike and Cumberland Gap Road together with the proposed Lynchburg-to-Tennessee railroad as being "calculated, I think, to strengthen the bonds of union, and increase the combined resources of the different parts of the state." Some good roads were needed east of the Blue Ridge as well, he asserted, but he hesitated to urge any particular route "as the creation of a railroad might interfere with its prospects."[34] The prospect of railroads in the Trans-Allegheny was too remote to require such circumspection.

In 1840 the Staunton and Parkersburg road was at last under construction. The next year Crozet reported that it had been completed 26¾ miles west of Staunton and 25 miles east of Parkersburg, plus portions in between totaling 73½ miles. He still was not satisfied with the location between Tygart's Valley and Weston and found the road needed more bridges than expected. "The western streams rise so high and float so much timber and ice, that the bridges require all much elevation and long spans." Moreover, there were problems in obtaining land for tollgates. "Few persons are willing to sell one acre, and a resort to condemnation never fails to produce high prices; it is not unfrequently cheaper to purchase amicably several acres than to condemn one." In September 1842 Crozet called the 93 miles from Staunton to Tygart's Valley "an excellent road."[35]

A third long road westward was the Kanawha Turnpike, starting at Covington and ending at Guyandotte (Huntington) on the Ohio River, essentially today's U.S. 60. Crozet had spent much time and labor on its location west of Charleston during the late 1820s, and he saw it again in May 1837. Starting at the Ohio River and traveling eastward, Crozet found it in "good order" as far as Big Sewell Mountain (Rainelle). But shortly after Crozet's inspection, the sky virtually fell in. "The rains fell upon the 14th and 15th May," reported Joseph C. Cabell. "The Kanawha river rose 25 feet in the course of one night," sweeping away the road "for considerable distances," along with "eleven important bridges." Six weeks of concentrated effort were required for the James River and Kanawha Company to put the road and bridges back in order. Crozet did not see the road again until he examined the whole line of the James River improvement in 1840 and pronounced it "in good travelling order." "The Great Greenbrier bridge, now 14 years old, is yet in fine condition," he said, "the pride of western Virginia."[36]

The legislature sent Crozet to examine twenty other turnpikes in the period 1837–43, all of them located west of the Blue Ridge, eight of them in what is now West Virginia. Only two of the twenty extended from the Valley eastward across the Blue Ridge: the Staunton and James River, from Staunton to Scottsville on the James, and the Pittsylvania, Franklin, and Botetourt Turnpike, essentially today's U.S. 220 from Martinsville to Fincastle. A brief look at three of the twenty provides a reasonably complete spectrum: the Staunton and James River, the Lexington and Covington, and the Valley Turnpike.

The Staunton and James River Turnpike opened in 1831, crossing the Blue Ridge at Rockfish Gap (Afton Mountain) and descending it to Scottsville, thus providing access to the James River navigation for Valley farmers. Crozet viewed it in June 1840, when it was undergoing repairs. "Now that the James river canal reaches beyond Scottsville, I should consider a re-location of the worst part, and stone capping most expedient, so as to allow of much larger loads," he observed. "Of what advantage, otherwise, will the Valley turnpike be in this direction, if the same loads cannot continue from it to Scottsville?" By 1842 both the James River Canal to Lynchburg and the Valley Turnpike had been completed, but Crozet judged the condition of the Staunton and James River Turnpike "not commensurate with its increased importance."[37] This road was a purely private enterprise, assisted by the state only in its purchase of two-fifths of the original stock and dependent for income entirely on tolls. Gate turning by wagoners, poor management, winter ice, rains and floods, and other problems kept the company on the edge of bankruptcy, as were all but a few turnpike companies. In a geographical position to become a vital and prospering link between the Valley Turnpike and the James River Canal, the Staunton and James River Turnpike was unable to grasp the opportunity. The solution in time was the Blue Ridge Railroad, built by the state under Crozet's direction.

The road that connected the Kanawha Turnpike with the Shenandoah Valley was also a private turnpike company, the Lexington and Covington, chartered in 1831. The company had built it well, said Crozet, and the bridges were good and firm. "It is only to be regretted that so much skill of construction," he added, was "not bestowed upon a more favourable location." The ascent across North Mountain west of Collierstown, which Crozet had advised the company against, would remain forever a bottleneck to traffic because of its steep grade and sharp turns.[38] The principal engineer had no way of requiring the companies to accept his professional advice, much to his frequent dismay.

Joseph Reid Anderson, native of Botetourt County and member

of the West Point class of 1836, had resigned from the army in 1837 and accepted appointment as assistant engineer on the Staunton and Parkersburg road. The next year he went to the Valley Turnpike as its superintending engineer and built one of the most durable and renowned turnpikes in the nation, 92 miles from Winchester to Staunton. The twenty-five-year-old Anderson had a thousand men at work because the legislature backed the project solidly; the people of the Valley, of course, had wanted a railroad from Staunton to Winchester, where the existing Winchester and Potomac Railroad would connect Valley farms with the B&O Railroad and the Baltimore market. Richmond, thus threatened with northern competition, threw support to a first-class turnpike, which could never compete with a railroad or a canal in cost per ton-mile. In this way Richmond and Lynchburg protected their hold on the Valley trade.[39]

Anderson's specifications for the Valley Turnpike show that in every respect he was in complete agreement with Crozet. He accorded first priority to careful location of the line to obtain the best grades, ground, and exposure. He, like Crozet, asserted that "there is no part of the construction of a road more important to be well executed than its drainings," for water was even more damaging to the road than traffic. Well-made side ditches, cross drains, gutters, and culverts were indispensable to keep the surface as dry as possible. As for the macadamized surface, Anderson specified that when the road had "become settled and compact, it is to receive a covering of broken stone or metal, for a width of twenty feet, leaving on each side a space of two feet, called the shoulder, between the edge of the metal and the ditch." The average thickness of the broken stone was to be 9 inches, "put on at two different times in separate strata," the first 6 inches thick, and later, when the road "by the travel on it becomes sufficiently consolidated, the second stratum three inches thick is to be applied."[40]

When Crozet visited the Valley Turnpike the last day of August 1840, 70 miles of the 92 were finished. He noted the superiority of the surfacing but observed that it obviated the necessity for having built so many expensive culverts, apparently used in preference to gutters. "A stone-capped turnpike affords the greatest facility for making gutters, since the road, being covered with broken stones all along, open drains may be made of any size, without adding one dollar to the cost." The Valley Turnpike had cost $3,853 per mile, plus $29,000 for engineering services, labor, and land damages, plus another $31,000 for bridges—all told around $415,000. Crozet had estimated the cost in 1837 at $2,500 per mile, but labor costs had been increased by the "proximity of three great improvements, the Ohio and Chesapeake canal, the Baltimore and Ohio railroad, and the James river canal, and by the rapidity with which the work was pushed," in addition to the unneeded culverts.

Crozet was also concerned about maintenance of the road because some wagoners loaded as much as 9,500 pounds on their vehicles and did considerable damage. He urged that the Valley Turnpike be protected by requiring wagoners to use 4-inch tires. "From well established facts, each trip of such a wagon, loaded with 25 barrels of flour, will wear out the capping to the amount of about 1⅓ cents per mile; whereas, the same load, with tires of 2½ inches only, would occasion a wear of the surface of 2 cents per mile, an important difference, when the low rate of tolls is considered."[41]

In November 1842 President James Pennybacker of the Valley Turnpike Company reported to the Board of Public Works much trouble with the lattice bridges, three in particular, across Middle River, North River, and Shenandoah River. The last mentioned was completed in December 1841, but "discovering as we did . . . that the bridge would go down unless timely supported from below," the company withheld about $2,000 still due the contractor. The company then built two trestles about 30 feet from either abutment, but the bridge still sank between the trestles. Blocks and wedges were used to raise the bridge to its original height. Then came high water, the river rising "higher than it had been known for 30 years." At one o'clock in the morning the bridge broke in two, and half of it was carried downstream to lodge on an island. "We have decided on erecting another bridge," reported Pennybacker, "and through the politeness of Capt. Crozet we have received his suggestions of the plan of a substantial and cheap bridge." Crozet examined also the other bridges, weakened but not yet fallen, "and with a promptitude characteristic alike of the gentleman and man of business, furnished us with a detailed statement of what was proper to be done."

Reporting his experience with the Valley Turnpike to the Board of Public Works, Crozet said, "I am sorry that I have to report that all the wooden bridges have proved more or less defective; they were of the construction known as the lattice plan, the many defects of which have been so well demonstrated by numerous failures, that it is a matter of wonder that this plan is yet so often chosen. . . . Probably this plan has been favoured on account of its being within the comprehension and capacity of any common carpenter, which I would myself rather consider an objection, as it not unfrequently becomes a guarantee of inferior workmanship and a cause of failure." He then shifted his attention to the economics of turnpike transportation. The advantages of the turnpike, he said, could be best understood from some basic facts. A six-horse wagon on the old road could carry 18 barrels of flour from 16 to 18 miles per day; now a four-horse wagon could carry 24 barrels from 20 to 24 miles, and the wagon lasted longer. Two tons of pig iron formerly required five or six horses; now four animals could haul 3 tons. Crozet expected the average cost per ton-mile of hauling goods on the Valley Turnpike to be about 15 cents, which experience proved correct.[42]

The Valley Turnpike represented the ultimate in road transportation in the antebellum years. For long hauls, it could not compete with the railroad or the canal in cost per ton-mile, and the Valley was denied a railroad in order to protect the interests of the James River Canal. But the shorter turnpikes or public roads that connected producers with canals, railroads, or the main turnpikes were vital. In response to the pressures of logrolling, the legislature was forced to support the building of a large number of them in every region after the federal government's withdrawal of such support in 1830. Crozet spent much time examining such lines for location, grades, drainage, and other important attributes. He seldom complained about such duty in remote areas because even though he gave priority to long extended lines reaching to neighboring states, he still sympathized with the local farmer who lacked access to market. Crozet also urged the opening of still-virgin farmlands in the Trans-Allegheny by means of good roads. His task was enormous, and he did it well. From the viewpoint of the legislature, handing out funds for a multitude of turnpikes in the Trans-Allegheny was a means of quieting dissent in that section. Nevertheless, the Virginia General Assembly in March 1843 decided the office of principal engineer was no longer needed.

Governor John M. Gregory informed the legislature in his message of 5 December 1842 that during the fiscal year ending 30 September the state's income from turnpike, canal, navigation, and bridge companies had come to a mere $3,314, while the interest alone on the debt for internal improvements amounted to $353,320. With such a deficit, the Board of Public Works had to ask the state treasury for $238,500 in order to meet immediate demands. "When the country shall have recovered from the calamitous shock which has universally paralyzed its energies for several years past," Gregory wrote hopefully, some of these improvements "will in some degree reward their proprietors for their long continued exertions and sacrifices."[43] Retrenchment was the order of the day in the view of a majority of the legislators. In the spring of 1842 Crozet's annual salary of $3,000 was cut to $2,000. The report Crozet submitted to the Board of Public Works dated 7 December 1842 turned out to be his last. On 27 March 1843, just before he was to take to the field again, the legislature passed an act terminating the office of principal engineer, to be effective the same day. Crozet's salary up to that date was paid, and that was the end of it.[44]

What is to be said of Crozet's second tour of duty as principal engineer of Virginia between 1837 and 1843? In 1837 when he was brought back from Louisiana, the James River and Kanawha Canal Company was predominant in the field of internal improvements, and its leaders had little interest in Crozet's advice. Even so, by the early 1840s the company had become somewhat paralyzed by internal division and had difficulty in visualizing, let alone implementing, its reach westward. Cabell wanted an all-water route, while the stockholders, perhaps more wisely, wanted a railroad to penetrate the land west of Covington, if not west of Buchanan or even Lynchburg. Meanwhile, $350,000 of much needed funds were diverted up North River from Balcony Falls to Lexington. As a point of departure for the Kanawha Valley, Lexington was inferior to Covington; but it potentially could tap the Valley trade from Staunton more efficiently than the Staunton and James River Turnpike. In the end, neither the turnpike nor the North River Navigation was effective. The bulk of Valley produce moved down the Shenandoah Valley to Winchester.

The legislature, instead of allowing Crozet to concentrate his energies on lines of transportation leading to neighboring states, sent the principal engineer hither and yon surveying, locating, and examining routes of peripheral importance. They came to resent paying his high salary, especially during the worsening depression, and cut it by a third in 1842. It was their own fault, however, that they did not get more for their money, for his remarkable talents, energy, integrity, and concern for the public interest could have accomplished much more had the legislature not hobbled him by prescribing his every mission. In addition, when he finally was requested to examine the

James River Canal in 1840, he did so with a critical professional eye, as was appropriate, and clearly earned the hostility of Cabell and other friends of the canal. Crozet's ouster in March 1843 was passed off by the legislature as just another retrenchment measure, but it was obvious that retrenchment was not the only motive of those who voted to terminate the office of principal engineer. The hostility of the James River interest had prevailed against Crozet a second time.

The new chief executive of the state was soon aware that Virginia was the loser. Governor James McDowell of Lexington said in his first annual report as president of the Board of Public Works in December 1843, "The office of principal engineer being abolished, the superintendents having charge of the roads were called upon" to report their condition and estimate their needs. Moreover, during the summer of 1844 McDowell and other members of the board personally visited "each of the principal improvements . . . in order to supply to the extent of their ability the place of that indispensable officer." As a result, the governor was convinced that the General Assembly had made an egregious error in abolishing the office of principal engineer, and he told the legislature so.[45] The Virginia legislature, seldom inclined to admit mistakes, made no response.

After suddenly losing his job in March 1843, Crozet endured six essentially disappointing, worrisome years. He and Agathe shared a comfortable house in Richmond with their daughter Claudia, who had married Dr. Charles S. Mills, a physician and the son of Nicholas Mills, a prominent Richmond businessman. Their son, Alfred, graduated from West Point in 1843 and entered the army. Crozet had a number of close friends and some interesting work to do. Even so, there were times when he seriously considered leaving Virginia and returning to France.

7

The Academic Life Renewed, 1837–49

Upon his return to Virginia from Louisiana in 1837, Crozet became interested in a movement to convert the state arsenal located outside the village of Lexington into a military college. In later years, after the college had been established as the Virginia Military Institute, the superintendent of the school, Colonel Francis H. Smith, credited his professor of modern languages, Major John Thomas Lewis Preston, with having originated the idea, but Preston disclaimed this honor. Some writers have looked to Crozet as the architect of the school's academic program and military organization. Whatever the case, Smith and Preston were close associates of Crozet in the VMI enterprise, and all three are regarded as founders of the Institute.

Preston had published a series of letters in the Lexington *Gazette* in 1835 under the signature "Cives," proposing that a military college be established at the arsenal with the specific object being "to supply the place of the present [state] Guard, by another composed of young men, from seventeen to twenty-four years of age, to perform the necessary duties of a guard, who would receive no pay, but, in lieu, have afforded to them the opportunities of a liberal education." The General Assembly of Virginia, in response to this and other entreaties, passed an act on 22 March 1836 establishing a Board of Visitors for the new institution, but no further progress was made that year toward actually establishing the college. A second act, passed exactly a year later, led Governor David Campbell to appoint as members of this new board Colonel Crozet, General William Ligon, General George Rust, Jr., General Peter C. Johnston, and ex officio, Adjutant General of Virginia Bernard Peyton.[1]

Crozet's experiences as a student at the Ecole Polytechnique, as an officer in Napoleon's artillery corps, as a professor of engineering at the U.S. Military Academy, and as president of Jefferson College undoubtedly served to recommend him highly to the initial organizers of the new military college. The primary reason for his appointment to the first Board of Visitors may have been his position as principal engineer of the state of Virginia; there was a parallel with the U.S. Military Academy where the first superintendent was the chief engineer of the U.S. Corps of Engineers. However, there does not appear to have been any thought given to appointing Crozet to the post of superintendent of the new college.

The governor's letter dated 30 May 1837 announcing Crozet's appointment to the board informed him that it was considered "expedient for the Board of Visitors for the Military School to be established at Lexington . . . [to] convene at an earlier date than the first of September." Complying with the governor's wishes, the board met in Lexington on 7 August to enter into discussions with a committee appointed by the Board of Trustees of Washington College, also located in Lexington, regarding a proposal by the General Assembly that the new school should be "part and branch, under certain conditions, of Washington College." This arrangement had been included among the provisions of the original act of the General Assembly which reorganized the Lexington arsenal into a military school.[2]

At their first meeting, the visitors commenced their business by electing Crozet president. Then they dispatched a letter to the Washington College trustees, meeting nearby at the college, sounding them out on the question of a connection between the two schools. Two days later the visitors were pleased to receive a message from the trustees welcoming a reciprocal arrangement between the two schools whereby students of one might receive instruction at the other without charge; however, the trustees rejected outright the plan to make the military school "a part and branch of the college." Other problems quickly followed. For example, to the dismay of the Board of Visitors, close inspection of the old arsenal buildings revealed that the facilities were unsuitable for cadets and their professors. The difficulties that confronted Crozet and the other members of the board from all quarters worked quickly to dampen their initial enthusiasm. Reluctantly they informed the governor on 9 August that "we feel ourselves therefore compelled by these circumstances to suspend for a while the organization of the military school, yet entertaining a lively hope that the general assembly will place within our reach the means of bringing into existence the proposed institution." In his annual message to the General Assembly, Governor Campbell stated, "I entirely concur in the opinion of these highly intelligent gentlemen, that the state would derive great benefit from the permanent establishment of a military school . . . and that the appropriation proposed by the visitors for erecting additional buildings ought to be made."[3]

Two years elapsed before the General Assembly passed another act, on 29 March 1839, reorganizing the Lexington arsenal into a military school and providing funds sufficient for the undertaking. Shortly thereafter, the governor reappointed Crozet, Ligon, Johnston, and Peyton as visitors of the military school and expanded the board by adding General Thomas H. Botts and Lexington residents J. T. L. Preston, Hugh Barclay, Dr. Alfred Leyburn, Colonel Charles P. Dorman, and James McDowell. Leyburn and Dorman were influential members of the House of Delegates; McDowell recently had served in the house and would be elected governor of the state in 1843. Dorman was a member of the House of Delegates for nine terms, serving on the committee of schools and colleges and the committee on the militia laws. He had introduced the original bills, in 1836 and 1837, calling for the reorganization of the arsenal, and Leyburn had introduced petitions from Lexington citizens supporting this plan.[4]

When the board met again in Lexington on Thursday, 30 May 1839, Crozet was reelected president. By the afternoon of the next day, all the members of the board had arrived from their homes across the Commonwealth, and work began in earnest on the reorganization of the Lexington arsenal into a military college. The first order of business was the repair of the arsenal buildings. The board quickly resolved, "On motion of Doct. Leyburn . . . that Gen'l Botts & Col. Crozet be a committee to ascertain the extent of repairs necessary to be made at the public Arsenal, and prepare, and report a memorial addressed to the Governor of Virginia, asking that the necessary repairs be made by the Executive out of the contingent-fund."[5]

Meetings of the new board were held every day the following week, 3–8 June, to draft a set of "Rules and Regulations for the organization and government of the Institute." In his biography of Crozet, Couper credited him with having suggested the West Point regulations as the model for those of the new institution in Lexington, stating that the final draft of the VMI regulations reflects "throughout [Crozet's] connection with education at [West Point], the

Ecole Polytechnique, and in Louisiana." This general conclusion is probably correct; however, close inspection of the written regulations contained in the original minutes book suggests that a number of visitors participated in the drafting process and contributed ideas. While some of the pages of the draft regulations are unquestionably in the hand of Crozet, a number appear to be in the handwriting of Dorman and others. In the early minutes of the board, for example, there is a list of courses to be taught in the second year: mathematics, algebra, geometry, analytical geometry. This appears in the characteristically fine hand of Crozet. Above this line, Dorman inserted the following additonal courses: trigonometry, mensuration, descriptive geometry. It is a minor point, because Crozet brought to the group an impressive knowledge of the essential elements of military and engineering education which surely guided the group's deliberations; however, it is evident that Crozet did not determine the entire content of the regulations or the course of studies.[6]

At the same time that the board was occupied with establishing the curriculum and the rules and regulations of the new school, it considered the appointment of a principal professor to lead the institution. Crozet favored Joseph Reid Anderson, an 1836 honor graduate of West Point who was then directing the construction of the Valley Turnpike. With the board's approval, Crozet offered the post to Anderson, but he declined. In doing so, Anderson suggested the name of Francis H. Smith, an 1833 graduate of West Point who was known to Anderson from his cadet days and who was currently teaching mathematics at Hampden-Sydney College in Virginia. The board corresponded with Anderson and Smith, but the members remained undecided.[7]

At the end of the week of meetings in June that resulted in plans for the organization of the school, the board made its final decision regarding a principal professor. The son of Anderson, Joseph R. Anderson, Jr., later recorded a story that had been told many times and had been confirmed for him by Smith. The younger Anderson wrote that "some of the gentlemen of the Board canvassing the relative merits of *Mrs.* Smith and *Mrs.* Anderson, [were] urged by Crozet to quickly decide the question as to which one of these two charming ladies should be the *Superintendent* of the *Virginia Military Institute*." The minutes of 8 June 1839 show that "the Board proceeded to the appointment of a Principal Professor of the Institute. Whereupon Francis H. Smith of Hampden-Sydney College was unanimously elected." According to Anderson, Smith "had a great admiration for [Crozet], occasioned by the reputation he had made at West Point, which was familiar to Smith; and when he found [Crozet] had been made President of the Board, he knew that his influence would be a strong one, and that the new School would take West Point for its model . . . and, therefore, he accepted his election the more willingly." Crozet, in turn, must have been delighted to bring to the new school a West Point graduate who had excelled in mathematics.[8]

Also on Saturday, 8 June, the board appointed William Dold of Lexington as clerk of the board and commissioned him to prepare a "fair copy" of the minutes and regulations that had been drafted. When it was completed, this copy was sent to Crozet in Richmond, in care of William Kenney of Staunton, as a preliminary to final approval and printing, and Crozet reviewed it for errors. Before departing Lexington, the board resolved "That Gen'l Thomas H. Botts, Col. C. P. Dorman & Col. Claude Crozet, or either of them proceed to the city of Richmond and present to the Governor the memorials of this board, on the subject of the immediate repairs to the Lexington arsenal." Confident, then, that the enterprise was finally launched, the board concluded its business and adjourned.[9]

The work of 3–8 June 1839 had been a group effort, and all members could feel just pride in having played an active role in the establishment of the new institution. Much credit for their success must be given to Crozet as president of the board, for his broad experience and organizing talents can be seen throughout the deliberations. It was also a high-water mark for Crozet as a founder of VMI. From this moment on, although Crozet retained the presidency of the board until 1845 and his influence among its members and in Richmond was highly regarded, others began to determine the direction and development of the young institution. Occupied fully with his work as state engineer, Crozet slipped into the shadows of the history of VMI. For example, arrangements for the acquisition of military supplies, including caps from West Point, muskets, and two 6-pounders, were made by Peyton. Much of the correspondence with Francis H. Smith before he left Hampden-Sydney was conducted by Preston. After the opening of the Institute on 11 November 1839, the driving force was, and would remain for fifty years, Superintendent Smith. He and the local visitors transformed the vision of Crozet into the reality of bricks, mortar, blackboards, and gray-clad, gilt-buttoned cadets.[10]

One of the advantages in having a group of local visitors, namely Dorman, Leyburn, McDowell, Barclay, and Preston, was that they could meet as an executive committee to address concerns and issues requiring immediate attention. Another advantage was that their presence provided a local base of support for the new institution in a town not undivided in its attitude toward VMI. Meetings of the Lexington members to conduct VMI business, with or without other members present, rarely included Crozet.

Despite his rigorous and demanding schedule of work as principal engineer of Virginia, Crozet managed to attend most of the early meetings of the Board of Visitors. Beyond noting his presence, however, the minutes are silent regarding his specific contributions to the important deliberations that preceded the opening of the Institute. It is easy to imagine that other board members sought his advice on many questions. Certainly in the development of the curriculum, which in the early days emphasized mathematics and French, Crozet provided valuable recommendations. Many of the authors of the mathematics texts selected for the cadets had been his professors at the Ecole Polytechnique. Even more important was his belief, shared enthusiastically by Smith, that VMI should and could be more than simply a parochial military college training officers for the state militia. Both men envisioned the school becoming a source of teachers and engineers for Virginia and the rest of the South, as well as educated officers for local militia units. The written record contains few identifiable traces of Crozet's thoughts, suggestions, or actions. What it does show is that others, especially Dorman and Preston, and later Smith, played the leading role in preparing the new school to receive its first cadets and professors.

The board's work culminated in ceremonies held on 11 November 1839, when all its members assembled in Lexington with the newly appointed principal professor, Major Francis H. Smith, to receive and examine seventeen regular and six irregular (paying) cadets. Pleased with the academic proficiency and high spirits of these young men, the board proceeded to assume formal responsibility for the arsenal buildings. The minutes indicate that General Peyton was appointed by his colleagues "to receive from the Commandant of the Lexington Arsenal, the Grounds, Buildings, Arms, & all other property belonging to said Arsenal. Whereupon the board proceeded to said arsenal and having the same surrendered to them by the commandant, placed the Grounds, Buildings, Arms & other property in the hands of Maj. Francis H. Smith principal professor of the Va. My Institute." It may be assumed that Crozet witnessed these proceedings with great satisfaction.[11]

In the next six months Smith emerged as the central figure in the developing story of VMI. His voluminous correspondence reveals that the burden of the new institution was placed squarely on his shoulders and that he quickly assumed responsibility for it. The board, which adjourned on 13 November, did not meet again until 15 April 1840, when Smith presented his first quarterly report. Crozet was in the chair, and the only other members in attendance were the Lexington members. A month later the full board met with Crozet presiding to review the progress of the Institute and to examine the cadets in mathematics and French. The next meeting was held on 1 July 1841. This meeting, occurring in late June and early July, became a regular annual session of the board, and for a number of years it was the only formal meeting of the Board of Visitors.[12]

Because of his engineering work, Crozet was frequently in the field and unable to attend to Institute business. This was sometimes awkward for Smith, who was keenly aware of the need for dependable and timely communications with Richmond. When Smith submitted his first annual report to the governor on 11 November 1840, he directed it through General Peyton, noting, "Apprehending the absence of Col. Crozet I have directed it to you, that there may be no delay in its reception as it is proper it [should] be communicated with the Governor's message. Should Col. C[rozet] be in town will you do me the favor to hand it to him, & explain to him the reason of my not sending it to him directly." Learning that Crozet was in Richmond at the time, Smith hastened to send him a letter via Dr. Leyburn, explaining, "The letter I sent to Gen. Peyton to render its receipt more certain, in consequence of the apprehension that you should be out of the City. The state of our funds will appear good—that is we are above debt." Although relations between the two men remained warm, the press of business and the distances that separated them resulted in decreasing contacts after 1840.[13]

On one subject, discipline in the VMI corps of cadets, Smith made a point of keeping Crozet fully informed of serious infractions of the regulations. He sent his quarterly and annual reports to Crozet for submission to the governor, and he sent him various merit rolls of the cadets. Nevertheless, much of the business of the Institute was conducted by Smith directly with Dorman, Peyton, and, before long, with Captain William H. Richardson, who was appointed adjutant general of the state in 1842 after serving as state librarian for three years. Perhaps it is natural that this should have occurred because in the all-important political arena, although Crozet had much influence with the governor, he was no match for such members of the General Assembly as Dorman, Leyburn, Peyton, and Richardson. In the final analysis, it was in the political arena that the future of VMI would be assured or cut short.[14]

Money appropriations, the lifeblood of the Institute, were in the hands of the Virginia General Assembly, where VMI was championed by Dorman and Leyburn. Dorman corresponded frequently with Smith, informing him of events in the legislature and offering timely advice. At one critical moment he wrote, "The Doctor [Leyburn] & myself think it would not be proper to ask for a money appropriation at this Session. We shall struggle hard for the Library fund." There is no evidence that either of them consulted with Crozet, the board president, on this matter. However, when Crozet's influence was needed, board members did not hesitate to ask him to lobby for a particular project. When, for example, Smith tried in 1840 to obtain funding from the state auditor for publication of a mathematics textbook that he proposed to write, General Peyton reported, "I have . . . mentioned the subject to Crozet, who seems much pleased with the scheme, & I asked him to call at the [State] Auditor's office, read the letter, & urge it upon the Board [of the Literary Fund], which I will also do myself."[15]

When Crozet lost his job as principal engineer of Virginia in March 1843, Smith wrote to express his "regrets at the action of the legislature in reference to your office." Crozet was indeed embittered by the blow and planned to return to New Orleans where he owned property and had relatives. Angry with the Virginia legislature, he wrote Smith in the late summer of 1843, "I have been thrown aside as a common useless tool." He vowed, "I will depend altogether on myself and no longer on the judgment of public men." Bound by conscientious feelings of duty and a genuine concern for the welfare of VMI, he chose to attend the meeting of the Board of Visitors in late June and early July 1843 rather than Alfred's graduation at West Point. Alfred was commissioned a second lieutenant in the Seventh Infantry and was ordered to a post in New Orleans where he remained until 1845.[16]

Before leaving for New Orleans, Crozet wrote Smith to say, "I yield to the necessity of lightening my burden of books" and offered for sale to VMI over four hundred volumes of mathematics, philosophy, chemistry, military engineering, science, civil engineering, and literature, at a price of $1,384. "I must . . . get what funds I can without the losses which sales of stocks would produce at this time," he admitted. General Richardson "and other friends expect that justice will be done me by the next Legislature," he added. "I am not quite so Sanguine: I know how easy it is to tear down and how difficult to build up again, especially when an increase of the budget is involved."[17]

Crozet was right. The economy of Virginia and the nation remained depressed for months to come. He delayed his departure for New Orleans through the remainder of 1843 and all of 1844. He missed three minor meetings of the VMI Board of Visitors late in 1843 but did attend the regular annual meeting from 26 June to 4 July 1844, signing the minutes of the board for the last time. At the annual session of the Board of Visitors held on 30 June 1845, Crozet's active involvement with VMI ended altogether when "on motion of Gen'l Dorman, Gen. Johnston was elected president of the board."[18]

It was the end of Crozet's connection with the Institute, but it was not the end of Crozet's friendship or correspondence with Smith. The loss of Crozet from the Board of Visitors was deeply felt by Smith, who admired his accomplishments, his education in France, and his reputation as a teacher at West Point, and who greatly appreciated the support that Crozet had given him in his first years at the Institute. Smith wrote to Crozet in 1845, "I hope you will permit me to add that nothing has transpired since the establishment of the Institute, which its friends have more cause to lament, than your separation from it." He concluded this letter by saying, "I feel this perhaps more than any one else, for there were helps rendered by you in the duties which devolved upon me . . . which have always operated for the good of the school. Altho' the state of your adoption has not rendered you the credit to which your eminent services have entitled you, the time will come when your services in the organization and control of this favored institution of the state will be more generally known and appreciated."[19]

Because both men had received excellent training in mathematics, they corresponded on that subject from time to time during Crozet's period of unemployment. "During the hours of immense leisure, I am now burthened with," Crozet wrote Smith in 1843, "I have occupied myself with those Subjects best calculated to while away time." A detailed presentation of a mathematics problem in one of Crozet's finely penned letters delighted Smith, and he showed it to cadets in his class. For Smith, the presentation "was [a] most beautiful exemplification of the principles which I was endeavoring to impress on them [the cadets]." He told Crozet, "I will preserve it and value it highly."[20]

Crozet's avocation led him into a contract with Richmond publishing company Drinker and Morris, which published his textbook entitled *An Arithmetic for Colleges and Schools* in 1848. The book proved sufficiently popular that a second edition was published in 1858 by E. H. Butler and Company of Philadelphia. In the summer of 1846 Crozet wrote Smith about the latter's second edition of a translation of Jean Biot's *Descriptive Geometry*, offering suggestions for clarifying the subject for the reader. Aware that Biot was a professor of mathematics at the Ecole Polytechnique, where descriptive geometry had been taught by the inventor of the subject and Crozet's former teacher, Gaspard Monge, Smith especially appreciated these suggestions.[21]

In 1845 Crozet found a new position, as principal of the Richmond Academy. This academy, founded in 1803 and defunct by 1851, had a precarious career. The General Assembly enacted a statute in 1803 appointing a Board of Trustees for the academy consisting of the governor and twenty-three others, with authorization to raise funds and establish a "seminary of learning in or near Richmond." They raised over $3,000 by subscription and another $1,000 by lottery, then "made the fatal blunder of selecting the wrong site, outside the city limits in Henrico County, on a hill known afterwards as Academy Hill, a quarter of a mile beyond the city almshouse."[22] Ground was broken in spite of protests from many citizens about the location, the basement was built, and there the project stopped. Governor John Tyler's efforts to renew it in 1810–11 were in vain, and the site became "an unsightly ruin." Thomas Ritchie, editor of the Richmond *Enquirer*, tried his hand at reviving it in 1815, with the same results. Finally in May 1833, John Brockenbrough, new president of the Board of Trustees, persuaded the city council to guarantee a loan of $20,000 to get it started once more, on condition that it be relocated in the city. The site chosen was the southeast corner of Marshall and Tenth streets, and the school opened its doors in 1835, in debt, unsupported by the legislature, and dependent on tuition payments for income. Socrates Maupin, principal from its opening until 1838 when he resigned to establish his own school, was a pillar of strength for the Richmond Academy. However, his successor, William Burke, endured seven years of seemingly endless troubles. For one, a long dispute with the city over water supply charges finally ended in the school's defeat. Then in 1842 the city council discovered it had no obligation to guarantee the $20,000 loan. The deteriorating school buildings could not be repaired, and in 1845 Burke departed. This was the condition of the school when Crozet became its head.

Margaret Meagher, who told the story of the Richmond Academy in her *History of Education in Richmond*, said that with the coming of Crozet as principal, the academy "secured a foothold for a season." He generously put some of his own money into needed maintenance and persuaded the city council to give $1,000 to forestall further deterioration. He obtained free water for the students at the nearby home of his son-in-law, Dr. Charles Mills. He taught classes in "the mechanic arts, including engineering, construction, and architecture." Among his students was Edward T. D. Myers, who later became noteworthy as an engineer. Meagher quoted an unnamed contemporary as having said about Crozet, "He had a way of distilling in those things with which he was associated, a homely solidity that ensured thoroughness, respect and permanence."[23] His students expressed their appreciation by presenting him in 1847 with a small silver loving cup engraved with his name. In the fall of 1848, the beginning of his last year at the Richmond Academy, Crozet proposed a plan for the financial soundness of the school, but under his successor the school rapidly declined. The last classes were taught there in the spring of 1850, and in the summer of 1851 the city bought the property. In 1853 it became a civic cultural center known as the Athenaeum.

Although Crozet had returned to academia, his interest in Virginia's internal improvements had by no means waned. The economy of the country entered a recovery phase during his first year at the Richmond Academy, and renewal of interest in various transportation projects ensued. In 1845 the Baltimore and Ohio Railroad, frustrated by the refusal of Pennsylvania to allow crossing of its southwest corner, considered building across western Virginia to Parkersburg rather than to Wheeling. Citizens of the Valley, enlivened by the prospect of access to the Baltimore market, berated the Virginia legislature for dragging its feet on extending the James River Canal to

Buchanan. An internal improvement convention at Fincastle in Botetourt County in July 1845 threatened to seek out Baltimore if Richmond continued to neglect Virginia west of the Blue Ridge.[24] In August a convention at Abingdon of delegates from Virginia and Tennessee petitioned both legislatures for a southwestern turnpike from Salem to Bristol leading toward Knoxville, built at public expense by each state. Former Virginia governor Wyndham Robertson declined the presidency of the convention because he was personally devoted to Crozet's favored project for this line, a railroad.[25] In November another convention at Fincastle urged a southwestern turnpike, completion of the canal to Buchanan, and a railroad west from Covington to the Ohio River. The times were becoming exciting once more; decisions were going to be made, and Virginians west of the Blue Ridge did not want to be left in the lurch again by Richmond.

In response to the many queries about internal improvements that came to his desk at the Richmond Academy, Crozet wrote a long letter late in 1845 which was published on the front page of Lexington's *Valley Star*. He described all the possible railroad routes to the Ohio River and concluded that the Baltimore and Ohio could not build to Parkersburg because of the difficult terrain. His own preference was for a railroad from Buchanan westward by way of the New River to the Kanawha Valley and Point Pleasant, preceded by a railroad from Richmond crossing the Blue Ridge through a tunnel at Afton Mountain to Staunton and from Staunton southward via Lexington to Buchanan. The alternate route for a railroad from Staunton by way of Covington to the Ohio River he thought less favorable.[26] Later, during the postwar years, the New River route was to become the line of the Norfolk and Western Railroad, while the Covington route would be used by the Chesapeake and Ohio Railroad.

Crozet's personal commitment to the Richmond Academy was apparently not strong, for in the spring of 1846 he was planning to leave Richmond after all, returning not to New Orleans but to France. He did not go, for the Mexican War broke out "just as I was preparing to depart for Europe," he wrote Smith. His trunks were actually packed, but "that and the Oregon question, made me unpack them."[27] Moreover, his son Alfred was in the war and had taken part in the battles of Palo Alto and Resaca de la Palma in May. Soon afterward he was transferred to Jefferson Barracks, Missouri. Crozet still intended to go to France "as soon as things are settled"; however, although the Mexican War was soon over, Crozet stayed with the

Richmond Academy, for a total of nearly four academic years. In the fall of 1847 Smith suggested that Crozet might be reappointed to the VMI Board of Visitors, but Crozet objected that his connection with the Richmond Academy would prevent it, because one man representing two schools would involve a conflict of interest, in his view. If, however, he should be reappointed principal engineer, "which his Excellency may intend to urge," it would be another matter.[28] Governor William Smith instead recommended Colonel Charles Dimmock for the position. Dimmock had been a West Point cadet while Crozet was a professor there, graduating in the class of 1821. He had resigned from the army in 1836 and was a member of the VMI Board of Visitors with Crozet in 1844. In December 1847 Richardson informed Smith that Crozet was being considered for the position of chief engineer of the Danville Railroad Company, a job that Crozet would have left the academy gladly to accept.[29] However, the Danville Railroad job went to another engineer, Andrew Talcott.

Talcott, seven years younger than Crozet, graduated second in his class at West Point in 1818 and undoubtedly studied engineering under Crozet. He remained in the army nearly twenty years, engaged in various engineering works, including Fortress Monroe, Fort Calhoun, and the Dismal Swamp Canal in Virginia. In 1836, like Dimmock, he left the army to become chief engineer of the Erie Railroad, followed by other engineering projects. While Crozet was at the Richmond Academy, Talcott was working at the Portsmouth navy yard, and probably he renewed his acquaintance with Crozet at that time. In January 1848 Crozet offered Talcott quarters in his house while Talcott conducted an examination of the James River and Kanawha works at Richmond. Talcott was a frequent guest at Crozet's home during the next several years.[30]

The question of his being offered the Danville Railroad position was no vital matter to Crozet, partly because of his friendly relationship with Talcott and partly because he was involved in other pursuits at the time, such as the mathematics textbook published in 1848. In addition, the General Assembly by an act of 15 March 1848 commissioned Crozet to prepare a comprehensive report on the state of internal improvements in Virginia, published by C. Sherman in Philadelphia in 1851, and also to prepare a map of internal improvements in Virginia to accompany the report. The map, 21 by 32 inches, in color, was engraved in Philadelphia in December 1848.

The availability of accurate maps was a matter of great importance to Crozet from the time of his arrival in Virginia in 1823. The General Assembly in 1816 in establishing the Board of Public Works also authorized an official map of the state. Governor Preston engaged John Wood, a Scottish engineer who had emigrated to Virginia. Wood pioneered in the mapping of western counties before his death in 1822. His successor was Herman Böÿe, a German engineer who completed the work by 1826 in the form of a 61½ by 93-inch map engraved on nine sheets, which according to E. M. Sanchez-Saavedra was "the most elaborate state map produced in America before 1850."[31] Replete with geographical errors, the Böÿe map "proved to be more of an ornament than a useful tool."

When Crozet returned to Virginia from Louisiana in 1837, the Board of Public works agreed that the Böÿe map was inadequate, and in April 1838 the legislature authorized Crozet to "cause to be prepared in some cheap and convenient form . . . a lithograph map of all railroads, canals, M'Adamized and turnpike roads constructed or surveyed in this state." Crozet finished the map in six months, and 500 copies were distributed. Crozet was aware of the many inaccuracies in this hurried work and continued to press for legislative funding of a complete revision of the Böÿe map, but not until economic conditions had improved in the late 1840s did the legislature act. The map he prepared in 1848 was another hurried work, not the thorough and adequately funded project he wanted to do, but at least it was an updated version of the 1838 map. It was etched on copperplate and engraved by one of the leading experts in the nation, Peter S. Duval of Philadelphia.

Crozet's preparation of this map involved him in an exchange of views with Francis Smith in which for once they disagreed. Smith's proposal for the practical way to obtain a much needed accurate map of Virginia went back to the spring of 1843, when Crozet lost his job as principal engineer. In April, immediately after the legislature terminated the office, Smith wrote a letter of application to the Board of Public Works, "for the loan of a theodolite and other similar instruments for the use of the cadets of that institution, accompanied by the suggestion that as the legislature has abolished the office of principal engineer, it would be in the power of one of the professors, assisted by the graduating class during two months of the year, to make any survey that might be required by the Board of public works, without expense to the state."[32] The board, aware of the strong appeal to the legislature of the final clause, complied without hesitating and in the bargain sent Smith a full set of the annual reports of the Board of Public Works.

Smith proceeded to work out a plan for having trigonometrical maps of parts of Virginia prepared by cadets and VMI professors. In February 1847 the Literary Committee (predecessor of the state board of education) adopted the plan. When Crozet learned of this, he objected that the cadets were not qualified, and he more than likely took initiatives that led to his being commissioned by the legislature in the spring of 1848 to make a state map. But the last had not been heard of the proposal to have VMI cadets and professors make their map, for a bill providing for it was before the legislature. "Crozet is doing all he can to defeat it," Richardson wrote to Smith in March 1849. "Told me yesterday it would take 60 years."[33] By that spring, when Crozet was fifty-nine, a new door was opened to him when he was offered the position of chief engineer of a newly created state corporation, the Blue Ridge Railroad Company. The challenge of building a long tunnel under the crest of the mountain range and the railroad leading to it would carry Crozet to the peak of his career as a civil engineer.

8

The Blue Ridge Railroad and Tunnel, 1849–57

Crozet was gratified to learn upon his return from Louisiana that the Virginia legislature had just passed an act on 30 March 1837 requiring a survey for a railroad from Gordonsville extending the Louisa Railroad across the Blue Ridge at Simmons Gap to Harrisonburg. The Louisa Railroad, begun in 1836, started at Taylorsville, on the Richmond and Fredericksburg Railroad twenty miles north of Richmond, and extended westward. After Crozet made the survey in the summer of 1838 and found the terrain at Simmons Gap too difficult to grade, he and W. B. Thompson made another survey the next summer. Crozet reported that "the most favorable pass is at Rockfish Gap," located a few miles south of Simmons Gap. A tunnel about a mile long would save about 14 miles, he estimated; a possible alternative plan could employ tacking (switchbacks) across the ridge.[1] Ten years elapsed before his suggestions showed any promise of materializing.

When the Louisa Railroad was extended beyond Gordonsville in 1848, after an eight-year pause, it turned southwestward toward Charlottesville rather than continuing west toward Harrisonburg, at least partly because of Crozet's reports. Facing the still formidable crossing of the Blue Ridge at Rockfish Gap, the managers of the railroad appealed for help from the state, this time with fairly prompt success. In March 1849 the legislature passed an act providing for the construction by a state corporation to be known as the Blue Ridge Railroad Company of seventeen difficult and expensive miles of track, from Mechum's River at the eastern base of the Blue Ridge range to Waynesboro at the western base. The project would include as its principal feature the Blue Ridge tunnel recommended by Crozet in 1839. The legislature stipulated that no more than $100,000 should be spent in any one fiscal year on the entire project, anticipating completion in three years.

The Blue Ridge Railroad Act was passed 5 March. The next day, the legislature incorporated the railroad Crozet had long advocated, the Virginia and Tennessee, to run from Lynchburg through the southwest valley to Bristol. Crozet had directed the original survey of this route in 1831 and at first could not decide which job he would seek, but on 22 March he wrote to the Board of Public Works applying for the Blue Ridge Railroad and tunnel position. Within two days he received notice of his appointment as chief engineer of the Blue Ridge Railroad Company at a salary of $3,000 plus "all the necessary expenses . . . other than lodging and board," which Crozet considered "a very reasonable compensation."[2]

During the summer of 1849 Crozet and his assistants located the exact line of the tunnel and the approaches to it. In round figures, the tunnel was to be 4/5 of a mile long, the railroad down from the west portal to Waynesboro was to be about 3 miles long, and the railroad down from the east portal to Mechum's River was to be about 13 miles long. The tunnel was to be excavated in a straight line, estimated at 4,250 feet between portals located in deep cuts. "It passes nearly 700 feet below the Apex of the mountain," Crozet noted, "a depth which precludes the thought of assisting its construction by means of shafts." Only two headings could be driven, one from the east and one from the west, to meet somewhere in the middle. The tunnel would be for a single track, 16 feet wide, and 20 feet high above the level of the rails. Its shape would be elliptical, rather than a semicircular arch, which would save excavation estimated at $12,800 for the whole length. Below the rails, excavation of "about one foot more" would accommodate ballasting and crossties.

The tunnel, although the most important feature of the entire project, was "not by any means the most difficult part of my operations," Crozet reported. Although the final 5 miles between the tunnel's eastern portal and Mechum's River were easy terrain, the 8 miles of railroad between the east portal and Blair Park were another matter. "I have operated over a good deal of ground," he wrote, "but I never saw any section of the same extent more complicated and rugged."[3] The tunnel's east portal opened in a "deep, contracted, and precipitous chasm," requiring "an immediate turn, upon emerging out of the Tunnel, along the face of a very declivitous hillside, and on the brink of a rapid torrent." A huge rock embankment would have to be built with materials from the tunnel excavation, upon which trains would negotiate a curve with a very short radius of only 546 feet. This embankment would be a problem until and even after the day when the Board of Public Works, whose members constituted the Blue Ridge Railroad Company, transferred the line in 1858 to the Virginia Central Railroad, called the Louisa Railroad until 1850.

Continuing eastward, the next obstacle was Robertson's Hollow (often called Robinson's Hollow), about 140 feet deep, requiring two deep cuts and an embankment which Crozet estimated would be about 70 feet high but when built was fully 80 feet.[4] One of these two cuts, Crozet suggested, "might be substituted by a short tunnel, without adding to the cost." This was done, and Crozet always referred to it as the "third tunnel," or the "short tunnel," because it was a mere 100 feet long. When the Chesapeake and Ohio Railroad took over the line after the Civil War, it was called the Little Rock tunnel.[5] Although it presented some difficult construction problems, it saved much of the expense involved in either a deep cut or a circumvention. Two miles farther downslope, a steep spur required another tunnel about 800 feet long which would be called Brooksville tunnel. The problems involved in building this one would prove staggering, later meriting lengthy description in the classic study of railroad tunneling by Henry S. Drinker.[6] East of Brooksville tunnel was Dove Spring Hollow, requiring two deep cuts and an embankment somewhat shorter than Robertson's Hollow. Thence the line "keeps as usual along a steep broken and rocky hillside," said Crozet, continuing the report of his 1849 survey, "cutting across several ridges until it comes to a long spur," the location of Greenwood tunnel, about 500 feet long. Thence to Blair Park the ground improved gradually, with the exception of a deep cut required near there which would be known as Kelly's Cut and would prove as troublesome as any feature of the route.

The nine-year period required for construction can be divided conveniently into three periods marked by turning-point events. The first period was from the beginning of organization in March 1849 until April 1853, when the Virginia Central Railroad, having arrived at Mechum's River in the summer of 1852, began to press for a temporary track across the mountain by tacking with two switchbacks on the east slope and one on the west, while the tunnel was being completed. The second period was from April 1853 until March 1854, when the temporary track was completed and the first trains operated across the Blue Ridge. The third period was from the beginning of railroad service on the finished portions of the Blue Ridge Railroad combined with the sections of temporary track built by the Virginia Central Railroad until completion of the work at the end of 1857. This period included the "holing through" of the main tunnel on Christmas Day, 1856, not so much a turning point as an expediting signal.

At the main tunnel, as the work was begun in 1849, the partnership of John Kelly and John Larguey contracted to excavate at $3.50 per cubic yard. With an estimated 55,000 to 60,000 cubic yards to be excavated, the cost of digging the main tunnel was expected to be around $200,000. Penetration at the east end, rapid at first, soon encountered rock of excessive hardness that wore out drills rapidly and slowed progress to as little as 19 feet per month. Moreover, drillers and blasters at the east end were going uphill, because the tunnel was 56 feet higher at the west end. This was in accordance with the 70-feet-per-mile gradient Crozet estimated would be required overall; furthermore, a slope in the tunnel was desirable so that train smoke would naturally escape westward and water would naturally escape eastward. At the east heading, the force of gravity favored the flooring crew, who normally worked at a convenient distance behind the heading crew but here often caught up, with resultant crowding. Water was no problem here because it ran out the east heading, but smoke from black-powder blasting charges was a constant irritation.

Penetration at the west heading was also rapid at first, and it continued so because little hard rock was encountered for some time. Crozet even wished for some, because the tunnel roof was "full of fissures and very dangerous."[7] Large masses falling from the roof required timbering for safety, preparatory to later arching with bricks. Where arching was required—at the end 797 of the 4,281 feet had required it, 483 feet of it starting at the west portal—the excavation of roof and sides had to be made that much larger to accommodate the bricks. At the west heading, flooring crews seldom crowded the heading crews because of the comparative difficulty of removing flooring slabs up the grade. Blasting smoke was a problem, for there would be no natural ventilation until the tunnel had been holed through, an event that did not occur until six years after the work began. Water was an even more persistent problem in the west heading, because it had to be pumped out.

Kelly and Larguey discovered within six months of starting the excavation at the main tunnel that they were losing money so fast they would be forced to abandon the contract. Instead of simply increasing the amount of money paid per cubic yard removed, the Board of Public Works entered into an entirely different arrangement with the partners on 15 March 1851. Kelly and Larguey became "virtually superintendents of the work, the Board defraying all the expenses and allowing them in lieu of salary 10 per cent on the cost of $200,000, with a sliding scale deducting 2 per cent on all excess above $200,000." This cost-plus contract protected the partners as well as the state, "making economy and diligence to the interest of the contractors."[8] If the work did cost $200,000, Kelly and Larguey would earn $20,000; if $400,000, then only $16,000. Actually, the final cost of the tunnel was $488,000. This agreement was so satisfactory in the main tunnel that Crozet was sometimes inclined to recommend its adoption on other parts of the work, notably the Brooksville tunnel. Had not John Kelly, also the contractor on this work, been so unpredictable in his behavior, it probably would have been done.

Crozet established his operational headquarters at Brooksville, not a town or even a village, but a large inn on the Staunton and James River Turnpike near the location of Brooksville tunnel. Work began on the railroad in March 1850, with the entire project divided into eleven sections for contract purposes. Section 1 was the main tunnel. Sections 2, 3, and 4, east of the tunnel, were contracted by Mordecai Sizer; 5 and 6 by John Kelly; and 7 and 8 by J. J. Randolph. Sizer's sections included Robertson's Hollow and the short tunnel; Kelly's included Brooksville tunnel, Dove Spring Hollow, and Greenwood tunnel, as well as the big cut at Blair Park; Randolph's consisted of the easy terrain from Blair Park to Mechum's River. John Kelly was by far the most fully occupied contractor on the work; his industry, ability, and above all his personal dedication to the task even to the point of willingness to assume heavy financial risk more than compensated for his occasional unpredictability. Sections 9, 10, and 11, starting at the west portal of the main tunnel, went down to the west abutment of a long bridge across South River at Waynesboro. After some uncertainty about who was to build the bridge, the Virginia Central Railroad or the Blue Ridge Railroad, the state built it. Section 11 became the bridge itself plus the 1,200-foot embankment needed for an approach to the east abutment. The west slope sections and the bridge were contracted by Walker, Gallaher, and Ives.

R. S. Walker and H. L. Gallaher were also contractors for the bridge and the Waynesboro cut, the latter needed only for borrowing earth and rock for construction of the embankment approaching the east end of the bridge. Walker withdrew in 1852, and Gallaher continued alone (Ives was a silent partner); he had completed about two-thirds of the embankment when the Virginia Central Railroad pressed in 1853 for the temporary track across the mountain. Gallaher had troubles not only with maintaining a sufficient labor force but also in finding suitable timber within economical transporting distance to erect the three 70-foot spans upon the abutments and two midstream piers he had constructed of stone. The search for timber ended in failure, and Crozet was required to take over the bridge himself. He contracted with Joseph Reid Anderson of the Tredegar Iron Works in Richmond to build an iron bridge instead, on the plan of Wendel Bollman, bridge builder for the B&O Railroad. Bollman, who rose from tracklayer in 1829 to high-ranking company executive by 1852, had just built at Harpers Ferry "a single suspension truss bridge of wrought iron, 124 feet in clear span." Tested with three locomotives and tenders across the entire span, nearly 137 tons, the bridge floor deflected less than 1¾ inches.[9] The Tredegar built prefabricated sections of the Waynesboro bridge and shipped them on the Virginia Central Railroad to the construction site as soon as the temporary track was passable. The embankment was completed in January 1854 and the bridge within a few weeks after that, all in time for the first scheduled trains across the mountain in March.[10]

Back on the east side of the mountain, work on the Brooksville tunnel was dangerous from the beginning. "Far from finding granite," Crozet reported, "nothing but a soft rotten slate is discovered in the deep cut, causing immense and dangerous slides." When the tunnel was begun at the head of the cut approaching the west portal, the roof "fell down in large masses to such a dangerous extent that the men had refused working in it." Not until early 1851 was the driving of the heading resumed. Crozet recommended that Kelly be granted an allowance for timbering, not provided for in his original contract. Then, to Crozet's astonishment, Kelly insisted on "excavating and timbering the whole tunnel at once" and refused to have "anything to do with brick arching." Standard procedure was to replace temporary timbering with permanent brick arching a few feet at a time as the excavation progressed. Moreover, Kelly's excessively heavy timbering cost around $12 per running foot, two or three times what Crozet thought adequate, all to be taken down and bricked by someone else. In time, Kelly agreed to do it Crozet's way. By early July

1851 over half of the 830-foot length of Brooksville tunnel had been excavated; but over five more years would be required to complete this tunnel and open it to trains because at about the midway point, roof falls became incredibly dangerous. One roof fall was so deep that a lamp on the longest pole available could not illumine the top of it, and it took some days to get the frightened men back to work. Because brick arching was essential, Crozet contracted with Joseph Dettor for making bricks.[11] When at last Dettor had made a sufficient supply, Crozet judged them inadequate in quality and diverted the best of them to arching Greenwood tunnel. But Dettor, meanwhile, had the contract, and Crozet was legally, though regretfully, bound to him.

Progress was slowed at the Brooksville tunnel by human factors as much as geological. Crozet found getting along with his staff much easier than getting along with contractors. "A more diligent, intelligent and gentlemanly corps I never had with me and I am happy to say that I have not yet heard a dissenting opinion about them," Crozet reported in the fall of 1849. Two of his assistant engineers, A. M. Dupuy and E. T. D. Myers, stayed with him three or four years. Myers had been his student at the Richmond Academy and returned to be present at the holing through of the main tunnel on Christmas Day, 1856.[12] Dupuy supervised work on the 8 miles of line west of Brooksville, and Myers the 9 miles east of it. Crozet seldom criticized his staff members, although critics of Crozet among the general public accused him of both unwarranted staff cutting and retaining unneeded staff members. Crozet said, "Though I have allowed myself to be influenced by the meddlesome reports directed against me, on the part of persons wholly unacquainted with the important requirements of such a difficult work, I have not gone, in retrenchment of aids, beyond the direct necessities of the business. . . . I reduced their number whenever I found it practicable; but procured immediately an adequate addition when requisite. . . . You may depend, gentlemen, that I shall consult the interest of the State and practice sound economy."[13]

Labor relations were another time-consuming aspect of Crozet's work. As on the James River Canal when construction began in earnest after 1835, the preponderance of white workers were Irishmen brought in from New York and New England. Crozet found them strong and vigorous but troublesome from beginning to end of the task. An annalist of Augusta County told of a fight between the

County Cork Irish, who were tunnel workers, and "Fardowners" (Ulstermen) who lived in Fishersville and sought jobs on the Blue Ridge Railroad.[14] "On Mr. Sizer's sections," Crozet advised the board in March 1850, "a strike has taken place among his irishmen, who are prowling about the mountain, harmlessly so far." But matters soon turned violent. Joseph Farrow, a foreman, drunk on a Sunday, shot and killed one of the Irish workers. Friends of the victim, threatening vengeance, left their work and escorted the body to Staunton for a lengthy wake and burial. When such incidents occurred, it was often days before laborers returned to the job. The project itself was dangerous, and workers who were injured received little or no compensation. When Michael Curran, an Irish tunnel worker, lost his hands in a premature explosion of black powder, Kelly asked the board to continue his regular wages while he was under medical care. "The Board have no authority to apply the public funds in the manner desired," was noted on the reverse side of Kelly's letter.[15] Curran was by no means the only laborer on the project to suffer from the lack of workmen's compensation.

Crozet was the frequent target of querulous interrogations from two sides: from the public on the one hand and from the legislature on the other. Some of the "meddlesome reports" from the general public appeared early in the project. Crozet was inclined to give them time and thought, being a sensitive man and by nature incapable of ignoring criticism. Moreover, he regarded himself as an agent of the state and responsible for proper handling of the taxpayers' money; in his view, petitioners were taxpayers and deserved to have answers to their questions. In the case of the public, Crozet was inclined to respond with patience and a substantial measure of consideration for their viewpoint. In the case of the legislature, he had no such inclination, for he regarded legislators as having every reason to be better informed than the general public. Too often they evidently were not, much to Crozet's annoyance.

John Bell and eight other citizens of Staunton and Augusta County sent the Board of Public Works in February 1853 a seven-page handwritten petition, complaining in detail of delays for which they held Crozet responsible. "His whole management of that work, is marked by almost a total want of the practical qualifications," they charged. First, the work between the tunnel and Waynesboro should have been completed before December 1852. "The Bridge would have been ready at the proper time, but for the child like management of Col Crozet, first giving plans, and then withdrawing them." As for the tunnel itself, "if left to the management of Col Crozet, God only knows when it will be completed." In attempting to ventilate it and clear the smoke from blasting, "he tried experiment after experiment, of his own origin, without any success whatever." They regarded Paul Stevens as an unappreciated genius whom Crozet employed to improve the ventilation and then "threw every obstacle in his way," forcing Stevens to abandon the contract "in a then unfinished state." They charged Crozet with shabby treatment of William Crouse of Waynesboro, the contractor for pumping water out of the tunnel. "We have no feelings of personal hostility towards Col Crozet," they ended self-righteously, "but on the contrary are actuated (we trust) by much higher and nobler motives." [16]

Crozet, in Richmond when he read this, dashed off a one-page reply to the board, at first regarding it as not worth much time and trouble. "Setting out from erroneous premises, it must, of necessity, land upon wrong conclusions," he remarked. However, when he reflected that Bell and his cohorts had secured signatures of twelve other citizens from Waynesboro and forty-eight more from Augusta County, Crozet changed his mind. Before retiring for the night, he had written on long legal paper in his fine, diminutive handwriting a twelve-page refutation, point by point.

He regretted, he told the board, "the necessity of occupying some of your valuable time, and employing a considerable portion of mine, which might be more profitably bestowed on my work." As for the three-month delay at the end of 1852, Crozet reminded the board that he was then waiting on the legislature to decide whether or not to appropriate $300,000 for the work of 1853, in amendment of the original $100,000 per year rule. As for the bridge and the railroad on the west side of the mountain, "the contractors themselves were the delinquents, generally for want of funds." The problem of timber for the bridge was also a delaying factor, until the decision was made in favor of an iron bridge. Stevens had turned out to be incompetent and a troublemaker; as for Crouse, he and Crozet worked together quite satisfactorily. Ventilating the tunnel was a more challenging problem than pumping out the water. Crozet, wishing to save the state the expense of a powerful steam engine, tried a device described in *A Rudimentary Treatise on Blasting and Quarrying*, by Major General Sir John Burgoyne, "sold by all the book-Sellers in Richmond." It consisted of "an inverted tub, moving up and down, in another tub, filled with water, traversed by a pipe, through which air is alternately introduced and ejected." Paul Stevens, a mechanic who worked for Sizer, claimed to have built "twenty of them," and in spite of his skepticism, Crozet hired him. Crozet's doubts were justified when Stevens abandoned his attempt and returned to Sizer. Crozet then hired William Crouse, who with Crozet's help succeeded in building a working Burgoyne ventilator, powered by mules on a treadmill, and the smoke problem was reduced for good. Why, Crozet wondered, could people not learn the facts for themselves, when they were "near enough to make their own inquiries and know all about it!"[17]

When Crozet was writing this reply to his critics, Charles Ellet, Jr., was preparing to move to Richmond, having been offered the position of chief engineer of the Virginia Central Railroad by its president, Colonel Edmund Fontaine. Ellet, twenty years younger than Crozet and in his early forties, was an engineer of substantial reputation. He had worked in his teens on the Chesapeake and Ohio Canal with Benjamin Wright, had studied in his early twenties in France at the Ecole des Ponts et Chaussées, and in 1835, with Wright's support, was appointed engineer on the James River and Kanawha Canal. However, Ellet managed to provoke the hostility of Joseph Cabell, who apparently forced him out of the company.[18] Leaving Virginia in 1839, Ellet built the Fairmount suspension bridge across the Schuylkill at Philadelphia in 1842 and another bridge 1,101 feet long across the Ohio at Wheeling. Completed in 1849, the Wheeling bridge was the world's longest suspension bridge at the time.[19] Crozet was quite interested in the prospect of a close professional relationship with Ellet and was disappointed when it failed to develop.

Ellet arrived in April 1853 and immediately urged a change in the plans for crossing the mountain. Mechum's River was reached by the Virginia Central Railroad in the summer of 1852, and the Blue Ridge Railroad had already laid track from there to Greenwood Depot 8 miles west. The plan was to use stagecoaches for passenger traffic west of Greenwood via the Staunton and James River Turnpike while the main tunnel, the approach tunnels, and the railroad were being completed. Then, persuaded by Ellet, the Virginia Central Railroad suddenly announced plans to build a temporary railroad track over the mountain, employing two tacks, or switchbacks, on the east slope and one on the west slope, and provide service to Waynesboro and Staunton as quickly as possible. There were several short unfinished sections of the Blue Ridge Railroad on the east slope, useful as connecting links for the temporary track. Ellet obtained permission from the Board of Public Works to complete them with the Virginia Central's work force and expected Crozet to press his contractors to expedite their work. In order to save time, the new permanent track was to be laid without ballast and would be ballasted afterward by the state. The Board of Public Works resolution agreeing to this arrangement stated further, "For the above work, the contract prices, allowed on the Temporary track, are to be paid to the Company for such work as may be done by the said company's force, to be measured by the Engineer of the Board of Public Works."[20] This agreement laid the groundwork for confusion, conflict, and misunderstandings, of which there was no lack from start to finish.

At the west heading of the main tunnel, mechanical pumps were sufficient for water removal until a large spring was struck, necessitating more ingenious measures. Crozet brought in 1,800 feet of $3\frac{1}{8}$-inch pipe and by late summer 1853 succeeded in siphoning out about two-thirds of the water with reputedly the longest siphon on record, while the mule-powered pumps removed the remaining third. The siphon and the Burgoyne ventilating apparatus "attracted considerable attention at the time from their novelty" and were a credit to Crozet's resourcefulness.[21]

Instability of the roof at the west heading continued to be a problem, and much time was spent on heavy timbering. Crozet urged the blasters never to use holes deeper than one foot. "I am in constant dread of a serious accident, which would, in all probability, irretrievably disperse the hands," he wrote. "Those who are now engaged in this hazardous work are entitled to high credit and I have advanced their pay to $1.50 during the continuance of this danger." Hope for firmer rock was shattered when they "encountered veins fully as dangerous as the section we had left behind: here water mixed with red clay indicates fissures rising to the very top of the mountain; the rock presents itself as an inverted wedge, far more dangerous and difficult to manage than crumbling materials; for so long as you perforate through the base of the wedge, it remains supported, but is apt to come down at once, when the perforation is entirely through it."[22] This section of about 200 feet in mid-tunnel was a worrisome problem for the west heading crews, who were required to timber and then arch it for 272 feet in 1854.

Outside the tunnel, the temporary track was in operation starting in the spring of 1854, ascending and descending grades as steep as

300 feet per mile in places. The railroad trains were operable but at a cost much too high for longer than temporary service. Relations between Ellet and Crozet were often strained. Friction was unavoidable, with the Virginia Central Railroad pressing for completion of detached sections of the state railroad while building their own connecting links. Crozet reordered his priorities with some difficulty, but some of his contractors resisted the new pressure. Ellet was shocked to learn in the late fall of 1853 that it was doubtful whether any of Crozet's contractors, "except perhaps one, will permit force to be put upon their work to aid in pushing it through; and that one of them, Mr. Kelly, certainly will not permit it."[23] However, the 1853 Christmas season apparently brought a measure of goodwill, and the work was progressing by early January 1854. Crozet thought that now there would be "no great difficulty in preparing the State work for its new visitor." Even so, Crozet complained that the Virginia Central was using his contractors' supplies of crossties, spikes, and chairs (iron brackets that held the rails in place) and credited Anderson and the Tredegar Iron Works for making an extra production effort to keep them going. "It will be impossible, until the tracks are all laid, to know exactly the quantity that may have been used by both parties."[24] Crozet's attitude toward Ellet and his temporary track project was altogether reasonable and conciliatory.

Greenwood tunnel, 538 feet in length, was completed in January 1854, "through dangerous ground requiring a heavy arch," at a final cost of $74,000, or $138.30 per running foot.[25] When Ellet examined it for the Virginia Central Railroad, he agreed it could be regarded as safe for a time, but not for long, because it was "lined and supported by an arch of brick that cannot be depended on." Water oozing through the brick would soon freeze and thaw and loosen the arch. He urged that it be "lined inside with a course of well burned, hard brick, of the very best quality."[26] Crozet could hardly have been surprised at Ellet's opinion, after the difficulties he had experienced with Joseph Dettor.

At the Brooksville tunnel, Kelly had finally agreed to construct the brick arching and contracted for brick with Robert Harris, who fortunately was able to produce better brick than Dettor. In the summer of 1853 Crozet reported that the arch at the east portal was completed and he no longer feared the "awful impending mass" at that point, where "enormous pressure had actually crushed timbers one foot square." He praised Kelly for having accomplished this "without the least accident" but reported that Kelly's financial losses at Brooksville at this point had run to about $4,000. A huge slide at the Brooksville tunnel had required extra labor, and Kelly's obstinate refusal to allow Crozet access to his books made ascertaining the basis for cost adjustments difficult. "Unless I had an assistant at each cut all the time, it cannot be obtained, without his willing co-operation," Crozet told the board.

Despite his frustration, Crozet expounded upon Kelly's cost problem to the Board of Public Works in September 1853.

> Some of the old contractors took their work when prices were at 75 cents per day; They cannot now obtain an adequate force under $1.25 per day. This is particularly the case with John Kelly: you have seen his work and witnessed the hardness of the rock for which he receives 55 cents per cubic yard; you cannot wonder that he is reluctant to increase his force by raising his price to $1.25: I have notified him that he must do so, or his contract would be forfeited: this is my duty; but if the warning is unheeded, as I apprehend it will be, what must be done? dismiss him and get another contractor? very little would be gained by this measure, even if sustained in equity. . . . Policy and justice alike would seem to recommend a modification of the contract; either a proportionate increase of prices or a cancelling of the contract and an arrangement similar to that in the Main Tunnel, where Kelly & Larguey are, in fact, mere agents.

Crozet repeated this suggestion to the Board of Public Works several times, meanwhile assigning a clerk to verify Kelly's vouchers for labor removing the big slide. Kelly agreed at first but later abruptly denied the clerk access to the accounts. "What has induced him to make these tardy objections I can only conjecture," Crozet told the board. "I have all along done justice to the energy and skill of Mr. Kelly, and he would be a most desirable contractor, but for the frequent jarrings which he allows himself to create."[27] As a result, agency status was not accorded Kelly at Brooksville.

Two miles upslope Crozet was increasingly satisfied with the adoption of the short tunnel at Robertson's Hollow. "The rock is so excessively hard, that it takes 30 or 40 drills for a hole of about 2 feet in depth, and that continuing the open cut would have consumed 10 or 12 months and been ruinous to the contractors." The short tunnel was built by a succession of contractors and was completed in January 1854 by Gallaher and McElroy. The final cost was $12,390, or $123.90 per running foot.[28]

After completion of the short tunnel there remained only the main tunnel, the embankment at its east portal, some heavy work at Robertson's Hollow and Dove Spring Hollow, together with the Brooksville tunnel and Kelly's Cut, to complete. Crozet thought it "somewhat curious" to note the difference in cost of the several sections, ranging from $6,000 to $100,000 for a section of about a mile. "Of course the most expensive are the last to complete," he observed, because the legislature was always slow to provide the funds.[29]

The Waynesboro bridge was also finished in February 1854 and passed a severe test of being loaded with over 300 tons, or a ton and a half per running foot, "which caused but a slight deflection." There remained only the completion of a few portions of the Blue Ridge Railroad tracks to place the entire temporary track in operation. In December 1853 Crozet visited Ellet in Richmond and informed him that Crozet had been given "the power, which he had not before," to permit the Virginia Central to aid Crozet's contractors. Ellet reported further that Crozet was "now satisfied with all my suggestions . . . and my purpose is to press the work simultaneously at all points—promising his cordial co-operation." Ellet still regarded himself as the man in charge and Crozet as obligated to follow his lead.[30]

During the course of the next month, cooperation between Crozet and Ellet disintegrated. Workers being in short supply, the state road and the Virginia Central Railroad competed for them. "My contractor, Mr. Carpenter, cannot depend on a large force; his hands leaving him occasionally to go on the Temporary track," Crozet wrote Ellet. "I do not discover any accusation in this—There is quite a difference between your *taking* his men and their *leaving* him, if he does not allow them as much as others, which is their right." After attempting to rectify other misunderstandings, Crozet concluded, "You are certainly aware that the Temporary track has been made the occasion of most unjust vexations and persecutions against me; I regret it particularly because it has changed the character of the relations which I had hoped would be established between us, when you were appointed to your present office. I hailed then with pleasure the coming of an Engineer of your eminent abilities; and had anticipated the most gratifying professional intercourse; it being so rarely my lot to meet with one."

Ellet responded promptly, revealing that he had believed Crozet had been opposed to the temporary track, which Crozet strongly disavowed. Crozet had recommended the use of switchbacks as far back as 1839 and considered the idea sound. "When I said that 'the temporary track has been made the *occasion* of most unjust vexations &c' observe I did not say the *cause*, which is widely different." Because Ellet had "labored under a mistake produced by misrepresentations," said Crozet, he was "quite excusable." He continued, "It was only when my work was invaded . . . that I began to be ill-satisfied . . . your rejection of my offer of co-operating without applying to the Board, which is now explained, was most unpleasant to me. . . . on the contrary, I was satisfied with what you were doing, and never answer the often repeated question of inquisitive people 'What do you think of the temporary track?'"

Crozet's well-meant effort to establish a cordial relationship with Ellet was soon rebuffed. On a visit to the Waynesboro cut, Ellet was informed by Gallaher that hands were in short supply, partly because Crozet had "withdrawn" the state force. "You have very unfortunate informers," Crozet declared. "I was far from anticipating a return to your unfriendly style—if you will not listen to informers and will apply to me freely in all cases, you will ever get correct information." "I have no 'informers,'" Ellet replied stiffly. "I perceive that you . . . choose to let off your vexation upon me. And that you can do with perfect security. I shall not retort in any manner." Crozet ignored Ellet's self-righteousness and left the door open. "I practice Engineering as I pursue the study of other Sciences, as a rational enjoyment," he replied, "and it is on that account that I was pleased to hear of your coming; and I hope that the mistakes of a day will not impair the realisation of my anticipation."[31] No friendship between the two men developed, to Crozet's disappointment. Ellet's biographer, in assessing his personality, wrote, "Like his father he was often harsh and irritable, and could seldom bring himself to tolerate honest differences of opinion." Ellet himself recognized his own shortcoming; he confided in a letter to his wife, "I have no society whatever outside of my own family," and "there is a drawing-off-ness about me which prevents . . . forming intimate association."[32] The exchange of letters between Ellet and Crozet in 1854 confirms this self-assessment.

In dealing with labor unrest, Crozet often expressed his admiration for the courage of the tunnel workers in facing the hazards of the work. When it came to striking for higher wages, however, he would set his face against them and refuse to yield as long as possible. As conscientious guardian of the taxpayers' money, in so far as he had discretion in spending it, he did not wish to open the door to spiraling costs. In the spring of 1853 a major strike of Irish workers at the main tunnel occurred, after Paul Stevens, who had failed to build a ventilator system, had been dismissed by Mordecai Sizer. "While engaged at the Tunnel," Crozet reported, "I am told that he tampered with the hands, telling them that they did not receive enough, that $1.50 per day was the price for working in a Tunnel &c." In April 1853 Stevens wrote to the tunnel workers from Cincinnati, urging them to come there and work at $1.50 a day excavating a tunnel. The workers "adopted $1.50 as their due in the heading," said Crozet, "and struck immediately."[33] Kelly offered them $1.25 in the heading and $1.12½ in the bottom; a large number rejected the offer and left for Cincinnati. As Crozet learned later, these workers had been misled by Stevens's misrepresentation of going wages in Cincinnati, so they went on strike for three weeks there and ended getting $1.25 a day in the tunnel heading, no more than they would have earned in Virginia. Larguey, unlike Kelly, had been willing to pay $1.50 at the heading and $1.25 in the bottom, saying that "the Tunnel is long, smoky and wet, that he did not wish to stop, &c." An adamant Crozet replied, "If, at last, we have to go up so high, let it be with new comers, who have not been guilty of embarrassing us and stopping work without warning." Crozet urged the board to advertise for 200 workers in newspapers in Baltimore, Philadelphia, New York, and Boston. "I suggest a good deal of trouble for you," he told the board, "but this is an important crisis, and I agree with Kelly, not Larguey, that concessions will be ruinous.... We hold in our hands, as it were, the fate of the System of improvements; were it for the Tunnel alone, I would incline to yield, but the consequences to other works frighten me."

The newspaper advertisements proved futile. In May, Crozet went to Harrisonburg to recruit some of the Valley Turnpike hands who were let go as that work ended, but they had no desire to work in the tunnel. Later in the summer, Crozet was ready to turn to the hiring of slave labor. "A gentleman, Mr. Robt. P. Smith, assures me that he can get me a force of 50 or 60 negroes to work at the Tunnel, if I will allow him for them Irish wages, and insure their employment for the year of their hire, which I have promised, subject to your ratification," Crozet wrote the board. Smith delivered to Crozet his force of blacks at the agreed price of $1.00 per day each and was attempting to secure fifty more when the contractors for the temporary track appeared, offering higher wages. Immediately the report was spread that $1.25 per day was the price allowed for blacks, which Crozet refused. Returning to white workers, Crozet found himself "under the injurious necessity of raising the price all round 12½ cents per day; that is $1.25 cents in the bottom and $1.37½ in the heading, which has retained the force, but not increased it, as yet."[34] Ellet reprimanded his temporary track contractor for this disruptive act.

The hiring of black labor was not thereby curtailed, by any means. In December 1853 Crozet signed a contract for the hire of blacks with George A. Farrow and David Hansbrough, who agreed to furnish "from forty to fifty able bodied negro men to be employed on the Blue Ridge railroad and Tunnel, chiefly under the management of Kelly and Larguey." The board agreed to pay $1.12½ per day each, plus $35 per month each for two white overseers hired by Farrow and Hansbrough. The board also agreed to be liable for injuries to black workers; of course, the owner, not the slave, received the payment. Owners preferred healthy workers to payments for injuries to them, and it was "distinctly agreed and understood that said negroes shall not be employed in loading or blasting on said work."[35] Two of these blacks were killed in an accident on the railroad a few months later, and Crozet, upset by inaccurate reporting in the newspapers, reported in detail to the board the results of his own investigation. Near the west portal of the main tunnel, several blacks had been assigned the task of loading flatcars on a train, which then backed down the grade toward Waynesboro. The coupling of the lead car snapped, separating all five cars from the engine, and the cars rolled freely, without brakes, down the slope. Some blacks prudently heeded shouted orders to jump off immediately, but three did not. As the cars ran across Waynesboro bridge at around 40 mph, they were seen laughing at their adventure, unaware that a flatcar was standing on the track around a curve. The collision killed two and seriously injured the third. It was the sort of accident that was nearly impossible to avoid, and public recriminations resulting from slipshod newspaper reporting were hardly in order.[36]

If blacks seemed to be vulnerable to accidents, the Irish appeared to be more vulnerable to sickness. In the late spring of 1854 Crozet reported "much sickness & many deaths, and the irish never work until their departed friend has been buried; this has been a serious cause of interruption during the whole winter." In July cholera broke out in the Irish shantytown on the east slope near the tunnel, with "awful fatality." Seventeen died in one week, and many "scattered in every direction." The epidemic abruptly moved from the east side to the west side of the mountain, where more died and others scattered. Fortunately the epidemic was hit and run; by the first of September the tunnel area was "perfectly healthy," and work had resumed. Among the 100 black tunnel workers, noted Crozet, "not one case of the disease has occurred . . . it seems to have marked the Irish especially for its prey."[37]

Crozet, Kelly, and Larguey agreed that Irish workers should be replaced with blacks as much as possible. "It was difficult last year to hire negroes for the Tunnel; but now the nature of the work is better understood and I think we can obtain a greater number," Crozet informed the board. But by the end of 1854, Irish labor was no longer as scarce as in 1853 and could be employed at a dollar a day, so neither the Irish nor the trouble they caused Crozet disappeared. The workers struck again for higher wages in March 1855. "We are trying to ferret out the ringleaders," Crozet reported. "I regret that we did not hire Negroes at Christmas."[38] In the spring of 1856 the annual spring migration of tunnel workers to jobs in the North occurred on schedule, to Crozet's annoyance. Another strike was rumored on the west side of the mountain, and he was becoming weary of the perennial labor problem.[39]

By the time of the railroad accident that killed the two blacks in April 1854, the trains had been crossing the mountain to Waynesboro and Staunton for a week or two. The first work train carrying five flatcars loaded with ties arrived in Staunton in mid-February 1854. The first passenger train made the crossing in late March, a trip marred by an accident in which one man was killed and a woman badly burned by falling against a stove. The temporary track was built not only over the crest of the Blue Ridge for a distance of 8 miles but also around the Brooksville tunnel, which presented construction problems long after the other two approach tunnels had been completed. Ellet urged Fontaine to insist that the state pay for the Brooksville temporary track, because it "will make a considerable portion of the state work available, which, without it, would have been long unproductive to the state and useless to the public."[40]

The completion of the temporary track signaled a new phase in the developing Blue Ridge Railroad and tunnel project. With train service now available, public pressure for early completion of the main tunnel eased somewhat, though by no means completely. To Crozet, it meant a little more freedom to stress construction with a view to public safety. The dangerous 200-foot section beginning

1,200 feet into the west heading of the main tunnel was passed by October 1854. Immediately workers raised the brick arch, which Crozet called "a most delicate operation" because, in order to make room for the abutments, it was necessary to remove "the treacherous rocks on which the timbering rests, which might be brought down." The work was completed without incident.

Crozet's hope that the two headings would meet in the summer of 1855 depended on an adequate supply of bricks. Robert Richardson, a Waynesboro brickmaker, bid $8.20 per thousand against eight higher bidders, and his work earned Crozet's praise. "There is no better hand at this business," he said. When in late summer 1855, 952 feet of the tunnel remained to be perforated, at 35 feet per month, chances for completion of the perforation by October 1856 seemed assured. Crozet urged the Virginia Central Railroad to order track from England immediately, because the Tredegar Iron Works had abandoned rail production in the face of British competition. Rails would be needed not only for the open road but also for the tunnel, "so that the road may be used at once on the day we remove the last cubic yard of rock."[41]

The drillers and blasters at the headings met each other on Christmas Day, 1856, and the "holing through" was finally accomplished. Crozet and a number of assistant engineers were present at the event. By no means had the last cubic yard of rock been removed, however; the entire year 1857 was required to remove the flooring in preparation for laying the track and to complete the arching.

Progress at Brooksville tunnel continued, although with enormous difficulties, while the temporary track around it was put into use. In August 1854 Crozet reported that just under the highest point of the ridge there was "a space where, as soon as exposed to the air, the rock crumbles and falls from an unknown height in immense bodies." Converting the tunnel to a cut would cost "no less than $200,000, to say nothing of the immense slides to be apprehended." As for going around the ridge, it would require two very large embankments, one of them at least 100 feet high. He did not believe it could be done for less than $100,000, "whereas the Tunnel itself, at the highest figure may cost $60,000." Actually, the hazards at Brooksville tunnel were still greater than he realized in August 1854. Completing it would require two more years, and the final cost would amount to nearly twice his figure. In March 1855 the cavity over the center of the tunnel finally extended all the way to the surface and daylight, 140 feet above the tunnel below it. "We can hear the rocks falling from an unknown height upon the timbers under which the men are at work, with a rumbling noise resembling that of distant thunder," Crozet reported. The avalanches continued for a time, but all things considered, Crozet believed, "this is rather favorable, as we shall be able to manage the work more understandingly." Finally in March 1856 Crozet was able to report that a powerful brick arch 3 feet thick had "made this threatening place now quite secure," and the tunnel was ready for trains to pass through it in September. The total cost was $114,000, or $131.90 per foot, actually less than the Greenwood tunnel per foot.[42]

The year 1855 saw the work suddenly slowed by a financial crisis during which the state's bonds fell below par. The Board of Public Works could not meet its payments, and the work would have been halted except for the willingness of some contractors such as John Kelly to continue it on their own, anticipating repayment at some future date. In March 1855 Crozet told the board it was "fortunate that we were enabled to continue the work" at Brooksville and the main tunnel, for stoppage could have resulted in unchecked roof falls. With the coming of a more general and serious downturn of the national business cycle in 1857, there was no easing of financial stringency for the Blue Ridge Railroad and tunnel project until its completion.[43]

The spring of 1855 brought sorrow to the Crozets with the death of their only son, thirty-three-year-old Alfred Armand. After the Mexican War, he had continued to serve in the army at posts in Missouri and Texas. The army granted him sick leave in 1854, during which time Alfred resigned his commission. Late in the year his resignation was returned to him, presumably for his reconsideration. "He is," wrote Crozet in late January 1855 to Thomas Green, a Washington lawyer, "determined not to return to his regiment, on the wild banks of the Rio Grande, with his young wife."[44] Crozet could sympathize with his son but nevertheless believed "his connection with the Army more congenial to his habits" than another employment. Crozet hoped that Alfred would consider remaining in the army if offered a more attractive assignment and asked Green to direct him to "the proper bureau in order that I may be introduced to the proper officer." The news of Alfred's sudden death in a Cincinnati hospital on 23 April came as a shock to Crozet and Agathe. Alfred's body was buried in Richmond beside his sister Adele.[45] There was now left to Crozet and his wife only their second daughter, Claudia, the wife since 1839 of Dr. Charles Mills of Richmond.

At intervals during Crozet's work on the Blue Ridge Railroad and tunnels, he found time to work on a new map of internal improvements. Early in 1849 the legislature at long last had authorized the Board of Public Works to take steps toward revising the Böÿe map. Crozet persuaded the board to let him create a series of skeleton base maps that could be filled in gradually by subsequent local surveys. In November 1851 he reported his progress to the board from his Blue Ridge Railroad headquarters at Yancey's Mill. Although many Virginia counties had been surveyed, others had never been. Taking locally produced county maps and piecing them together as a jigsaw puzzle was a futile procedure. "Not only the boundaries of adjacent counties do not coincide, but, in a great many instances, they differ so widely that no one would recognize them as meant for the same line of division," he noted. The act of the legislature had called for the clerk of every county created since 1 January 1824 to send the Board of Public Works an official report on its boundary lines, together with a copy of the "plates, notes, and papers accompanying such report."[46] Only in "few, very few, instances" did the county clerks comply, Crozet complained. Therefore, he appointed Andrew Talcott to obtain a number of basic latitudes and longitudes by astronomical observation. By late 1851 Talcott had done this for Washington, Richmond, Winchester, Harrisonburg, and three stations on the Danville Railroad; but he was still to perform this service for Staunton, Warm Spring Mountain, White Sulphur Springs, Covington, Gauley Bridge, Parkersburg, Abingdon, and a few more places. Also at work on the drawing of the map were Captain William I. Vaisz and a fellow officer of the Hungarian army, Captain Anthony Kanalassi. Vaisz had fought the invading forces of Czar Nicholas I in 1849, making him in Crozet's eyes "one of the sons of the noble Hungarian nation, which defended so bravely the outpost of European freedom." Because Vaisz was a graduate of the Polytechnic School of Vienna and a fellow engineer, Crozet would have made him an assistant had Vaisz had a better command of English. Instead, Crozet managed to secure jobs for both Vaisz and Kanalassi on the map project, and he supervised their work when he had the opportunity.[47]

The results of the efforts of Crozet, Vaisz, Kanalassi, Talcott, and a young German army officer, Ludwig von Bucholtz, who was employed after the untimely death of Kanalassi, was the production of two maps: first, the Crozet map of 1855, and second, a new version of the Böÿe nine-sheet map of 1825, "corrected by order of the Executive" and issued in 1859.[48] When the new Crozet map was issued in 1855, many of the same former errors were still uncorrected. Crozet then suggested in March 1856 the creation of "a special bureau, to use the Washington term," well-financed and directed by the Board of Public Works, to "cause the most indispensable surveys to be made."[49] Increasing financial stringency in 1857 and the growing political crisis that followed hampered further efforts, and the map question drifted, although the state did issue the "corrected" Böÿe map in 1859. Meanwhile, completing the Blue Ridge Railroad demanded most of Crozet's attention.

The short tunnel of 100 feet at Robertson's Hollow was built rather than a cut at that point due to the peculiar lay of the land. Ordinarily a narrow ridge would be cut through, as was the case at Kelly's Cut. East of Greenwood tunnel, Crozet had noted in his survey of 1849, "the difficulties diminish gradually and the division ends in Blairpark, just below a thorough cut which also saves expense and distance." In Kelly's section 6, the cut was 200 feet long, 15 feet wide, and 100 feet deep, and it proved to be one of the most troublesome engineering features of the line. When the Virginia Central Railroad reached Mechum's River in 1852 and then decided in 1853 on the temporary track across the mountain to Waynesboro, Ellet and Fontaine became impatient with the slow progress at Kelly's Cut. The Virginia Central persuaded the Board of Public Works to allow them to take possession of it so they could press Kelly, now in their employment, to finish it more rapidly. This did not produce the desired results. "Had Mr. Kelly been left in undisturbed possession of his work, it would, by this time be nearly if not quite completed," Crozet wrote in February 1854. But Ellet's plan was to "lay the track through the cut, in its present unfinished state, and, it being about 12 feet high at its lower end, to descend from it along some of the waste material spread in a slope for the purpose, leaving the cut to be finished afterwards."[50] Crozet could not imagine how this could be managed while the road was in use, nor could Kelly, who refused to undertake it. Eventually the Virginia Central Railroad decided on a temporary track around the cut similar to the one around Brooksville tunnel. Also in time the Virginia Central persuaded Kelly to abandon his contract at the cut and awarded it to James Goodloe, who performed no better, if as well. Late in April 1856 Fontaine informed Crozet that

Goodloe was now willing to surrender the work to Kelly and to work under him. Kelly assured Crozet that with Goodloe's help, he could complete it in time for the Brooksville tunnel, and Crozet considered the matter closed. Two days later, in Richmond, Crozet heard that Goodloe was in town, insisting on his exclusive contract, "unrelenting in his complaints, attacks and threats," behavior Crozet found "inexplicable."[51] Kelly's reputation for obstinacy was now overshadowed by his successor's vacillation. Goodloe was eased out, and Kelly resumed the work at the cut.

In the spring of 1857 Crozet reported that Kelly's Cut would "not be ready much before the opening" of the main tunnel, already holed through and being bottomed. Winter and spring rains repeatedly filled the upper side of the cut with 4 to 5 feet of water, limiting excavation to the lower end. Finally, the summer of 1857 saw completion of work at the cut. In September, H. D. Whitcomb, Ellet's successor as chief engineer of the Virginia Central, was sent to inspect the line. Whitcomb was concerned that Kelly's Cut was still liable to slides and urged removal of about 4,000 cubic yards of rock, which would take thirty or forty men about six weeks. Meanwhile, he also urged retention of the temporary track for a time, just in case.[52]

By September 1857 Crozet was ready to leave the completion of the work in the hands of others. Whitcomb was satisfied that the main tunnel was "perfectly safe for the present," and the first trains would be able to use it in October. He was not so certain about the embankment at the east portal; a portion of it was still subject to sliding, possibly "for a year to come." As for the railroad, Whitcomb found it "in excellent order, reflecting credit upon those entrusted with its construction." A few features, however, deserved comment. Kelly's Cut, threatened with rock slides for sometime to come, needed more rock removed. The stone could be used to shore up the embankment at Dove Spring Hollow. Robertson's Hollow embankment was still sliding on the lower side and needed about 2,000 cubic yards of rock taken from adjacent cuts. All of these corrections, he thought, should be paid for by the state.[53]

A few weeks after Whitcomb's report, Crozet left the work and went to Georgetown, where a new employment opportunity was opened to him, working with Montgomery C. Meigs on the Washington aqueduct. At sixty-eight years of age, he was by no means ready to retire. He did not sever his connection with the Blue Ridge Railroad altogether but continued to "visit the work and give directions, though at some inconvenience." He stopped doing so as soon as he "found that what remained to be done was too simple to need any farther instructions." In February 1858 the Board of Public Works requested Crozet to come and accompany Charles Fisk and Whitcomb on a final inspection, but he declined. "If there were no other Engineer to represent professionally the Board of Public Works, I would feel it to be my incumbent duty to attend," he replied, "but the selection of Mr. Fisk, who is every way qualified to judge and inspire confidence, relieves me from the necessity."[54]

Charles B. Fisk made his inspection and reported in detail to the board, having understood that four questions were at issue: (1) Was the main tunnel wide enough? (2) Was the east portal embankment safe? (3) Was the Robertson's Hollow embankment stable? (4) Was Kelly's Cut sufficiently wide and safe?

As for the main tunnel, he reported that of the 4,281 feet of its length, 797 feet (18.6%) had been arched in three separate and detached lengths. Starting at the east portal, 2,792 feet were unarched, then 272 feet arched; next a 20-foot unarched section followed by a 42-foot arch; next, unarched for 672 feet; and finally, 483 feet arched to the west portal. While the tunnel heading was being driven through, 617 feet were arched, and another 180 feet were arched afterward. Where arched, the tunnel was as wide or wider than the average single-track tunnel in the United States; where unarched, it was "under the average" of them. "If the track is always properly adjusted there need be no difficulty in running trains safely through the tunnel with its present width," he concluded. Nevertheless, he thought some widening would be desirable in some of the unarched sections.

Fisk said that neither the east portal embankment nor the one at Robertson's Hollow could be regarded as stable. He suggested a remedy for each one by "benching and levelling a sufficient quantity of materials to resist by their weight, the thrust of the banks"; that is, to broaden the base of the embankment forming the material as a series of steps, with the level flat surfaces turning the thrust downward rather than outward. As for Kelly's Cut, he would remove a small quantity of materials from one point and widen a narrow place; otherwise he regarded it as acceptable. In sum, he recommended that the Board of Public Works pay the Virginia Central Railroad $10,000:

$6,000 for widening the main tunnel, $3,300 for benching and leveling the two embankments, and $700 for the finishing touches at Kelly's Cut.[55]

The work was finished, and with a high degree of professional competence. Unfortunately, Crozet left the work feeling bitter at having been subjected to unwarranted criticism from various sources; namely, Ellet, the general public, and the state legislature. "I think it might have been better for me to continue my supervision of the work," he wrote Board of Public Works Secretary Thomas H. DeWitt from Georgetown, "but it will not suffer in proportion as much as I did, to be, notwithstanding my exclusive attention to the State's interest, constantly harassed by the most unfair and insulting misrepresentations and I am glad the Board did not insist on my continuing to attend to this thankless business.—To do everything for the best interest of others and be rewarded and treated thus! and that by the very people whom I studied to benefit! but enough of this embittering subject."[56] He would have been pleased to know that twelve years after his death a new station at Blair Park was named Crozet.

9

Virginian to the End
1858–64

After his long years in the Virginia mountains building a railroad and tunnel to surmount the Blue Ridge, Crozet was ready for a change of environment. During the final phases of the work, he was invited to Washington by the secretary of war and offered the position of principal assistant engineer on the Washington aqueduct.

The engineer selected in November 1853 to make the survey was Lieutenant Montgomery C. Meigs (1816–92), who reported to the Fillmore administration in February 1853 his recommendation of an aqueduct all the way from the Great Falls. A bill appropriating $100,000 to begin the work passed Congress the day before Franklin Pierce was inaugurated, and Pierce's secretary of war, Jefferson Davis, assigned Meigs to superintend the project. In addition, Meigs was given the tasks of rebuilding the United States Capitol according to the plans of architect Thomas U. Walter and extending the Post Office building.[1] Although Meigs was involved in all three projects simultaneously, Crozet was involved only with the aqueduct.

Dividing his time between the Capitol, the Post Office, and the aqueduct, Meigs managed to make progress smoothly on all three during the remaining years of the Pierce administration. Meigs had no difficulties with President Pierce and enjoyed a most cordial relationship with Jefferson Davis, whom he admired greatly in the years before the Civil War. Little was done on the aqueduct during the summer of 1853 because of the prevalence of illness in the Potomac Valley, but ground was broken for the project at Great Falls on the last day of October by Meigs himself.[2] On 4 March 1857 President James Buchanan was inaugurated, and he appointed as his secretary of war John Buchanan Floyd of Virginia. Floyd disrupted Meigs's smooth progress on all three projects and eventually transferred him from Washington to the Dry Tortugas and Fort Jefferson, west of the Florida keys.

John Buchanan Floyd (1806–63) was the son of John Floyd (1783–1837), governor of Virginia between 1831 and 1834. The elder Floyd had reluctantly accepted Crozet's resignation at the end of his first term of service as state engineer, before his departure for Louisiana. The younger Floyd, trained in the law, left his Wytheville practice while still a young man in his twenties to take up life as a cotton planter in Arkansas, at which he failed. In 1837, the same year in which his father died and Crozet returned to Virginia for his second term as state engineer, Floyd returned to Virginia to resume the practice of law at Abingdon. In 1847 he was elected to the Virginia House of Delegates, where he urged state investment in railroads. In 1848 the legislature elected him governor for a three-year term beginning 1 January 1849.[3] When Crozet accepted in March the task of building the Blue Ridge Railroad and tunnel, Floyd was president of the Board of Public Works and Crozet's strong supporter. When Floyd became Buchanan's secretary of war in 1857, it was he who provided Crozet the opportunity for employment on the construction of the Washington aqueduct.

Meanwhile, during the spring and summer of 1857, Secretary Floyd and Captain Meigs were in conflict over the matter of awarding contracts on the aqueduct. Floyd put patronage considerations ahead of professional engineering qualifications in several instances, to Meigs's dismay. For his part, Floyd regarded Captain Meigs as politically naive. Although a mere captain, Meigs ranked high in the engineering profession and was something of a Washington institution in his own right after four years in the limelight during the Pierce administration. Nevertheless, he had to be careful to avoid the charge of insubordination to Floyd. President Buchanan was in the middle, occasionally making some ineffective gesture to mollify both Floyd and Meigs, wanting to retain the services of both.[4] This was the political background when Crozet entered the Washington scene in November 1857.

Meigs had probably heard of Crozet and his work on the Blue Ridge tunnel two years before. In the summer of 1855 Meigs went with his wife on a vacation trip to a place in the mountains west of Staunton at Buffalo Gap, at least partly to facilitate Mrs. Meigs's recovery from an illness. They traveled to Staunton on the Virginia Central Railroad, using the temporary track over the Blue Ridge because the tunnel was still in progress. Meigs commented in an entry in his diary on the train's surmounting "grades 270 feet per mile—1 in 19½."[5]

An avid diary keeper whose normal handwriting was little more legible than the shorthand he often employed, Meigs noted on 8 October 1857 that in an interview with President Buchanan and Secretary Floyd he was "authorized to push forward the aqueduct by all proper & legal means." On 14 November 1857 he noted that Floyd was "going to give me Crozet, a bitter man. This is to give me as assistant a man who was a professor at W. Pt. before I went there and an engineer in chief before I was heard of." Meigs apparently had forgotten whatever he may have heard of Crozet in 1855, for he added, "He is a former[?] Chf Engr of the State of Virginia." Four days later Crozet visited Washington and called on Meigs, who noted, "Crozet not determined or did not tell me of his determination to take Bryan's place."[6] The reference was to William H. Bryan, one of Meigs's assistant engineers. "When the Secretary sent for me I had not the least idea of his object," Crozet explained in a letter to Meigs. "However, I never coveted nor accepted any office unless vacant, or certainly to be vacated.... If, therefore, you think you can by any possibility retain your assistant if I decline, let me know, confidentially, and I will do it. If, on the contrary, a change is decided upon, I would accept."[7] In concluding, Crozet said to Meigs, "We are all dependent in some way or other, and as an old soldier I understand the value of discipline, without which no service can be efficiently rendered." As it turned out, Meigs did not replace Bryan with Crozet, but retained Bryan and hired Crozet. Meigs noted in his diary his receipt of this "very good letter from Col Crozet who offers to decline the place tendered if I can retain Bryan. Wrote in reply. He will come." So it was done. On 1 December 1857 Meigs and Crozet together called at the office of Secretary Floyd, where Crozet met Bryan and was appointed by Floyd "Principal Assistant Superintendent of the Washington Aqueduct."[8]

It would be interesting to know what thoughts went through Meigs's mind on this occasion, for the day before he had received two callers at his office, Bryan and H. L. Gallaher, a contractor on a portion of the aqueduct. This was the same Gallaher who had been engaged four years earlier in building the bridge across South River at Waynesboro, at the western extremity of the Blue Ridge Railroad, and with whom Crozet had experienced some difficulty. In July 1857

Meigs also had some difficulty with Gallaher, having to placate some alleged grievance, although he was essentially satisfied with Gallaher's work.[9] Therefore, what confidence Meigs may have placed in Gallaher's assertions remains problematical. Gallaher, in Bryan's presence, told Meigs that "Crozet is intriguing and not to be trusted ... & says he will displace me if he can do so by any intrigue."[10] At the appointment ceremony in Floyd's office the following day, it appeared that Meigs and Bryan were each inclined to keep his own counsel. Crozet entered this post as Floyd's man and was identified as such by Meigs throughout Crozet's nineteen or twenty months on the job. In many of Meigs's letters to his father he alluded to the pressure from Floyd to go along with his favoritism to certain contractors, but Meigs never associated Crozet with what he believed to be Floyd's dishonesty with the taxpayers' money. At least implicitly, Meigs recognized Crozet's integrity.[11]

Two days after the appointment of Crozet, Meigs wrote his mother about it. "He was professor of mathematics at West Point when I was one year old," he related in a tone of incredulity. "He was in the Austrian & Russian campaigns of Napoleon as Capt of Engineers. He is an intelligent & scientific man too old for use in the service he ought to do. But the Secretary ... being very fond of Crozet who was Chf Engr of Va when Sec of War was on the Board of Public Works he ... gave him to me.... Therefore at least he meant well."[12] Meigs was not always ready to attribute good intention to Floyd, but he did in this instance. Moreover, there is evidence that Meigs did, in fact, appreciate the value of Crozet's services and on a number of occasions genuinely enjoyed his company. In addition to riding and walking together to inspect the works in progress, there were occasional dinners, at which Crozet enthralled his hearers with stories of his experiences in Russia.[13]

Bryan, in effect, shared the position of principal assistant engineer with Crozet. Other assistant engineers included Charles G. Talcott, Albert L. Rives, W. R. Hutton, and Edmund T. D. Myers. Myers and Talcott were Crozet's friends without question, but Rives seems to have shared the negative attitude expressed by contractor Gallaher. Meigs confided to his diary on 24 January 1858, "Rives thinks Crozet a traitor. He is there much at the department. There should be no business between Secretary and him. Has bad reputation in Virginia." It is difficult to estimate how much credence Meigs accorded such backbiting reports, but on at least one occasion he was severely critical of Rives for irresponsibly absenting himself to visit his parents when a flood "destroyed several hundred barrels of cement & injured canal" at the construction site of Cabin John bridge. "I wish he would not indulge his filial affection at the risk of the public interest committed to him," was Meigs's sharp comment.[14]

Rather than finding Crozet handicapped by his age in carrying out his duties in the field, Meigs was gratified by Crozet's energetic attention to his tasks. On only one occasion, according to the remarkably full records left by Meigs, was he disappointed in Crozet's performance. This was entirely due to a misunderstanding of construction schedules, resulting in the late start of the masonry foundation for a large pipe vault. "In these three weeks nearly since the orders were given, I think that much more ought to have been done had my wishes been more carefully considered," he admonished, but it was perhaps not too late to avoid added charges from the pipe contractor.[15]

The aqueduct was sufficiently completed by the first of January 1859 to conduct the first water to the city. Two miles of masonry conduit 9 feet in diameter, plus a half mile of conduit 7 feet in diameter, received water from a 100-million gallon reservoir above Georgetown at 10:00 A.M. on January 3. "I had the satisfaction of sending to Georgetown and Washington a supply of water larger than they are likely to provide the pipes to distribute before the aqueduct can be completed to the Great Falls," Meigs wrote Mayor J. G. Berret of Washington. A 4-inch jet on the Capitol grounds dazzled spectators with a fountain 120 feet high, yet there remained much work to be done. "Large water mains are being ranged along the gutters of the south side of Pennsylvania avenue, commencing at the western end, and we may expect next summer to have a second protracted job of laying them under ground," noted a newspaper editor.[16] Congress passed an act on 3 March 1859 providing for the sharing of the water supplied by the federal government with the corporations of Georgetown and Washington. A month later, Meigs wrote further to Mayor Berret, "The population seems to have concentrated around the various public establishments, and to have extended along and from each side of the streets connecting them. The United States has provided large mains to all the public buildings, which are available to supply water to the distributing pipes to be laid by the city. These mains are so extensively distributed and so well placed that I do not think it will be necessary for the city, for some years to come, to lay any pipe larger than six inches in diameter."[17]

The follow-up work of constructing systems of distribution continued through 1859 and 1860 and was still in progress when Meigs was transferred to Fort Jefferson in September 1860. In the summer of 1859 there was a reduction in the staff of engineers, and Crozet was among those terminated. In his letter of notification to Crozet on 8 July 1859, Meigs was businesslike, as fitted the occasion. "The suspension of all contracts has been ordered, & I am compelled to notify all persons employed upon the work that their engagement cease today with the exception of Messrs. Whitelocke & McCullough. . . . In sending you this notice permit me to express my obligations to you for the assistance you have rendered me during the time we have been associated together in the conduct of this work &c." The remainder of the letter instructed him to turn in all drawings, records, and official correspondence to the office.[18]

Crozet was not taken by surprise with this turn of events, for he had seen it coming and had written to his friend, VMI Superintendent Francis Smith, in June. "It would not suit my views of propriety, to remain unemployed nearly a whole year waiting, on pay, for an adequate appropriation to resume the work," he told Smith, indicating that he had been offered that option. He admitted he was beginning to feel his age in "the labors of the field" and was interested in teaching at a new military college to be established at Alexandria, Louisiana, which later moved to Baton Rouge and became Louisiana State University. In his reply, Smith included a testimonial on Crozet's behalf, referring to his service as president of the Board of Visitors of VMI, which Smith said he could not "too highly estimate."

By October 1859, when Major William Tecumseh Sherman assumed the presidency of the new college, Crozet was aware he was not destined to receive the appointment, if indeed, engineering was to be taught there. He philosophized about it to Smith, saying, "A quiet retirement, with some pleasant occupation nearer to family and old friends, will be more acceptable than residence in a secluded spot, so far away."[19] He could not close without adding a generous personal word to Smith, "It must be a source of very proper pride for you to look back to the small beginning of the Institute over which you preside, and compare it to the standing to which you have raised it. . . . It has become the model upon which other institutes have been established in many States of the Union; even, as far as I can judge, the Louisiana institution [Louisiana Military Academy] is an exact counterpart of your own organization. It must be pleasant for you to reflect, that you will leave a monument to perpetuate the recollection of yourself and services."

From July 1859 until July 1860, Crozet did indeed live in quiet retirement at his home in Richmond with Agathe, enjoying the company of their daughter and her husband and their two grandchildren.[20] Crozet's time during this year was partly occupied with answering a questionnaire submitted to thirty-eight respondents which was part of a congressional report on the academic program at West Point. By the time the 350-page report was published in December 1860, Crozet had been in the field once again for six months, hard at work on the Virginia and Kentucky Railroad.

In March 1849 the Virginia legislature authorized the building of the Virginia and Tennessee Railroad from Lynchburg to Bristol on the day after its authorization of the Blue Ridge Railroad and tunnel. Crozet took a few days to decide for which of the two projects he would apply and chose the latter. William Beverhout Thompson, with whom Crozet made his first survey of the route across the Blue Ridge at Rockfish Gap, was chosen to be chief engineer on the Virginia and Tennessee Railroad. Thompson later became chief engineer on the Virginia and Kentucky Railroad, after a brief period of employment as engineer on the Baltimore and Ohio Railroad. Crozet was chosen as the controversial Thompson's replacement as chief engineer of the Virginia and Kentucky Railroad in July 1860, which resulted in a strained relationship between the two engineers.

The Virginia and Tennessee Railroad, begun in 1849, was completed in its entire 204-mile length in 1858. While its construction was in progress, the idea of building a branch line from some point on it reaching toward Kentucky received favorable notice, and in 1853 the legislature chartered the Virginia and Kentucky Railroad. The legislature decreed that "the line is to commence from some point on the Virginia and Tennessee line not further east than Abingdon, and to end at the Cumberland gap in the most extreme southwestern corner of the state."[21] The company was authorized a capital of $2.5 million, the cost of construction was estimated at around $19,000 per mile, and the distance 132 miles. No survey or location was attempted during four of the remaining five years of construction of the Virginia and Tennessee Railroad; then, in 1857, even before Crozet went to work on the Washington aqueduct, Thompson began work on the Virginia and Kentucky Railroad.[22]

During 1858 a controversy involving conflict of interest developed and began swirling around W. B. Thompson with increasing intensity. The Virginia and Kentucky Railroad made a contract with a New York construction firm, Dorr and Company, "for the construction & equipment of the entire line" at the price of $38,000 per mile, double the capital figure. Dorr and Company insisted as part of the contract that they "were to have an equal voice with the company in the selection and appointment of the engineer of the company." At first it appeared that Dorr and Company aimed to replace Thompson with another engineer, but later it appeared that Thompson was in their favor. At a stockholders' meeting on 12 June 1858, Benjamin Rush Floyd, president of the railroad company, approved two resolutions: one ousted Thompson as chief engineer for alleged collusion with Dorr and Company; the second resolved to invite Robert T. Bailey to be chief engineer of survey and construction and Charles B. Fisk to be consulting engineer. The turmoil that resulted ended with Floyd yielding the presidency to William Y. C. White, who restored Thompson to his position as chief engineer.[23]

The Board of Public Works in Richmond, concerned about the escalating cost of this railroad, urged the company to abandon the contract with Dorr and Company, which was done, and a new contract was made with Hawkins and Company, a North Carolina firm. However, the new contract was even worse, the $38,000 price per mile not even allowing for the building of "several expensive tunnels, of land damages, or engineering expenses, or compensation of officers, and other contingent expenses of general administration." The board therefore curtailed state payments for its shares of stock in the Virginia and Kentucky Railroad.[24] Hawkins and Company departed the scene, Dorr and Company returned, and the state rescinded the curtailment order.

A second controversy developed in 1859 over the eastern terminus of the Virginia and Kentucky Railroad. The state charter had provided only that it should be at a point "not further east than Abingdon," thus allowing the company some choice in the matter. The Virginia and Tennessee Railroad preferred that the eastern terminus be Bristol, so as to feed into the entire line of their railroad and make Bristol, not Abingdon, a railroad center. Actually, the Bristol terminal was to be located at the town of Goodson, adjacent to the west side of Bristol, where benefactor S. E. Goodson was willing to donate land for the purpose of building a depot. The stockholders were split, one group headed by W. Y. C. White supporting Abingdon, another headed by B. R. Floyd supporting Goodson. Thompson, supported by White, naturally favored Abingdon. While the controversy raged, work was paralyzed.

The dispute reached a dramatic climax with a meeting of the stockholders, called by the Board of Public Works, at Estillville (later Gate City), county seat of Scott County west of Bristol, on Monday, 2 July 1860. Benjamin Rush Floyd having died, some of the directors brought forth a big gun, his kinsman Secretary of War John B. Floyd, as candidate for president of the Virginia and Kentucky Railroad. W. Y. C. White nominated Colonel Isaac B. Dunn, who received 12 votes to Floyd's 625. Secretary Floyd, as president of the company, immediately persuaded the directors to appoint Crozet chief engineer of the railroad, which was done with their unanimous approval. Crozet was "vested with necessary powers—among other things to carefully review the profiles & routes to the Virginia & Tenn RR & report to the Directors."[25]

Floyd had no intention of becoming the active president of the railroad and promptly yielded to another who was elected by the board of directors the same day, Robert W. Hughes. With Hughes presiding, Crozet was unanimously confirmed as chief engineer at a salary of $3,000 per year and "authorized to form a corps of assistants and to proceed as soon as practicable with the location, construction and all other business pertaining to the Engineer's department."[26] Crozet went to work promptly, surveying the route west of Abingdon and that west of Goodson to their common meeting point about 34 miles to the west at Poor Valley. On 23 July his report to the president and directors of the Virginia and Kentucky Railroad was printed in the Abingdon *Democrat*. His conclusions were bad news for the local readers, because he supported the Goodson route.

With regard to the technical aspects of the problem, Crozet took issue with some of the results of Thompson's survey. For example, instead of a difference of 2.17 miles between the two routes, Crozet found the Goodson route only 0.43 mile longer than the Abingdon route. For another, he thought Thompson's estimated cost of tunneling much too high. Altogether, Crozet estimated the probable cost of the Goodson route at over $400,000 less than the Abingdon route. But this was not all. The state had an interest in the Goodson terminus, said Crozet, in that "the advantage on the link from Goodson to Abingdon [14.6 miles], would be lost to the State by terminating the contemplated road at Abingdon.... For, in fact, the connection with the Va. & Tenn. Railroad is not actually a terminus, but rather a mere junction; and I am not aware of any junction which has procured to its locality any more advantage than would have been derived from a common railroad station." For example, he suggested, look at the Virginia Central Railroad, which for a long time terminated at Taylorsville, 20 miles north of Richmond on the Richmond, Fredericksburg and Potomac Railroad, "without any show of improvement" at Taylorsville. Eventually the Virginia Central built a line parallel with the RF&P into Richmond at a cost of around $750,000, to bypass the control by the RF&P of the Virginia Central's access to the Richmond market. Crozet mentioned other examples in other states, then concluded, "Without adducing more such examples, I can safely assert, that, only those places which possess natural advantages of position will prosper by a railroad."[27]

President Robert W. Hughes could not have agreed more, and added his own comments to those of Crozet. "My individual feelings and interests would incline me altogether in favor of Abingdon," said Hughes, but every economic argument favored Bristol. "Over the fourteen miles back from Abingdon to Bristol, the Virginia & Tennessee railroad would have the power to lay charges so high as absolutely to prevent the trade from taking that direction;—to say nothing of the additional 26 or 28 miles required to be travelled; and the double handling that would be necessary at Abingdon and at Bristol.... We should be in the same helpless condition in which the Va. Central Railroad constantly found itself, when it terminated on the Richmond and Fredericksburg road.... Looking therefore at this question as one of business and duty, I for one am forced to decide for Goodson."[28]

Three days later Hughes presided over a meeting of the board of directors of the Virginia and Kentucky Railroad held at Jonesville in Lee County, which voted unanimously for Goodson as the eastern terminus. Crozet was instructed by the same meeting "to locate the part of the line from Goodson to Estillville as speedily as practicable" and to "prepare a plan for a depot building at Estillville" and to superintend its construction. The directors also accepted the offer of S. E. Goodson "to give to the Va & Ky R.R. company three acres of land or three or four Town lots for depot purposes at the town of Goodson."[29] At Abingdon, W. B. Thompson rallied supporters to oppose the board's decision and published in the Abingdon *Democrat* a lengthy negative and defensive criticism of Crozet's report. At the next meeting of the board, on 16 August at Estillville, however, the directors resolved that they had "entire confidence in the skill and ability of Col. Crozet to locate correctly and report truly in relation to the line to Goodson at which point the Eastern Terminus has been fixed."[30]

This crisis past, Crozet then settled into his work of surveying and locating the line of the railroad, which of necessity operated on a shoestring budget. In mid-October Crozet wrote to the president of the Board of Public Works requesting permission to use a "transit, with a vertical arc" that he had seen in the office when last in Richmond. "Our company, as you well know, is not much in funds and, at this time, could not purchase an instrument which, however, is much needed for the location."[31] He would plan to obtain it on a forthcoming trip to Richmond. A month later, a contract was signed with W. J. Hawkins and Company when they presumably underbid the principal contractor, Dorr and Company, for the grading and masonry of sections 13 and 23 of the railroad. The printed contract was quite detailed and specific as to the obligation of the contractor to submit to the authority of the chief engineer in every aspect of the work.[32]

On 14 March 1861 Crozet's wife Agathe died of "old age" at Claudia's home at the age of seventy-eight, according to the cemetery records. She was buried two days later in Shockoe Hill Cemetery beside Adele and Alfred.[33] Claudia was now the only member of Crozet's immediate family left to him, and for the remainder of his days his residence was at her home in Midlothian. This did not mean, however, that he was ready for the rocking chair. There was a railroad to be built, and he was needed to build it. When he returned to the job at Goodson early in April, Crozet encountered greater frustrations than a scarcity of funds or instruments. Building supplies were becoming next to impossible to obtain, partly due to funding problems and partly due to the mounting confusion resulting from the outbreak of war in April 1861. On 6 April, Crozet wrote to President R. W. Hughes of the railroad company that he hoped to see him soon at Goodson, where, Crozet said, he could judge for himself "the no-progress of the work." Stacks of crossties were rotting in the weather, unusable until a hundred barrels of cement, ordered early in November, were delivered. The cement was being held in the depot of the Virginia and Tennessee Railroad, subject to storage payments, because the "ordering power has not paid the freight."[34] Within days after Crozet wrote this complaint, Virginia seceded from the Union as a result of President Lincoln's decision to mobilize troops, and the Old Dominion was at war. As it gradually became clear that Kentucky would not secede from the Union, work on the Virginia and Kentucky Railroad ground to a halt. It was resumed in the postwar years, after Crozet's time.

Work on the railroad continued to occupy Crozet until midsummer of 1861. From Wytheville in July, he wrote to Major John Tyler, Jr., a son of the former president, reiterating his wish to do something for his adopted home, Virginia. Tyler had suggested that Crozet call on President Jefferson Davis, a graduate of West Point in the class of 1828. Davis, Crozet discovered upon visiting him in his office, already knew about him "as much as I could tell him; since, at the time he entered West-Point, my course of instruction both in the mathematical & Engineering department was still in operation." Crozet told Davis that if he "could be useful in any dept. other than active Service," he would be "at his disposal." Crozet thought "that the organization of a Southern M[ilitar]y Academy would probably for me [be] the most suitable field of usefulness."[35] When in August 1861 Colonel Francis Smith was called from VMI to Richmond for duties there, General Richardson considered asking Crozet to be acting superintendent of the military college in Lexington, but he stopped short as "his age apparently made him ineligible."[36]

In his letter to Tyler in July, Crozet also offered his comment on the military situation in northwestern Virginia, then still a part of Virginia.

> I am sorry to learn that we have met with a check in the N. West. It is to be regretted we could not occupy that district in time to nip the rebellion there in the bud, and keep in the right track timid men, who would be guided by the first plausible man, who would excite their fears. I hope, however, that by some prompt and well concerted movement, we may yet cut off, surround and capture the invaders among the intricate localities of that country—for it is not by the number of the killed, but by the capture or definite repulsion of enemies that the success of a war is decided—this requires conveying and concentration of forces—we were unfortunately too much scattered in that quarter.— God speed our cause.

Crozet's military experience dated back to the Napoleonic wars, but his long years of experience in building roads, canals, and railroads were not unrelated to his military concepts. Both were up to date.

In the late summer of 1861, with no railroad to build, no new school to plan and organize, not even VMI to superintend, Crozet was forced to resign himself to inactivity at his daughter's home in Midlothian. The destruction by war of so much that Crozet had labored so long to build must have dismayed him. The president of the Valley Turnpike Company, for example, reported to the Board of Public Works after the Valley campaign of "Stonewall" Jackson, "When our army came up the Valley, they destroyed every large bridge . . . on the road, and nearly every small bridge from Winchester to Harrisonburg."[37]

When in June 1862 McClellan's threat to Richmond was fended off by the Seven Days' battles, Crozet at Midlothian was relatively safe, on the opposite side of Richmond from the scenes of conflict. With the coming of the new year, Crozet decided it was time to write his last will and testament, which he wrote with his own hand and filed with the Hustings Court in Richmond on 5 February 1863. It was over three legal pages in length, in a handwriting that shows not a trace of shakiness. If handwriting is an indication of health, Crozet must have been still vigorous at seventy-three.

The will was thoroughly characteristic of its author. He began with the request that the funeral should be "performed without unnecessary display, which, while of no service to the dead, is a tax upon the living, frequently for the benefit of undeserving individuals." Let the money saved "be appropriated to the relief of some indigent persons," he instructed. He bequeathed all of his property, consisting of "some real estate in the City of Jefferson, near New-orleans; Bank and railroad stocks in Virginia; Lots and houses in the City of Richmond; some servants and other personal property," to his son-in-law, Dr. Charles S. Mills, "as Trustee, in Trust, for the sole and separate use, benefit and enjoyment of my daughter, Claudia Natalia Mills." He added further that in the event Claudia should die without a will and having been preceded in death by both her husband and her children, "the said property shall belong to her next of kin residing in America . . . to the exclusion, however, of my niece Anna Crozet, now Mrs. Felix Roman." His reason for excluding Anna may be only surmised; perhaps it was for no other reason than that she was financially secure. Those who were not to be excluded he named: "my nephew Adolphus Crozet and my niece Mary his sister . . . and possibly my sister Eliza Magne and her children Paul and Marie Magne, at present in Paris, France, but who may return to Louisiana." If they remained in France, that should be regarded as "evidence of a more prosperous situation than that of the other branch." His failure to include his brother William, father of Adolphus and Mary, suggests that William had died sometime shortly after 1860, when he was listed in the census report. Further stipulations included directions that his properties in Louisiana, "now in possession of the enemy," should be sold as soon as practicable and "the proceeds applied to the purchase of some other real estate nearer my daughter's residence." With regard to his two servants, Phoebe and Josephine, their situation should remain "as at present, as long as they live in the confederacy." If either or both of them should wish to leave, they should be allowed to do so, "after admonishing them of the probable consequences to themselves of taking such a step." He did not want them to leave the security of a home where they were cared for to the hazards they would encounter elsewhere.[38]

Crozet died on 29 January 1864 at Midlothian, the country residence of Claudia and Dr. Mills. He was buried in Shockoe Hill Cemetery beside Agathe, Alfred, and Adele. The coffin containing his remains was removed from that spot during World War II and reinterred on Founders' Day at VMI, 11 November 1942, in a plot in front of Preston Library.[39] On 2 December 1948 a small, plain granite monument was erected to mark the new gravesite at VMI and inscribed:

> COLONEL CLAUDIUS CROZET
> BORN IN FRANCE   DEC. 31, 1789
> DIED IN VIRGINIA JAN. 29, 1864
> SOLDIER   SCHOLAR   EDUCATOR   ENGINEER
> CHAIRMAN OF THE FIRST
> BOARD OF VISITORS   V.M.I.
> 1837 . . . 1845

First among those people who have made an effort to prevent Crozet's name from lapsing into obscurity was General Williams C. Wickham, who became president of the Virginia Central Railroad in 1866, succeeding Colonel Fontaine, and president of the Chesapeake and Ohio Railroad in 1869. Wickham, in naming a new railroad depot between Mechum's River and Blair Park around which a town was to develop, said flatly in 1876, "The name will be Crozet or nothing."[40] Wickham certainly wished to recognize Crozet's work in building the Blue Ridge Railroad and tunnel; moreover, having been a Confederate general, Wickham also remembered that Crozet was loyal to Virginia when the war came.

A Chesapeake and Ohio Railroad official of a later generation, James Poyntz Nelson, lamented the obscurity into which Crozet had fallen by the 1920s. At the unveiling of a restored stone tablet at the tenth milestone of the Manchester and Petersburg Turnpike on 7 November 1924, Nelson spoke to a small gathering, linking Crozet with George Washington. "Had the vision of Washington and Crozet been carried out before our great Civil War," said Nelson, "and if these two people had been brought closer together by having highways, there would today be no West Virginia."[41] Present to unveil the stone tablet was Adele Crozet Mills, who revealed the inscribed words: "In memory of Claude Crozet, Scholar, Soldier, Teacher, Engineer."

Nelson referred also in his speech to the "interesting sketch of the life of Crozet by General John D. Imboden," which was perhaps the most frequently quoted source of information about Crozet until Couper wrote his biography. John Daniel Imboden (1823–95) was a native of Augusta County and practiced law in Staunton in the 1840s and 1850s. He became acquainted with Crozet in the summer of 1849 after Crozet began work on the Blue Ridge Railroad and tunnel. Crozet visited Staunton frequently on business, and he and Imboden became good friends.[42] During the war Imboden became a Confederate general especially famed for the "Imboden Raid" in West Virginia before Gettysburg. Later, when he had returned to practicing law, he was asked to contribute an essay on Crozet to the section on Virginia in W. F. Switzler's *Report on the Internal Commerce of the U.S.* (1886).[43] Apparently Imboden wrote essentially what he remembered Crozet had told him about himself and made very few errors. In his final paragraph, he sketched Crozet's character.

> He was irritable in business matters and intolerant of pretenders of all sorts, and especially of quacks in his own profession . . . he was not a popular man. He was a thorough republican; neither birth nor rank weighed a feather in his scales. He was scrupulously honest, despising kings, hating imperialism, detesting Napoleon, whom he regarded as finally a traitor to his country and to mankind, though he admired his

genius. Abhorring war and loving liberty and peace, he entered more thoroughly and understandingly into the political and social life of Virginia than foreigners are wont to do, and had he been native born he would have been distinguished in the true sense as a man of the people, an upholder of the laws which restrain their passions and protect their rights.

The record of Crozet's life seems to verify the essentials of Imboden's estimate of the man, although perhaps with some qualifications. In business matters Crozet was by no means always "irritable"; his efforts to mollify associates such as Ellet and Kelly show that he could exhibit patience. Critics such as Gallaher and Thompson would have disagreed with this statement, but they were at cross-purposes with Crozet, not aiming at a common goal. Although Meigs did not hold Crozet's sponsor in high regard, he respected and apparently liked Crozet. As for Crozet's republicanism, there was no question of it. When Captains William Vaisz and Anthony Kanalassi of the Hungarian army arrived at the Blue Ridge Railroad in 1849, Crozet could not do too much for Kossuth's freedom fighters. He also had high regard for Vaisz as a graduate of the Vienna counterpart of the Ecole Polytechnique and as a "brother engineer," an aspect of *fraternité* that was important to Crozet.

He did indeed enter "thoroughly and understandingly into the political and social life of Virginia." In his reports to the Board of Public Works, he often was given to long essays on the economy and resources of Virginia and fervently urged their development as a means of recovering Virginia's lost position of preeminence in the nation. His political influence was strong with several governors, but Virginia governors were no match for the legislature in any of Virginia's antebellum constitutions. On the social side, Crozet's work in higher education was noteworthy. Colonel Smith was always ready to acknowledge his debt to Crozet for assistance in the early years of VMI, and the Institute remembers Crozet as a principal founder. The Richmond Academy probably reached the peak of its productive years under Crozet, and West Point honors him as a positive contributor to its programs in engineering and mathematics.

When Crozet and his wife Agathe came to the United States in 1816, they were in search of a new home. West Point did not become that home, but by 1825 or 1826 Crozet was certain that he had found it in Virginia. An unfortunate turn of events uprooted him again in 1831, but by 1836 he was convinced that living in Louisiana was a "sad exile" for him, and he was overjoyed to return to Virginia in 1837. There were still misfortunes ahead of him, especially in 1843, but save for his brief residence in the District of Columbia, he never left the Old Dominion again. Claudius Crozet truly loved Virginia, and in return Virginia has made him one of its own.

Notes

Bibliography

Index

Notes

1

1. Vital information on Crozet and the Crozet family may be found in the following sources: Last will and testament of Claudius Crozet, Chancery Court Records, Richmond; "Testament ... Pierrette Varion ...," 1801, Claudius Crozet Collection, VMI Archives, Preston Library, Virginia Military Institute (hereafter VMI Crozet Collection); "Rapport fait au ministre, Ministère de la guerre, 10 September 1812," dossier of Captain Crozet, Archives de la Guerre, Service Historique de l'Armée, Vincennes (hereafter AGSHA); "Livre d'immatriculation," no. 1625, Archives, Bibliothèque Centrale de l'Ecole Polytechnique, Paris (hereafter ABEP); "Extrait de Registre de Baptême, Mariage, et Décés de la Commune Darnal, Canton de Villefranche, Department du Rhône, dossier of Captain Crozet, AGSHA.

2. Jean-Nicholas-Pierre Hachette, *Correspondance sur l'Ecole Impériale Polytechnique*, 2d ed., 3 vols. (Paris, 1813–16), 1:90, 158 (hereafter cited as *Correspondance*); Robert R. Palmer, *The Improvement of Humanity: Education and the French Revolution* (Princeton, N.J., 1985), 242–57.

3. Ecole Impériale Polytechnique, "Liste des Elèves admis à l'Ecole Polytechnique en l'an 14 ... ," [1807], ABEP, carton: 1805; Jean-Gérard de Lacuée, *Rapport sur l'Ecole Impériale Polytechnique* (Paris, 1806), 3–4.

4. "Tableau des Elèves l'Ecole Impériale Polytechnique des l'Ouverture de l'année scholaire au 1er Frimaire an 14, 1805," ABEP, carton: 1805; Ecole Polytechnique, *Livre du Centenaire, 1794–1894*, vol. 1, *L'Ecole et la Science* (Paris, 1895), 31–35.

5. *Correspondance*, 1:161–62.

6. Ecole Polytechnique, *Extrait, du Registre des délibérations du Conseil d'administration de l'Ecole Polytechnique, An 14—1806, Du 3e jour complémentaire an 13* (n.p., 1806), 3–5, ABEP.

7. Lacuée, *Rapport*, 3, 4, 5, 12, 13.

8. Joseph Brunet, Jr., "Science and the Early *Ecole Polytechnique*, 1794–1806" (Ph.D. diss., University of Kentucky, 1969), 210; *Livre du Centenaire*, 1:40–43; Maurice Crosland, *The Society of Arcueil* (Cambridge, Mass., 1867), 193–96.

9. Ecole Impériale Polytechnique, *Programme générale de l'Ecole Impériale Polytechnique* (Paris, 1806), 7–8; *Programme générale de l'Ecole Impériale Polytechnique* (Paris, 1807), 10.

10. "Compte du mois de frimaire . . . an 14," 1806, ABEP, carton: 1806.

11. Ibid.

12. Ibid.

13. For recent biographical sketches of professors of the Ecole Polytechnique during Crozet's student days, see Jean Dhombres, "Biographies," in Ambroise Fourcy, *Histoire de l'Ecole Polytechnique* (1828; rpt. Paris, 1987), 143–93.

14. Crozet to Francis H. Smith, 16 Sept. 1843, Superintendent's Incoming Correspondence, Archives Division, Preston Library, Virginia Military Institute, Lexington; Jānis Langins, *La République avait besoin de savants* (Paris, 1987), 53–68; Emmanuel Grison, "Les cours de chimie de Berthollet an Pluvoise An III," *La Jaune et la Rouge* 429 (Nov. 1987): 36–38.

15. Frederick B. Artz, *The Development of Technical Education in France: 1500–1850* (Cambridge, Mass., 1966), 153; "Compte du mois de frimaire . . . an 14," 1806, ABEP, carton: 1806; Fourcy, *Histoire*, 258–59.

16. "Refectoire No. 29," "Chefs de Chambre, 4e Compagnie," and "Liste général des élèves des 2 Divisions réunies par l'ordre alphabétique," 1805, ABEP, carton: 1805.

17. *Correspondance*, 1:201–2.

18. "Liste des Elèves admis à l'Ecole Polytechnique en l'an 14 présentant la comparaison de Nos d'admission, de passage à la 1ère Division et de passage dans les Services Publics, avec les noms des Examinateurs qui les on examinés," 1805, ABEP, carton: 1805; "Mouvement journalier depuis le 1er frimaire an 14 jusque & inclus le 31 Décembre 1806, 1ère division de la 4ème Compagnie," 1805, ABEP, carton: 1805; "Ecole Impériale Polytechnique, Tableau présentant l'ordre alphabétique des Elèves des deux Divisions à leur mérite sur chaque partie et l'instruction d'après les Examen intérieurs," 1806, ABEP, carton: 1807.

19. Crosland, *Arcueil*, 200.

20. "Sortie de l'Ecole," 1807, ABEP, carton: 1807; "Ministère de la Guerre, 6e Division, Bureau du Personnel, Paris," 22 Oct. 1807, VMI Crozet Collection; David D. Chandler, *The Campaigns of Napoleon* (New York, 1966), 279; Alfred Fierro-Domeneche, "Jean-Jacques Basilien, Comte de Gassendi," *Dictionnaire Napoléon* (1987).

21. "Le Ministre Secrétaire d'Etat de la Guerre, 6e Division, Bureau de Personnel de l'Artillerie, Paris," 11 April 1816, VMI Crozet Collection; William Couper, *Claudius Crozet: Soldier—Scholar—Educator—Engineer (1789–1864)* (Charlottesville, Va., 1936), 9–10; Chandler, *Campaigns*, 708; Ulrich Troubetzkoy, "Colonel Claudius Crozet," *Virginia Cavalcade* 12, no. 4 (1963): 5, 7.

22. Couper, *Crozet*, 10; Simon Schama, *Patriots and Liberators: Revolution in the Netherlands, 1780–1813* (New York, 1977), 625-26. For example, when in 1826 Crozet examined the lower Appomattox River to its confluence with the James, he recommended constricting the channel in order to maintain its depth "by means of jetties made of fascines united by wattles, and loaded by

alternate courses of gravel." Crozet added, "Such works are used to a great extent and success in Holland, and on the Rhine, where I have seen them sunk to a depth of 30 feet." (*Annual Report of the [Virginia] Board of Public Works* 11 [1826]: 99–103).

23. "Extrait des Minutes du Greffe de la justice de Paix . . . de Villefranche, Department du Rhône," 22 June 1812, dossier of Captain Crozet, AGSHA; "Ministère de la Guerre, 6e Division, Bureau de l'Artillerie, Paris," 31 July 1812, VMI Crozet Collection; "Le Ministre Secrétaire d'Etat de la Guerre, 6e Division, Bureau du Personnel de l'Artillerie, Paris," 11 April 1816, VMI Crozet Collection.

24. "Situation des Troupes," 1–15 Sept. 1812, AGSHA, carton: C2 526.

25. Chandler, *Campaigns*, 790–810; Couper, *Crozet*, 12; Troubetzkoy, "Crozet," 5. The authors wish to acknowledge the assistance of Professor Donald D. Horward of Florida State University who discovered the evidence that Crozet was captured at the battle of Borodino.

26. Crozet to [Baron Evain], 30 Aug., 5 Sept. 1814, dossier of Captain Crozet, AGSHA.

27. Citation, "La décoration du Lys," 1814, and Ministry of War, Bureau of Personnel, to Crozet, 29 Oct. 1814, VMI Crozet Collection; Order to Captain Crozet, 11 Oct. 1814, dossier of Captain Crozet, AGSHA.

28. Order from Baron Dessalles to Captain Crozet, 19 March 1815, Order to Colonel Dessalles, 19 March 1815, VMI Crozet Collection.

29. Orders from Ministry of War, Bureau of Personnel, to Captain Crozet, 28 March 1815, Order from General Neigre to Captain Crozet, 13 June 1815, and "Service militaire aux Armées," 11 April 1815, VMI Crozet Collection; "Etat des Services Militaires de M. Crozet (Claude)," Crozet to Baron Evain, Maréchal de Camp, chef de la 6ième Division, 30 Aug., 5 Sept. 1814, and "Relevé de Services de Crozet," Ministère de la Défense, dossier of Captain Crozet, AGSHA; Troubetzkoy, "Crozet," 6.

30. "Lettre de Licenciement," 1 Nov. 1815, VMI Crozet Collection; Crozet to the duc de Feltre, 1 April 1816, and "Rapport fait au Ministre," Ministère de la Guerre, 11 April 1816, dossier of Captain Crozet, AGSHA.

31. "Mariage M. Crozet & Mlle. Decamp," 5 June 1816, "Extrait du Registre des Actes de Mariage de l'an 1816, Préfecture du Département de la Seine, Ville de Paris," "Régiment de Monsieur, 4ème Hussards, Certificat de Mort (Le Sieur Pierre Camp)," 24 Oct. 1814, "Partage de la succession de M. Decamp," Dec. 1814, VMI Crozet Collection.

32. Claudius Crozet, *A Treatise on Descriptive Geometry for the Use of the Cadets of the United States Military Academy* (New York, 1821), xii; Crozet to Col. F. H. Smith, 26 Aug. 1846, VMI Crozet Collection.

33. Crozet to Minister of War, 9 June 1816, and "Note pour le Bureau de l'Artillerie," 3 April 1820, dossier of Captain Crozet, AGSHA.

34. Couper, *Crozet*, 20; *Biographie Universelle*, s.v. "Bernard, Simon"; *DAB*, s.v. "Bernard, Simon"; Stephen E. Ambrose, *Duty, Honor, Country: A History of West Point* (Baltimore, 1966), 64-67; Edgar Denton III, "The

Formative Years of the United States Military Academy, 1775–1833" (Ph.D. diss., Syracuse University, 1964), 139–40.

2

1. Swift to Winfield Scott, 26 Nov. 1822, Board of Public Works Papers, Virginia State Library, Richmond.

2. Swift to William H. Crawford, 10 Sept. 1816, Records Relating to the United States Military Academy, Adjutant General's Office, Record Group 94, M–91, roll 1, frame 27, National Archives.

3. Harrison Ellery, ed., *The Memoirs of General Joseph Gardner Swift, LL.D., U.S.A. First Graduate of the U.S.M.A., West Point, Chief Engineer U.S.A. from 1812 to 1816* (Privately printed, 1890; copy in USMA Library, West Point, N.Y.), 143–45, 149.

4. Augusta Blanche Berard, *Reminiscences of West Point in the Olden Times* (East Lansing, Mich., 1886), 26.

5. Thomas C. Griess, "Dennis Hart Mahan" (Ph.D. diss., Duke University, 1968), 69. See also Edwin L. Dooley, Jr., "Claudius Crozet: Disseminator of French Technical Education to the United States," *Proceedings of the Consortium on Revolutionary Europe, 1750–1850* (Athens, Ga., 1986), 449–59.

6. Swift to Captain Alden Partridge, 20 Sept. 1816, Swift to Crozet, 20 Sept. 1816, Records Relating to the USMA, RG 94, National Archives. See also MS AGOMA (Adjutant General's Office of Military Affairs), cited in *The Centennial of the United States Military Academy at West Point, New York, 1802–1902*, 2 vols. (Washington, D.C., 1904), 2:71; Couper, *Crozet*, 22.

7. Richard S. Kirby, "Graphic Communication, Books on Drawing and Descriptive Geometry," in *The First One Hundred and Fifty Years: A History of John Wiley and Sons, Incorporated, 1807–1957* (New York, 1957), 84.

8. "Extract of the report of Gen'l [Joseph G.] Swift Relating to the Military Academy at West Point, Laid before Congress Feb. 15th, 1817," enclosure in S. C. Crafts to Alden Partridge, 21 Feb. 1818, Alden Partridge Papers, box 4, USMA Library.

9. *DAB*, s.v. "Williams, Jonathan."

10. Denton, "Formative Years," 23.

11. Ambrose, *Duty, Honor, Country*, 35–37; Denton, "Formative Years," 66–79, 84, 86.

12. *Register of Graduates and Former Cadets, United States Military Academy* (West Point, N.Y., 1955), 131; *DAB*, s.v. "Swift, Joseph Gardner."

13. Swift Report, 15 Feb. 1817, Partridge Papers; Ellery, *Memoirs of Swift*, 151.

14. George Graham, Chief Clerk, Department of War, to Swift, 12 April 1815, Confidential and Unofficial Letters Sent by Secretary of War, RG 107,

Microfilm Publication M-7, National Archives; Denton, "Formative Years," 109, 126–27; Couper, *Crozet*, 7–12; Ambrose, *Duty, Honor, Country*, 66.

15. *DAB*, s.v. "Bernard, Simon." See also Ellery, *Memoirs of Swift*, 143–49, 177–80. In 1819 Swift participated in a month-long meeting of the presidentially appointed Board of Engineers at Georgetown. "The service on the board," he recorded in his memoirs (180), "left an impression on the minds of McRee and myself that Bernard was not the genius he had been reputed. . . . My opinion of Bernard is that he is an excellent bureau officer, a cold-hearted man; not in any sense a man of genius."

16. R. Ernest Dupuy, *Where They Have Trod: The West Point Tradition in American Life* (New York, 1940), 116–20, is strongly partial to Thayer but lacks documentation. Sidney Forman, *West Point: A History of the United States Military Academy* (New York, 1950), 40–45, is slightly partial to Thayer. Lester A. Webb, *Captain Alden Partridge and the United States Military Academy* (Northport, Ala., 1965), 102–5, is strongly partial to Partridge. Ambrose, *Duty, Honor, Country*, is objective. The best and most thorough discussion is found in Denton, "Formative Years," 156–76. No reference to this topic is complete, however, without mention of George Washington Cullum. Graduated from the academy in 1833, Cullum returned as adjutant during the superintendency of Robert E. Lee in the 1850s and was superintendent in 1864–66. In compiling the *Biographical Register of the Officers and Graduates of the U.S.M.A. from 1802 to 1850*, extended to 1890 in the third edition, he included a history of West Point as part of the third volume. This history was "largely a panegyric on the excellence of Sylvanus Thayer," notes Denton, and is considered the basis of the extensive memorialization of Thayer's name at the academy.

17. *DAB*, s.v. "Partridge, Alden"; Denton, "Formative Years," 104.

18. Ibid., 105–8.

19. Ambrose, *Duty, Honor, Country*, 57–61.

20. Ellery, *Memoirs of Swift*, 168–70.

21. Denton, "Formative Years," 143, 156, 162; Webb, *Partridge*, 49; George Graham to President Monroe, 21 July 1817, Letters Sent to the President by the Secretary of War, RG 107, Microfilm Publication M-27, National Archives.

22. Crozet to Swift, 5 Oct. 1818, in file folder marked "Crozet, Claude, 1790–1864," Special Collections, USMA Library.

23. Ambrose, *Duty, Honor, Country*, 77–79.

24. Crozet to Swift, 5 Oct. 1818, Special Collections, USMA Library.

25. Jared Mansfield to Captain John O'Connor, 12 Feb. 1819, Jared Mansfield Papers, USMA Library.

26. Crozet to John C. Calhoun, 16 June 1819, War Department Records, RG 107, National Archives, copy in USMA Library.

27. Ibid.

28. Mansfield to John O'Connor, 28 June 1819, Mansfield Papers.

29. Crozet to Calhoun, 16 June 1819, USMA Library.

30. Crozet to Calhoun, 2 July, 26 July 1819, Letters Received by the Secretary of War, Registered Series, RG 107, Microfilm Publication M-221, National Archives.

31. Denton, "Formative Years," 177.

32. Calhoun to Monroe, 30 Aug. 1819, Letters Sent to the President by the Secretary of War, RG 107, Microfilm Publication M-127, National Archives.

33. Ambrose, *Duty, Honor, Country*, 77–78.

34. Cadets Nathaniel H. Loring, Charles R. Holmes, and Charles R. Vining to Secretary of War Calhoun, 23 July 1819, in W. Edwin Hemphill, ed., *The Papers of John C. Calhoun*, 4 vols. (Columbia, S.C., 1969), 4:171. The other two cadets were Wilson M. C. Fairfax and Thomas Ragland.

35. General Order, Adjutant General's Office, 10 Nov. 1819, West Point Letters, Sylvanus Thayer Collection, USMA Library, cited in Ambrose, *Duty, Honor, Country*, 79.

36. Crozet to Calhoun, 30 Aug. 1819, Calhoun to James Monroe, 30 Aug. 1819, and General Order by Daniel Parker, Adjutant & Inspector General's Office, 23 Sept., 10 Nov. 1819, Hemphill, *Calhoun Papers*, 4:283–84, 287, 344–45; see also Calhoun to Henry Brush, 2 Feb. 1820, ibid., 629–30.

37. Cadet Charles R. Holmes to Calhoun, 29 Nov. 1819, ibid., 456; see also Cadet Wilson M. C. Fairfax to Calhoun, 17 Nov. 1819, Cadet Thomas Ragland to Calhoun, 17 Nov. 1819, Cadet Charles R. Vining to Calhoun, 20 Nov. 1819, and Cadet Nathaniel H. Loring to Calhoun, 23 Nov. 1819, Hemphill, *Calhoun Papers*, 4:414–15, 422, 427.

38. Thayer to Calhoun, 4 Jan. 1820, Calhoun to Alexander Smyth, Chairman of the Military Committee, 1 Feb. 1820, ibid., 549, 628.

39. See Ambrose, *Duty, Honor, Country*, 164; Denton, "Formative Years," 252–81.

40. Jared Mansfield to Calhoun, 20 Dec., 30 Dec. 1819, Hemphill, *Calhoun Papers*, 4:495–96, 524–26. Crozet and Simon Bernard, said Mansfield, were his sources of information about the Ecole Polytechnique.

41. Mansfield to Calhoun, no month or day, 1821, Mansfield Papers.

42. Crozet to Calhoun, 26 July 1819, RG 107, Microfilm Publication M-221, National Archives.

43. See Robert F. Hunter, "The Turnpike Movement in Virginia, 1816–1860" (Ph.D. diss., Columbia University, 1957).

44. Couper, *Crozet*, 29–31.

45. Ambrose, *Duty, Honor, Country*, 98–102; Griess, "D. H. Mahan."

46. Crozet to James Barbour, Secretary of War, 30 June 1825, War Department Records, Letters Received, RG 77, box 25, no. 867, National Archives.

3

1. *Revised Code of the Laws of Virginia*, 1819, 2:201–5.

2. See Carter Goodrich, "The Virginia System of Mixed Enterprise: A Study of State Planning of Internal Improvements," *Political Science Quarterly* 64, no. 3 (1949): 362–63.

3. Madison to Nicholas, 8 April 1816, B. H. Latrobe to James Madison, 8 April 1816, Board of Public Works Papers.

4. *DAB*, s.v. "Baldwin, Loammi"; see also Bernard Peyton to Baldwin, 24 Dec. 1816, Board of Public Works Papers.

5. Crawford to Preston, 28 May 1818, Board of Public Works Papers.

6. Scott to Peyton, 16 Nov. 1822, Crozet to Swift, 23 Nov. 1822, Swift to Scott, 26 Nov. 1822, ibid.

7. Long to Winfield Scott, 29 Nov. 1822, Calhoun to Hon. George Newlon, 4 Dec. 1822, and Extract of a letter from Thomas Jefferson to James Pleasants, dated Monticello, 21 Dec. 1822, ibid.

8. Scott to Peyton, 7 Feb. 1823, ibid.; see also James Pleasants to McRee, 29 Jan. 1823, ibid.

9. Cheves to Peyton, 27 March 1823, Scott to James Pleasants, 3 April 1823, ibid.

10. *Annual Report[s] of the Board of Public Works* (Richmond, 1816–73), 7 (1822): 14–15 (hereafter cited as *ARBPW*).

11. Ibid., 1823, 8:114.

12. See table listing estimates of public aid to canals between 1815 and 1860 in Carter Goodrich et al., *Canals and American Economic Development* (New York, 1961), 214. By 1860 the Virginia state government had invested in round figures $820,000 in the Chesapeake and Ohio Canal, compared with $5.5 million in the James River and Kanawha Canal.

13. *ARBPW* 1823, 8:122–27. On the Chesapeake and Ohio Canal, see also Walter S. Sanderlin, *The Great National Project: A History of the Chesapeake and Ohio Canal* (Baltimore, 1946).

14. *ARBPW* 1823, 8:133.

15. Ibid., 213–20.

16. Wayland F. Dunaway, *History of the James River and Kanawha Company* (New York, 1922), 10–19. Otis K. Rice, in his "Coal Mining in the Kanawha Valley to 1861: A View of Industrialization in the Old South," *Journal of Southern History* 31, no. 4 (1965): 393–416, asserts that Kanawha Valley coal was never able to reach eastern markets before the Civil War due to deficiencies of transportation.

17. Dunaway, *JR&K Co.*, 26–7, 43.

18. *ARBPW* 1823, 8:281–83.

19. Ibid., 1824, 9:91–92, 99; Crozet's Second Report on the Location of the Canal through the Blue Ridge, 15 Jan. 1825, ibid., 111.

20. Ibid., 1823, 8:221–30.

21. See note 34, Chapter 2.

22. J. H. Cocke, Jr., to J. H. Cocke, Sr., 24 June, 22 Aug. 1824, John Hartwell Cocke Papers, University of Virginia Library, Charlottesville. See also M. Boyd Coyner, "John Hartwell Cocke of Bremo: Agriculture and Slavery in the Ante-Bellum South" (Ph.D. diss., University of Virginia, 1961).

23. *ARBPW* 1825, 10:223–25, 242–50, 298.

24. Ibid., 10:227–30, 239–40, 268–77. For the connecting of this basin with the Midlothian coal mines by a 13-mile horse-drawn tramway, see Elizabeth D. Coleman, "Forerunner of Virginia's First Railway," *Virginia Cavalcade* 4, no. 3 (1954): 4–7.

25. *ARBPW* 1825, 10:278–88, 447–48, 475–83. See also Goodrich et al., *Canals and Economic Development*, 77–94.

26. *ARBPW* 1825, 10:486–91.

27. Ibid., 1826, 11:86.

28. Ibid., 90–91.

29. Ibid., 116.

30. Ibid., 1827, 12:229–33, 245–47.

31. D. I. Burr to Crozet, 4 Jan. 1828, cited, ibid., 308–9. Two experimental steam-powered, iron-hulled vessels were actually built for use on the James River Canal in the early 1840s but were removed after inflicting damage with their wakes. See Alexander C. Brown, "The Canal Boat 'Governor McDowell': Virginia's Pioneer Iron Steamer," *Virginia Magazine of History and Biography* 74, no. 3 (1966): 336–45.

32. *ARBPW* 1827, 12:332–34.

33. Ibid., 396–99.

34. Ibid., 399–402.

35. Ibid., 1828, 13:496–98.

36. Ibid., 527–29.

37. See Couper, *Crozet*, 51–52.

38. *ARBPW* 1829, 14:104–8.

39. Ibid., 1830, 15:111–17.

40. Ibid., 1829, 14:147–49.

41. Ibid., 1830, 15:153–55.

42. Ibid., 159.

4

1. Lexington *Intelligencer*, 17 May 1823, 2. On the role of the "Richmond Junto" in limiting legislative support of internal improvements, see Harry Ammon, "The Richmond Junto, 1800–1824," *Virginia Magazine of History and Biography* 61, no. 4 (1953): 395–418.

Notes

2. See Dunaway, *JR&K Co*, 75–76; Couper, *Crozet*, 48–49.

3. Dunaway, *JR&K Co*, 76–77; see also Fletcher M. Green, *Constitutional Development of the South Atlantic States* (Chapel Hill, N.C., 1930), 210–15; Dickson D. Bruce, *The Rhetoric of Conservatism: The Virginia Convention of 1829–30 and the Conservative Tradition in the South* (San Marino, Calif., 1982).

4. For a brief discussion of the dismemberment movement of 1830, see Charles H. Ambler, *West Virginia: The Mountain State* (New York, 1940), 239–42; see also his classic earlier study, *Sectionalism in Virginia, 1776–1861* (Glendale, Calif., 1910), 166–74. Otis K. Rice, *West Virginia: A History* (Lexington, Ky., 1985), reaffirms Ambler's view that better transportation could have prevented the division of the state in 1863. See also Robert Seager, *And Tyler Too: A Biography of John and Julia Gardiner Tyler* (New York, 1963), 76–77, for Governor Tyler's warning to the legislature on this subject.

5. Lexington *Intelligencer*, 14 Jan. 1825, 2.

6. Richmond *Enquirer*, 4 June 1830, 3.

7. Petersburg *Old Dominion*, cited in Richmond *Enquirer*, 6 July 1830, 2.

8. Richmond *Enquirer*, 17 Sept. 1830, 1.

9. Fincastle *Patriot*, cited in Richmond *Enquirer*, 21 Sept. 1830, 4.

10. Lynchburg *Virginian*, cited in Richmond *Enquirer*, 7 Dec. 1830, 1.

11. Richmond *Enquirer*, 7 Dec. 1830, 2, 11 Dec. 1830, 1, 14 Dec. 1830, 3.

12. Ibid., 15 Jan. 1831, 4; *ARBPW* 1831, 16:228–41.

13. The Garland Committee Report is found in *ARBPW* 1830, 15:241-69; also in Richmond *Enquirer*, 19 Feb. 1831, 4 et seq.

14. *ARBPW 1830*, 15:268–69.

15. Richmond *Enquirer*, 12 March 1831, 2, 31 March 1831, 2, 22 March 1831, 4.

16. Ibid., 22 March 1831, 4.

17. Richmond *Enquirer*, 26 March 1831, 3; Couper, *Crozet*, 56–57.

18. Richmond *Enquirer*, 26 March 1831, 3.

19. Ibid., 26 March 1831, 2, 5 April 1831, 2.

20. Ibid., 13 May 1831, 3.

21. Ibid., 17 May 1831, 3, 27 May, 1831, 3.

22. Couper, *Crozet*, 47.

23. Richmond *Enquirer*, 31 May 1831, 3, 3 June 1831, 3, 10 June 1831, 3.

24. Kanawha *Banner*, cited in Richmond *Enquirer*, 10 June 1831, 4.

25. Richmond *Enquirer*, 17 June 1831, 3.

26. Wright to Floyd, 9 Aug. 1831, Crozet to Wright, 6 Aug. 1831, *ARBPW* 1831, 16:452, 457.

27. Wright to Floyd, 9 Aug. 1831, ibid., 454–55.

28. Ibid., 459.

29. Richmond *Enquirer*, 12 Aug. 1831, 3.

30. Crozet to Wright, 6 Aug. 1831, *ARBPW* 1831, 16:458.

31. Cabell to Cocke, 30 Aug. 1831, Joseph C. Cabell Papers, University of Virginia Library, Charlottesville; see also Carol M. Tanner, "Joseph C. Cabell, 1778–1856" (Ph.D. diss., University of Virginia, 1948). For a brief biographical sketch of both Cabell and Cocke, see Philip Alexander Bruce, *History of the University of Virginia, 1819–1919: The Lengthened Shadow of One Man*, 2 vols. (New York, 1920), 1:147–64.

32. Cocke to Cabell, 3 Sept. 1831, Cabell Papers.

33. Rives to Cabell, 5 Sept. 1831, ibid.

34. Cabell to Cocke, 12 Sept. 1831, ibid.

35. Coalter to Cabell, 27 Sept. 1831, ibid.

36. Abingdon *Republican*, 20 Aug. 1831, cited in Richmond *Enquirer*, 30 Aug. 1831, 4.

37. Richmond *Enquirer*, 11 Oct. 1831, 4; *ARBPW* 1831, 16:379–86.

38. Richmond *Enquirer*, 18 Nov. 1831, 2.

39. Crozet to Floyd, 28 Oct. 1831, *ARBPW* 1831, 16:305; Couper, *Crozet*, 61.

40. Crozet to BPW, 16 Dec. 1831, *ARBPW* 1831, 16:376.

41. Ibid., 377–78.

42. Ibid., 395–408.

43. Ellery, ed., *Memoirs of General Joseph G. Swift*, 211.

44. The growing volume of public demand during the period 1830–31 and after included requests for roads and turnpikes as well. See Hunter, "The Turnpike Movement in Virginia, 1816–1860," in which petitions to the legislature from all quarters of Virginia were examined. See also H. J. Eckenrode, ed., *A Calendar of Legislative Petitions Arranged by Counties: Special Report of the Department of Archives and History* (Richmond, 1908).

5

1. The Pontchartrain Railroad was built by General Joseph G. Swift, whose first experience as a civil engineer was as chief engineer of the Baltimore and Susquehanna Railroad in 1828. Swift had left Louisiana before Crozet arrived there. See Ellery, *Memoirs of Swift*, 204–7.

2. See Stanley C. Arthur and George C. H. de Kernion, *Old Families of Louisiana* (New Orleans, 1931), 268–73.

3. *DAB*, s.v. "Roman, André Bienvenu"; see also Alcée Fortier, ed., *Louisinana*, 3 vols. (New York, 1914); Charles Gayarre, *History of Louisiana*, 4 vols. (New Orleans, 1903; rpt. New Orleans, 1965).

4. Baton Rouge *Gazette*, 12 Feb. 1831, 2.

5. Ibid., 14 Jan. 1832, 1; New Orleans *Courier*, 4 Jan. 1832, 3.

6. *Journal of the [Louisiana] House of Representatives*, 10th Leg., 2d Sess., 120–21.

7. New Orleans *Bee*, 17 Jan. 1833, 3.

8. Ibid., 22 Jan. 1833, 2.

9. *Journal of the [La.] House of Representatives*, 10th Leg., 2d Sess., 33.

10. Ibid., 34–35.

11. New Orleans *Courier*, 24 Jan. 1833, 3; New Orleans *Bee*, 24 Jan. 1833, 2.

12. Merl E. Reed, *New Orleans and the Railroads* (Baton Rouge, La., 1966), 5.

13. New Orleans *Bee*, 11 March 1833, 2.

14. Reed, *New Orleans*, 51–52.

15. Report of the Civil Engineer of the State, 16 Dec. 1833, New Orleans *Bee*, 11 Jan. 1834, 1.

16. Ibid., 10 Dec. 1833, 2; Baton Rouge *Gazette*, 14 Dec. 1833, supplement, n.p.

17. New Orleans *Courier*, 18 July 1833, 3.

18. Reed, *New Orleans*, 52.

19. New Orleans *Bee*, 11 Jan. 1834, 1; *Journal of the [La.] House of Representatives*, 10th Leg., 2d Sess., 24 Dec. 1833.

20. New Orleans *Bee*, 11 Jan. 1834, supplement, 2.

21. New Orleans *Bee*, 7 Feb. 1834, 2, 13 Feb. 1834, 2.

22. *Journal of the [La.] House of Representatives*, 10th Leg., 2d Sess., 12 Feb. 1834, 90–91.

23. New Orleans *Bee*, 27 Feb. 1834, 1.

24. "An Act Granting further powers to the Board of Public Works and for other purposes," approved March 10, 1834, reported in New Orleans *Bee*, 25 April 1834, 2.

25. New Orleans *Bee*, 5 March 1834, 2, 6 Jan. 1835, 2.

26. Ibid., 1 Sept. 1834, 2, 21 Nov. 1834, 2. On the latter date, the newspaper article, entitled "The Rail Road to Nashville," stated, "At a meeting called by public advertisement, at Bishop's Hotel, in the city of New Orleans on Thursday, the 20th day of November 1834, George Eustis, Esq., was called to the chair, J. W. Breedlove was appointed vice-president, Thomas Barrett and Joshua Baldwin Esqs, were appointed secretaries. The meeting was addressed by Judge Watts, M. W. Hoffman, B. Marigny, and J. Kilty Smith, Esqrs." The term "esquire" designated landed proprietors as well as attorneys.

27. Reed, *New Orleans*, 24.

28. New Orleans *Bee*, 6 Jan. 1835, 2.

29. Baton Rouge *Gazette*, 12 Feb. 1831, 2.

30. Earl F. Niehaus, "Jefferson College: The Early Years," *Louisiana Historical Quarterly*, 38, no. 4 (1955): 66–69. Robert Carter Nicholas was the

son of Virginia Governor Wilson Cary Nicholas (1814–16). The younger Nicholas settled in Donaldsonville, Louisiana, and became a sugar planter. He served in the legislature and as secretary of state of Louisiana.

31. Oliver P. Carriere, *A Sketch of the History of Jefferson College and Manresa House of Retreats* (Convent, La., 1974), 8.

32. Baton Rouge *Gazette*, 21 Dec. 1833, 2.

33. Niehaus, "Jefferson College," 77–78.

34. U.S. Census Report, 1860, Saint James Parish, Louisiana, Baton Rouge Public Library, Centroplex Branch; Crozet's will, dated 5 Feb. 1863, 4-page parchment manuscript, not bound in a will book, Chancery Court, 800 Marshall St., Richmond, Va.

35. This marriage is listed in Nicholas Russell Murray, *St. James Parish, Louisiana, 1809–1900* (Hammond, La., n.d.), 33; see also Couper, *Crozet*, 70. For information on the Roman family, see especially Arthur and Kernion, *Old Families*, 268–73. They mention several unnamed sons of A. B. Roman, and several of his five younger brothers and some of their sons and daughters, but never refer to the name Felix.

36. Simone de la Souchère Délery, "Some French Soldiers Who Became Louisiana Educators," *Louisiana Historical Quarterly* 31, no. 4 (1948): 853.

37. Niehaus, "Jefferson College," 76.

38. John D. Imboden, "Biographical Sketch of Colonel Claudius Crozet," in W. F. Switzler, *Report on the Internal Commerce of the U.S.* (1886), 17–19, cited in *Bulletin of the Virginia State Library* (Richmond, 1914), 95–97.

39. Niehaus, "Jefferson College," 77.

40. Edwin W. Fay, *The History of Education in Louisiana* (Washington, D.C., 1898), 49–50.

41. Huguer Jules de La Vergne to Crozet, 15 July, 21 Oct. 1835, La Vergne Papers, Louisiana State University, Baton Rouge. In the fall of 1835, among the students listed were two Roman boys, Charles and Felix (La Vergne to Crozet, 21 Oct. 1835). There was no indication here of Felix's age, but he was probably 14 in 1835. There was a Charles F. Roman listed in the Census Report of 1860, born probably in 1850, in all likelihood the son of Felix and Anna and named after his uncle Charles.

42. La Vergne to Ingalls, 26 April 1836, La Vergne Papers.

43. New Orleans *Bee*, 18 July 1836, 2.

44. Ibid., 19 Sept. 1836, 2.

45. *Journal of the [La.] House of Representatives*, 10th Leg., 2d Sess., 7 Jan. 1840.

6

1. Couper, *Crozet*, 72.
2. *ARBPW* 1837, 22:51.

3. Ibid., 1838, 23:12–13.

4. Ibid., 1837, 22:60. On early Virginia railroads, see also Charles W. Turner, "The Early Railroad Movement in Virginia," *Virginia Magazine of History and Biography* 55 (1947): 350–71.

5. *ARBPW* 1838, 23:6.

6. Ibid., 1839, 24:3–6, 22–26.

7. Ibid., 1840, 25:247–52. On Gilmer see also Robert Sobel and John Raimo, eds., *Biographical Directory of the Governors of the United States, 1789–1978*, 4 vols. (Westport, Conn., 1978), 4:1638–39. The Richmond Junto orchestrated the wide dispersion of internal improvement funds, in the view of Joseph H. Harrison, Jr. ("Oligarchs and Democrats: The Richmond Junto," *Virginia Magazine of History and Biography* 78, no. 2 [1970]: 184–98).

8. *ARBPW* 1840, 25:461–62; on the Southwestern Turnpike, see Hunter, "Turnpike Movement in Virginia," 210–16.

9. *ARBPW* 1841, 26:317, 321–22.

10. Dunaway, *JR&K Co*, 90–91; Tanner, "Joseph C. Cabell," 195–96. Richmond City Council, in order to save the charter, subscribed in 1834 to 7,500 shares at $100 per share. When Richmond property owners protested, the legislature took 5,000 shares on state account, reducing Richmond's commitment to $250,000 worth of stock in the James River and Kanawha Company. This increased the state's share to three-fifths, a practice extended to all internal improvement companies after 1835. However, the state refrained from assuming majority control on boards of directors of the companies.

11. For Crozet's full report on the James River Canal, see *ARBPW* 1840, 25:482–98. See also Christopher T. Baer, *Canals and Railroads of the Mid-Atlantic States, 1800–1860* (Wilmington, Del., 1981), for comprehensive data and maps; Virginia receives only peripheral treatment.

12. *ARBPW* 1841, 26:334–37.

13. Cabell to Cocke, 11 March 1841, Cabell Papers.

14. *ARBPW* 1841, 26:395–99.

15. Cabell to Cocke, 17 Jan. 1842, 8 Nov. 1842, Cabell Papers.

16. Cabell's long report is found in *ARBPW* 1842, 27:496–539.

17. Although Cabell disagreed with Wright about the proposed railroad for the western section of the James River and Kanawha line, he and Cocke were nevertheless close friends of Wright. On the occasion of Wright's death in August 1842, his son James wrote a long letter to Cocke, referring to pleasant family visits to Bremo and the friendship of his sister with Cocke's daughter (James Wright to John H. Cocke, 27 Aug. 1842, Cocke Papers). Cabell in writing to Cocke about it referred to "our excellent friend Judge Wright than whom a purer man never sunk into the grave" (Cabell to Cocke, 16 Sept. 1842, Cabell Papers).

18. Dunaway, *JR&K Co*, 154–55; Tanner, "Joseph C. Cabell," 195–96. The James River Canal was completed to Buchanan in 1851. Between 1853

and 1856 work was done on its extension toward Covington, then abandoned. See Alexander C. Brown, "The Tomb of a Dream: The Marshall Tunnel and the Unfinished Portion of the James River and Kanawha Canal," *Virginia Cavalcade* 22, no. 4 (1973): 18–29. For a delightful pictorial essay, see Kent Druyvesteyn, "With Great Vision: The James River and Kanawha Canal," ibid., 21, no. 3 (1972): 22–47.

19. *ARBPW* 1837, 22:88–89; ibid., 1857, 40:546. See also on the North River Navigation, Elizabeth D. Coleman and W. Edwin Hemphill, "Boats beyond the Blue Ridge," *Virginia Cavalcade* 3, no. 4 (1954): 8–13.

20. See *ARBPW* 1838, 23:409–11; ibid., 1839, 24:203.

21. Ibid., 1837, 22:97.

22. Ibid., 1839, 24:215–17.

23. Ibid., 1842, 27:615–17.

24. Both of these railroads were built by Moncure Robinson, Virginia-born engineer who wanted Crozet's job in the late 1820s. See, for example, Robinson to Randolph Harrison, 27 June 1827, Moncure Robinson Papers, Virginia Historical Society, Richmond. See also Charles W. Turner, "Early Railroad Entrepreneurs and Personnel," *Virginia Magazine of History and Biography* 58, no. 3 (1950): 325–34.

25. *ARBPW* 1842, 27:617–19.

26. Ibid., 1840, 25:503–7.

27. Peter C. Stewart, "Railroads and Urban Rivalries in Antebellum Eastern Virginia," *Virginia Magazine of History and Biography* 81, no. 1 (1973): 3–22.

28. *ARBPW* 1837, 22:226; ibid., 1838, 23:22–23.

29. Ibid., 1839, 24:24–25, 199–203.

30. Ibid., 1841, 26:324–32. The historical literature on the Baltimore and Ohio Railroad is extensive. A good starting point is the centennial history of Edward Hungerford, *The Story of the Baltimore and Ohio Railroad, 1827–1927* (New York, 1928), 2 vols. (vol. 1: 1827–61). Crozet's visit is not mentioned in this or any other study we have seen.

31. *ARBPW* 1841, 26:332–33.

32. Ibid., 1837, 22:90–94; ibid., 1838, 23:16–17. On turnpike construction principles and methods, see Robert F. Hunter, "Turnpike Construction in Antebellum Virginia," *Technology and Culture* 4, no. 2 (1963): 177–200.

33. *ARBPW* 1839, 24:22, 26–29, 208; ibid., 1840, 25:475–78.

34. Ibid., 1838, 23:18–21; ibid., 1839, 24:22–26.

35. Ibid., 1841, 26:340–42; ibid., 1842, 27:608–11.

36. Ibid., 1837, 22:144–45; ibid., 1840, 25:497–98.

37. Ibid., 1840, 25:499; ibid., 1842, 27:595–96.

38. Ibid., 1837, 22:97.

39. Ibid., 1839, 24:138–42. See also Charles B. Dew, *Ironmaker to the*

Confederacy: Joseph R. Anderson and the Tredegar Iron Works (New Haven, 1966), 8–9.

40. *ARBPW* 1839, 24:149–50.

41. Ibid., 1840, 25:500–502.

42. Ibid., 1842, 27:596–600.

43. Ibid., 355–58.

44. For the closing of the account, see *ARBPW*, 1844, 29:xiii. Crozet's annual salary of $3,000 was close to the average paid engineers of the first rank in the United States. See Mark Aldrich, "Earnings of American Civil Engineers, 1820–1859," *Journal of Economic History* 31, no. 2 (1971): 409–10.

45. *ARBPW* 1844, 29:259–74.

7

1. J. T. L. Preston, "Cives," cited in William Couper, *One Hundred Years at V.M.I.*, 4 vols. (Richmond, 1939), 1:18, 26.

2. Ibid., 25.

3. Ibid., 25–28; *Journal of the House of Delegates of the Commonwealth of Virginia* (Richmond, 1837), 13. See also Ollinger Crenshaw, *General Lee's College: The Rise and Growth of Washington and Lee University* (New York, 1969), 59–65.

4. Couper, *One Hundred Years*, 1:29–30; *Journal of the House of Delegates of the Commonwealth of Virginia* (Richmond, 1839), 15, 41.

5. Minutes of the Board of Visitors (2), 1839–53, Meetings of the Board, p. 1. The minutes of the early meetings of the Board of Visitors exist in two duplicative volumes in the Archives Division of Preston Library, VMI. The first volume appears to contain the working drafts of the minutes of the board; the second volume is a fair copy by various clerks and secretaries. The contents of the two volumes are virtually the same for the early meetings except for the inclusion in the working copy of the first set of regulations for the Institute. Hereafter, the first volume will be cited as Minutes of the Board of Visitors (1), and the second volume will be cited as Minutes of the Board of Visitors (2).

6. Minutes of the Board of Visitors (1), 5, 15; Couper, *Crozet*, 103. The Minutes of the Board of Visitors (1) contain sections written by Dorman, Crozet, Smith, Dold, and others.

7. Joseph Reid Anderson, Jr., "A Complete History of Virginia Military Institute," 1:17–18, typescript, Joseph R. Anderson, Jr., Collection, Archives Division, Preston Library, VMI.

8. Ibid.; Minutes of the Board of Visitors (1), 6.

9. Minutes of the Board of Visitors (1), 45; ibid. (2), 6, 7.

10. Adjutant General, U.S.A., Roger Jones to Peyton, 16 Sept., 18 Oct.

1839, letters nos. 3 and 4, Records of the Superintendent, Incoming Correspondence, 1839–42, VMI Archives.

11. Minutes of the Board of Visitors (2), 13.

12. Ibid., 25–27.

13. Smith to Peyton, 11 Nov. 1840, Smith to Crozet, 25 Nov. 1840, Records of the Superintendent, Outgoing Correspondence, 25 July 1840–8 Feb. 1844, 19, 21.

14. Smith to Crozet, 12 Jan., 9 March, 11 March 1841, Outgoing Correspondence, 1840–44, 42, 59, 66.

15. Dorman to Smith, 18 Jan. 1841, letter no. 8, Peyton to Smith, 30 Dec. 1840, letter no. 21, Incoming Correspondence, 1839–42.

16. Smith to Crozet, 21 April 1843, Outgoing Correspondence, 1840–44, 280; Crozet to Smith, 16 Sept. 1843, letter no. 8, Incoming Correspondence, 1843–44. See also Couper, *Crozet*, 111–12.

17. Crozet to Smith, 8 Nov. 1843, letter no. 9, Incoming Correspondence; also cited in Couper, *Crozet*, 113.

18. Minutes of the Board of Visitors (2), 87.

19. Smith to Crozet, 24 April 1845, letter no. 22, Records of the Superintendent, Outgoing Correspondence, 10 Feb. 1844–30 Dec. 1848, 120–21.

20. Crozet to Smith, 20 Feb. 1845, letter no. 22, Records of the Superintendent, Incoming Correspondence, 1845; Smith to Crozet, 24 April 1845, Outgoing Correspondence, 1844–48, 120–21.

21. Crozet to Smith, 26 Aug. 1846, letter no. 22, Records of the Superintendent, Incoming Correspondence, 1846.

22. Margaret Meagher, *History of Education in Richmond* (Richmond, 1939), 45.

23. Ibid., 47–49; Couper, *Crozet*, 121.

24. Lexington *Valley Star*, 24 July 1845, 1.

25. Ibid., 18 Sept. 1845, 1. Robertson, governor for one year (1836–37), was "noteworthy for the development of railroads in the state" (Sobel and Raimo, *Biographical Directory of the Governors*, 4:1637–38). The Richmond and Petersburg Railroad and the Louisa Railroad were chartered during his term.

26. *Valley Star*, 6 Nov. 1845, 1, 4 Dec. 1845, 1.

27. Crozet to Smith, 26 Aug. 1846, letter no. 22, Incoming Correspondence, 1846; Couper, *Crozet*, 119–20. For information about Crozet's residences in Richmond, see Robert B. Munford, Jr., *Richmond Homes and Memories* (Richmond, 1936), 120; Mary Wingfield Scott, *Old Richmond Neighborhoods* (Richmond, 1950), 115–17; Valentine Museum, *Richmond Portraits: In an Exhibition of Makers of Richmond, 1737–1860* (Richmond, 1949), 50–51. Crozet bought a house at 100 East Main St. in 1828, which he sold in 1832. After the marriage in 1839 of his daughter, Claudia Natalia, to Dr. Charles S. Mills, the Crozets lived with them at 310 North Twelfth St.

28. Crozet to Smith, 20 Sept. 1847, letter no. 22, Incoming Correspondence, 1847; also cited in Couper, *Crozet*, 121–22.

29. Couper, *Crozet*, 122–23.

30. Andrew Talcott Diary, Virginia Historical Society, Richmond, entries dated 14 Jan. 1848, 26 Dec. 1848, 6 Sept. 1849, 29 Dec. 1851, 24 Nov. 1852, 14 Feb. 1854, 8 April 1860. See also *DAB*, s.v. "Talcott, Andrew."

31. The story of mapmaking in Virginia is told in E. M. Sanchez-Saavedra, *A Description of the Country: Virginia Cartographers and Their Maps, 1607–1881* (Richmond, 1975). For the role of Crozet, see chaps. 6 and 7, pp. 55–86.

32. *ARBPW* 1843, 28:15; see also Couper, *Crozet*, 122–23.

33. Richardson to F. H. Smith, 13 March 1849, cited in Couper, *Crozet*, 125.

8

1. *ARBPW* 1838, 23:22–23; ibid., 1839, 24:24–25.

2. Crozet to BPW, 22 March, 24 March 1849, Board of Public Works Papers, Group 125, box 215, Virginia State Library, Richmond. This chapter is largely based upon Crozet's letters to the Virginia Board of Public Works, which agency was in fact the Blue Ridge Railroad Company.

3. Crozet Report to BPW, 30 Nov. 1849, ibid.

4. Crozet to BPW, 9 Dec. 1855, cited in Couper, *Crozet*, 149.

5. Report of Williams C. Wickham, vice-president, Chesapeake and Ohio Railroad, *Annual Reports of the Internal Improvement Companies of the State of Virginia to the Board of Public Works, for the Year 1873* (Richmond, 1874), 20.

6. Henry Sturgis Drinker, *Tunneling* (New York, 1878), 792–94.

7. Crozet to BPW, 15 Jan. 1851, Board of Public Works Papers.

8. Crozet to BPW, 17 Jan. 1854, ibid; Couper, *Crozet*, 133.

9. Edward Hungerford, *The Story of the Baltimore and Ohio Railroad, 1827–1927*, 2 vols. (New York, 1928), 1:152.

10. Crozet to BPW, 2 Aug., 3 Oct. 1853, 4 Jan., 8 Feb. 1854, Board of Public Works Papers.

11. Crozet to BPW, 8 March 1850, 15 Jan., 16 July 1851, ibid. The slight difference in lengths given for each of the several tunnels at different points in the text reflect changes in current estimates.

12. Crozet to James Brown, Jr., Secretary BPW, 6 Nov. 1849, ibid. Myers's name was one of three etched on a granite square which was for some years embedded in the east portal of Greenwood tunnel; the third name was John Kelly. That stone is mounted today on the face of the parapet of Crozet Hall at VMI.

13. Crozet to BPW, 2 May 1854, Board of Public Works Papers.

14. Joseph A. Waddell, *Annals of Augusta County, 1726–1871*, 2d ed. (Staunton, Va., 1902), 442; Couper, *Crozet*, 152. Father Daniel Downey, Roman Catholic priest in Staunton, was influential with the Irish workers and prevented even more violence. Crozet appreciated Downey's work. See Elizabeth Dabney Coleman, "The Story of the Virginia Central Railroad, 1850–1860" (Ph.D. diss., University of Virginia, 1957), 80.

15. Crozet to Brown, 26 March, 18 June 1850, Kelly to BPW, 8 March 1853, Board of Public Works Papers.

16. MS Petition to BPW, signed by John Bell and eight other citizens of Staunton and Augusta County, 28 Feb. 1853, box 216, Board of Public Works Papers.

17. Crozet to BPW, 11 March 1853, ibid.

18. Cabell to Cocke, 18 May 1842, Cabell Papers.

19. Gene D. Lewis, *Charles Ellet, Jr.: The Engineer as Individualist, 1818–1862* (Urbana, Ill., 1968).

20. Crozet to BPW, 10 Jan. 1857, Board of Public Works Papers. On the construction of the temporary track, see Coleman, "The Story of the Virginia Central Railroad, 1850–1860," 93–117.

21. Drinker, *Tunneling*, 484; see also Crozet to Thomas H. DeWitt, 19 Sept. 1853, Board of Public Works Papers; Couper, *Crozet*, 139. Drinker said 2,000 feet of 3-inch pipe, as did Couper, whose source was Drinker. The length and diameter cited here are from Crozet's letter to DeWitt.

22. Crozet to BPW, 4 Jan., 8 Feb. 1854, Board of Public Works Papers.

23. Ellet to A. Graham, President BPW, 5 Dec. 1854, ibid.

24. Crozet to BPW, 4 Jan. 1854, ibid.

25. Crozet to BPW, 17 Jan. 1854, 22 Oct. 1856, ibid.

26. Ellet to Col. Edmund Fontaine, President VCRR, 11 Feb. 1854, ibid.

27. Crozet to BPW, 2 Aug., 5 Sept. 1853, 2 Oct. 1854, ibid.

28. Crozet to BPW, 22 Oct. 1856, cited in Couper, *Crozet*, 156.

29. Crozet to BPW, 8 Feb. 1854, Board of Public Works Papers.

30. Ellet to A. Graham, President BPW, 9 Dec. 1853, ibid.

31. Crozet to Ellet, 18 Jan., 21 Jan., 30 Jan., 1 Feb. 1854, Ellet to Crozet, 31 Jan. 1854, ibid.

32. Lewis, *Ellet*, 30, 98.

33. Crozet to W. R. Drinkard, Secretary BPW, 22 April 1853, Board of Public Works Papers.

34. Crozet to BPW, 2 Aug., 5 Sept. 1853, ibid.

35. Blue Ridge Railroad, Contract for the Hire of Negroes, 23 Dec. 1853, box 216, ibid.

36. Crozet to BPW, 29 April 1854, ibid.

37. Crozet to BPW, 3 June, 1 Sept. 1854, ibid.

38. Crozet to BPW, 1 Dec. 1854, 31 March 1855, ibid.

39. Crozet to BPW, 16 June 1856, ibid.

40. Lexington *Gazette*, 30 March 1854, quoted in Couper, *Crozet*, 140–41; Ellet to Fontaine, 11 Feb. 1854, Board of Public Works Papers.

41. Crozet to BPW, 5 Nov. 1854, 1 March 1856, Board of Public Works Papers; Dew, *Anderson*, 14.

42. Crozet to BPW, 31 March 1855, Board of Public Works Papers; Crozet to BPW, 9 Dec. 1855, 22 Oct. 1856, cited in Couper, *Crozet*, 148, 157.

43. Couper, *Crozet*, 143–44.

44. Crozet to Thomas Green, 19 Jan. 1855, Thomas Green Correspondence (1815–71), Virginia Historical Society.

45. Couper, *Crozet*, 144.

46. Ibid., 154.

47. Crozet to BPW, 1 Oct. 1850, Crozet to Governor Floyd, 17 Oct. 1850, box 215, Board of Public Works Papers; Crozet to BPW, 22 Nov. 1851, *ARBPW* 1851, 36:464–66.

48. Sanchez-Saavedra, *Virginia Cartographers*, 81–86.

49. Crozet to BPW, 4 March 1856, cited in Couper, *Crozet*, 153–55.

50. Crozet to BPW, 30 Nov. 1849, 8 Feb. 1854, Board of Public Works Papers.

51. Crozet to BPW, 24 July 1856, ibid.

52. H. D. Whitcomb to President & Directors, Virginia Central Railroad, 21 Sept. 1857, ibid. Whitcomb was chief engineer of the Virginia Central until its consolidation with the C&O in 1867, and of that railroad until 1874 (Drinker, *Tunneling*, 484).

53. Whitcomb to President & Directors, Virginia Central Railroad, 21 Sept. 1857, Board of Public Works Papers.

54. Crozet to Thomas H. DeWitt, Secretary BPW, 8 Feb. 1858, ibid.

55. Charles B. Fisk Report to BPW, 20 Feb. 1858, box 217, ibid.

56. Crozet to DeWitt, 11 Jan. 1858, ibid.

9

1. Russell F. Weigley, *Quartermaster General of the Union Army: A Biography of M. C. Meigs* (New York, 1959), 60.

2. Ibid., 68.

3. *DAB*, s.v. "Floyd, John Buchanan."

4. Weigley, *Meigs*, 80–81, 87.

5. Pocket diary, entry for 5 Aug. 1855, Montgomery C. Meigs Papers, reel no. 1, Library of Congress.

6. Pocket diary, 14 Nov., 18 Nov. 1857, reel no. 1, Meigs Papers.

7. Crozet to Meigs, 24 Nov. 1857, cited in William H. Carter, "Claude

Crozet," *Journal of the Military Service Institution of the United States* 53 (July-Aug. 1913): 6; also cited in Couper, *Crozet*, 175.

8. Pocket diary, 1 Dec. 1857, reel no. 1, Meigs Papers.

9. Letter from Meigs, 3 July 1857, no addressee, Letterbooks, reel no. 17, ibid.

10. Pocket diary, 30 Nov. 1857, reel no. 1, ibid.

11. See Letterbook, Private Letters, 21 Sept. 1858–18 Aug. 1859, reel no. 19, ibid.

12. Meigs to Mother, 3 Dec. 1857, Letterbooks, reel no. 17, ibid.

13. Pocket diary, entries for 2 March, 10 April, 5 Dec. 1858, 27 Feb. 1859, reel no. 1, ibid.

14. Pocket diary, entries for 24 Jan., 12 June 1858, reel no. 1, ibid.

15. Meigs to Crozet, 23 April 1858, Letterbooks, May 1857-March 1861, reel no. 17, ibid.

16. Clipping from Washington newspaper (name omitted), 3 Jan. 1859, reel no. 14, ibid.

17. Meigs to Berret, 7 April 1859, Journals, 1857–60, reel no. 14, ibid.

18. Meigs to Crozet, 8 July 1859, Letterbook, Private Letters, 21 Sept. 1858–18 Aug. 1859, reel no. 19, ibid.

19. Crozet to Smith, 24 June, 6 Oct. 1859, Smith to Crozet, 7 July 1859, cited in Couper, *Crozet*, 175–78.

20. The granddaughter, Adele Crozet Mills, lived into the mid-1930s and discussed the writing of the first biography of Crozet with its author, Colonel William Couper.

21. Report of T. H. DeWitt, Secretary BPW, 30 Dec. 1858, *ARBPW* 1859, 41:viii, 582. For a brief sketch of southern railroads in the 1850s, see John F. Stover, *Iron Road to the West: American Railroads in the 1850's* (New York, 1978), 59–93.

22. Newspaper clipping (name omitted) attached to letter from Thomas J. Boyd to T. H. DeWitt, Secretary BPW, 27 Sept. 1857, in Correspondence, Reports, etc. 1857–58, entry 154 (Virginia and Kentucky Railroad Papers), Board of Public Works Papers.

23. *ARBPW* 1859, 41:xxi; Report of Stockholders' Meeting, Virginia and Kentucky Railroad, 12 June 1858, entry 154, Board of Public Works Papers.

24. *ARBPW* 1859, 41:xxiii–xxv.

25. Albert H. Dorr to T. H. DeWitt, 3 July 1860, Correspondence, Reports, etc. 1859 (Virginia & Kentucky Railroad), entry 154, Board of Public Works Papers.

26. Proceedings of the Board of Directors, Virginia & Kentucky Railroad, 2 July 1860, entry 154, ibid.

27. Abingdon *Democrat*, 23 July 1860, clipping in entry 154, ibid. On the extension of the Virginia Central Railroad from Taylorsville to Richmond, see Coleman, "The Story of the Virginia Central Railroad," 1–29.

28. Abingdon *Democrat*, 23 July 1860, entry 154, Board of Public Works Papers.

29. Proceedings of the President and Board of Directors, Virginia & Kentucky Railroad, at Jonesville, Va., 26 July 1860, entry 154, ibid.

30. Clipping from Abingdon *Virginian*, 10 Aug. 1860, in Proceedings of the President and Board of Directors, Virginia & Kentucky Railroad, at Estillville, Va., 15 Aug. 1860, entry 154, ibid.

31. Crozet to Alex R. Holladay, President BPW, 15 Oct. 1860, entry 154, ibid.

32. Articles of Agreement between W. J. Hawkins & Company and Enoch Taylor and Albert J. St. Clair, 23 Nov. 1860, 2 pp. (printed), entry 154, ibid.

33. Couper, *Crozet*, 180.

34. Crozet to Robert W. Hughes, 6 April 1861, Robert William Hughes Papers, Swem Library, College of William and Mary, Williamsburg, Va.

35. Crozet to Major John Tyler, Jr., 19 July 1861, John Tyler, Jr. Papers, Swem Library, College of William and Mary.

36. Couper, *Crozet*, 180–81.

37. Samuel Shacklett, President, Valley Turnpike Company, to BPW, Oct. 1862, ARBPW 1861–70, reel no. 16, Board of Public Works Papers, Preston Library, VMI.

38. "My Will, C. Crozet," Chancery Court, Richmond; Couper, *Crozet*, 181.

39. For many years there was no memorial marking the grave of the Crozet family except for the 1830 headstone over Adele's grave, its inscription weathered beyond legibility a century later. In 1942, when Crozet's casket was transported to Lexington, a monument was erected in Shockoe Cemetery to mark his former resting place and the graves of the rest of his family.

40. Couper, *Crozet*, 152.

41. James Poyntz Nelson Papers, Virginia Historical Society, Richmond.

42. See, for example, Crozet to Imboden, 18 Aug. 1849, John D. Imboden Papers, University of Virginia Library.

43. See reprint of Imboden's essay in *Bulletin of Virginia State Library* (1914), 95–97.

Bibliography

A Note on Sources

For the student life of Crozet, the essential manuscript source is the archival collections of the Bibliothèque Centrale de l'Ecole Polytechnique, formerly in Paris and now located at Paliseau. Over the period of nearly twenty years that research was conducted for this biography the archives of the Ecole Polytechnique have been transformed from a confused collection of original documents roughly arranged in cartons by year to a model of systematic arrangement and preservation. There are scattered references to Crozet in the student records preserved for the years 1805 to 1807, as well as in the alumni records. Especially helpful were various Listes des élèves admis à l'Ecole Polytechnique, the Livre d'immatriculation, the Registre des délibérations du Conseil d'administration de l'Ecole Polytechnique, and the Registre des délibérations du Conseil de perfectionnement de l'Ecole Polytechnique.

Also located in Paris, the holdings of the Service Historique d l'Armée at the Archives de la Guerre in the Chateau de Vincennes were of great value. Preserved in these archives are not only the dossier of Captain Crozet, containing much of his service record, but also the important "Situations des troupes" for the campaign of 1812 that show Crozet's movements with the Grande Armée and provide evidence of his capture at Borodino.

The Claudius Crozet Collection in the VMI Archives, located in Preston Library at the Virginia Military Institute, Lexington, contains original documents and manuscript copies of Crozet's service record, as well as a small number of personal items. The archives also contain the bound minutes of the VMI Board of Visitors, the incoming correspondence of the VMI superintendent, in which are found several original Crozet letters, and the outgoing correspondence of the VMI superintendent, in which are found copies of letters from Colonel Francis H. Smith to Crozet.

For the educational program at the Ecole Polytechnique during Crozet's years as a student, reports included in Jean-Nicholas Pierre Hachette, *Correspondence sur l'Ecole Impériale Polytechnique* were especially useful. This three-volume work contains lists of students admitted to the Ecole, lists of graduates, general information and news about the school, and reports on the scientific and mathematical work of its professors. The monumental *Livre du centenaire, 1794–1894*, published in the centennial year of the Ecole, 1895, was helpful, but a recently reprinted edition of Ambroise Fourcy, *Histoire de l'Ecole Polytechnique*, originally published in 1828, was of greater use, especially as it contains a register of alumni from 1794 to 1827, a new bibliography of studies of the Ecole Polytechnique, and biographical sketches of the leading personalities involved with the Ecole from 1794 to 1827. A detailed study of the courses offered at the Ecole during its early years is to be found in Jānis Langins, *La République avait besoin de savants.*

Several manuscript collections at the library of the United States Military Academy are useful for Crozet's years at West Point, notably the letters and papers of Jared Mansfield, Joseph G. Swift, and Alden Partridge. These are complemented by letters sent and received by the secretary of war, located in the National Archives, Washington, D.C., as well as by the published letters of John C. Calhoun.

Crozet's work as principal engineer of Virginia is found in the Virginia Board of Public Works papers at the Virginia State Library in Richmond, and the published *Annual Reports of the Board of Public Works* (1816–73). Special subdivisions of the extensive Board of Public Works papers, such as the Blue Ridge Railroad and tunnel papers and the Virginia and Kentucky Railroad papers, have been little used previously. Insight into the political opposition to Crozet is found in the letters and papers of Joseph Carrington Cabell and John Hartwell Cocke at the University of Virginia Library, Charlottesville. Evidence of Crozet's friendship with John D. Imboden is found in the Imboden papers in the same library.

Manuscript collections and even published government reports are conspicuous by their absence in Louisiana, due to destruction during the Civil War. Published reports of the Louisiana Board of Public Works and of the state legislature may be found in newspapers, which provide information about the work of Crozet as state engineer. The De La Vergne family papers, located at Tulane University, New Orleans, add some insight into Crozet's work as president of Jefferson College. Copies of these papers are located at Hill Library, Louisiana State University, Baton Rouge.

Letters and papers of Thomas Green, James Poyntz Nelson, and Andrew Talcott, located at the Virginia Historical Society, Richmond, shed some light on Crozet during his years as principal of Richmond Academy.

Crozet became involved in the construction of the Washington aqueduct following completion of the Blue Ridge Railroad and tunnels. The papers of Montgomery C. Meigs, located at the Library of Congress, are useful for the aqueduct. Crozet's final engineering project was the Virginia and Kentucky Railroad, for which the Board of Public Works papers are essential. Additional light is shed by the letters and papers of Robert W. Hughes and John Tyler, Jr., located at Swem Library, College of William and Mary, Williamsburg, Va.

Finally, Crozet's handwritten last will and testament, located at the Chancery Court in Richmond, provides valuable information about his personal life.

Manuscript Sources

Anderson, Joseph Reid, Jr., "A Complete History of Virginia Military Institute." Typescript. Joseph R. Anderson, Jr., Collection, VMI Archives, Virginia Military Institute, Lexington.
Board of Public Works, Commonwealth of Virginia, Letter Book A, 1816–32. Virginia State Library, Richmond. (245 pp.)
———, Letter Book B, 1837–40. Virginia State Library. (260 pp.)
———, Letter Book C, 1840–45. Virginia State Library. (320 pp.)
———, Papers, Applications for Position of Principal Engineer, 1816–23, unnumbered box. Virginia State Library.
———, Papers, box 3, 1823–31, Letters and Reports. Virginia State Library.
———, Papers, box 4, 1823–25, Accounts and Vouchers. Virginia State Library.
———, Papers, box 5, 1826–28, Accounts and Vouchers. Virginia State Library.
———, Papers, box 6, 1840–43, Accounts and Vouchers. Virginia State Library.
———, Papers, Railroads, box 2, 1849–51. Blue Ridge Railroad, Correspondence, Reports, Bids, Contracts, etc. Virginia State Library.
———, Papers, Railroads, box 3, 1852–54. Blue Ridge Railroad, Correspondence, Reports, Bids, Contracts, etc. Virginia State Library.
———, Papers, Railroads, box 3, 1855–58. Blue Ridge Railroad, Correspondence, Reports, Bids, Contracts, etc. Virginia State Library.
———, Papers, Entry 154, Virginia and Kentucky Railroad, Correspondence, Reports, Bids, Contracts, etc., 1857–80. Virginia State Library.
Cabell, Joseph Carrington (1779–1856), Letters and Papers, 1817–46. University of Virginia Library, Charlottesville.
Cocke, John Hartwell (1780–1866), Letters and Papers, 1817–65. University of Virginia Library.
Confidential and Unofficial Letters Sent by the Secretary of War, 1814–47. Records of the Office of the Secretary of War, M7, Record Group 107, National Archives, Washington, D.C.
Crozet, Claudius, Last Will and Testament, 5 Feb. 1863, 4 pp. MS, Chancery Court Records, Richmond.
———, Letters and Papers, VMI Archives, Virginia Military Institute, Lexington.
———, Letters and Papers, United States Military Academy Library, West Point, N.Y.
———, Letter to Robert T. Hubard, 3 Jan. 1843, 4 pp. University of Virginia Library.
De La Vergne Family Papers, folder 6 (1831–35), folder 7 (1836–40), Hill Library, Louisiana State University, Baton Rouge.
Dossier of Captain Claudius Crozet, Archives de la Guerre, Service Historique de l'Armée (AGSHA), Vincennes, France.
Green, Thomas, Correspondence, 1815–71, Virginia Historical Society, Richmond.
Hughes, Robert William, Letters and Papers, Swem Library, College of William and Mary, Williamsburg, Va.

Imboden, John Daniel (1823–1895), Letters and Papers, box 1 (1844–74), University of Virginia Library.
Jefferson, Thomas (1743–1826), Letters and Papers, University of Virginia Library.
Letters Received by the Secretary of War, Registered Series, 1801–70, M221, Record Group 107, National Archives, Washington, D.C.
Letters Sent to the President by the Secretary of War, 1800–1863, M127, Record Group 107, National Archives, Washington, D.C.
Livre d'immatriculation, Archives, Bibliothèque Centrale de l'Ecole Polytechnique (ABEP), Palliseau, France.
Louisiana Board of Public Works, 1833–42. Reports 1833–41. New Orleans, 1834–42. 9 vols. Report for January 1835 only. All others missing.
Mansfield, Jared (1759–1830), Letters and Papers. United States Military Academy Library, West Point, N.Y.
Meigs, Montgomery C., Letters and Papers, Library of Congress, Washington, D.C.
Minutes of the Board of Visitors, Virginia Military Institute, 1839–53. MS Bound Volume in VMI Archives, Lexington.
Partridge, Alden (1785–1854), Letters and Papers, United States Military Academy Library, West Point, N.Y.
Records Relating to the United States Military Academy, 1812–67, M91, Record Group 94, National Archives, Washington, D.C.
Registers of Letters Received by the Office of the Secretary of War, Main Series, 1800–1870, M22, Record Group 107, National Archives, Washington, D.C.
Smith, Francis H. (1812–90), Letters and Papers, VMI Archives, Virginia Military Institute Library, Lexington.
Swift, Joseph Gardner (1783–1868), Letters and Papers, United States Military Academy Library, West Point, N.Y.
Talcott, Andrew, Diary, Virginia Historical Society, Richmond.
Tyler, John, Jr., Letters and Papers, Swem Library, College of William and Mary, Williamsburg, Va.
United States Census Reports: 1830, Richmond, Va., National Archives Roll 19–195, 1840, Henrico County, Va., National Archives Roll T5–181, copies at University of Virginia Library; 1860, Saint James Parish, La., Centroplex Plaza Library, Baton Rouge.
War Department, Letters Received, 1819–25, Record Group 77, Oversized Letter Book, Entry 13, National Archives, Washington, D.C.

Public Records

Annual Report[s] of the Board of Public Works to the General Assembly of Virginia. Richmond: State Printer, 1816–73.
Journal of the House of Delegates of the Commonwealth of Virginia. Richmond: State Printer, 1816–60.

Journal of the Senate of the Commonwealth of Virginia. Richmond: State Printer, 1816–60.
Journal of the House of Representatives of the State of Louisiana. New Orleans: State Printer, 1828–36.

Newspapers

Abingdon, Va., *Democrat*
Abingdon, Va., *Republican*
Abingdon, Va., *Virginian*
Baton Rouge, La., *Gazette*
Charleston, Va., *Banner*
Fincastle, Va., *Patriot*
Lexington, Va., *Gazette*
Lexington, Va., *Intelligencer*
Lexington, Va., *Valley Star*
Lynchburg, Va., *Virginian*
New Orleans, La., *Bee*
New Orleans, La., *Courier*
Petersburg, Va., *Old Dominion*
Richmond, Va., *Enquirer*
Staunton, Va., *Spectator*

Books

Ambler, Charles H. *Life of John Floyd*. Richmond: Richmond Press, 1918.
———. *Sectionalism in Virginia, 1776–1861*. Glendale, Calif.: A. H. Clark, 1910.
———. *Thomas Ritchie: A Study in Virginia Politics*. Richmond: Bell Book & Stationery Co., 1913.
———. *West Virginia: The Mountain State*. New York: Prentice-Hall, 1940.
Ambrose, Stephen E. *Duty, Honor, Country: A History of West Point*. Baltimore: Johns Hopkins Press, 1966.
Anderson, Dice Robins. *William Branch Giles*. 1914. Rpt. Gloucester, Mass.: Peter Smith, 1965.
Arthur, Stanley C., and George C. H. de Kernion. *Old Families of Louisiana*. New Orleans: Harmanson, 1931.
Artz, Frederick B. *The Development of Technical Education in France, 1500–1800*. Cambridge, Mass.: MIT Press, 1966.
Baer, Christopher T. *Canals and Railroads of the Mid-Atlantic States, 1800–1860*. Wilmington, Del.: Regional Economic History Research Center, Eleutherian Mills-Hagley Foundation, 1981.

Berard, Augusta Blanche. *Reminiscences of West Point in the Olden Time*. East Saginaw, Mich.: Evening News Printing and Binding House, 1886.

Bruce, Dickson D., Jr., *The Rhetoric of Conservatism: The Virginia Convention of 1829–30 and the Conservative Tradition in the South*. San Marino, Calif.: Huntington Library, 1982.

Bruce, Philip Alexander. *History of the University of Virginia, 1819–1919: The Lengthened Shadow of One Man*. 2 vols. New York: Macmillan, 1920.

Carriere, Judge Oliver P. *A Sketch of the History of Jefferson College and Manresa House of Retreats, Convent, Louisiana*. Convent, La.: Manresa House of Retreats, 1974.

Chandler, David D. *The Campaigns of Napoleon*. New York: Macmillan, 1966.

Chitwood, Oliver P. *John Tyler: Champion of the Old South*. New York: Appleton-Century, 1939.

Couper, William. *Claudius Crozet: Soldier—Scholar—Educator—Engineer (1789–1864)*. Charlottesville, Va.: Historical Publishing Co., 1936.

———. *One Hundred Years at V.M.I*. 4 vols. Richmond: Garrett and Massie, 1939.

Crenshaw, Ollinger. *General Lee's College: The Rise and Growth of Washington and Lee University*. New York: Random House, 1969.

Crosland, Maurice. *The Society of Arcueil*. Cambridge, Mass.: Harvard University Press, 1967.

Crozet, Claudius. *An Arithmetic for Colleges and Schools*. Richmond: A. Morris, 1858.

———. *A Treatise on Descriptive Geometry for the Use of the Cadets of the United States Military Academy*. New York: A. T. Goodrich, 1821.

Cullum, Brevet Major-General George W. *Biographical Register of the Officers and Graduates of the U.S. Military Academy at West Point, N.Y., from Its Establishment, in 1802, to 1890, with the Early History of the United States Military Academy*. 3d ed., revised and extended. Boston and New York: Houghton, Mifflin & Co., 1891.

Dabney, Virginius. *Richmond: The Story of a City*. Garden City, N.Y.: Doubleday, 1976.

Dew, Charles B. *Ironmaker to the Confederacy: Joseph R. Anderson and the Tredegar Iron Works*. New Haven: Yale University Press, 1966.

Drinker, Henry S. *Tunneling, Explosive Compounds, and Rock Drills*. New York: John Wiley & Sons, 1878.

Dunaway, Wayland F. *History of the James River and Kanawha Company*. New York: Columbia University Press, 1922.

Dupuy, Richard E. *Where They Have Trod: The West Point Tradition in American Life*. New York: Frederick A. Stokes Co., 1940.

Eckenrode, Henry J., ed. *Richmond, Capital of Virginia: Approaches to Its History*. Richmond: Whittet & Shepperson, 1938.

Ecole Polytechnique. *Programme générale de l'Ecole Impériale Polytechnique*. Paris: L'Imprimerie Impériale, 1806.

Ellery, Harrison, ed. *The Memoirs of Gen. Joseph Gardner Swift, LL.D., U.S.A., First Graduate of the United States Military Academy, West Point,*

Chief Engineer U.S.A. from 1812 to 1818: 1800–1865. Privately printed, 1890.
Fay, Edwin Whitfield. *History of Education in Louisiana.* Washington, D.C.: Government Printing Office, 1898.
Fleming, Thomas J. *West Point: The Men and Times of the United States Military Academy.* New York: Morrow, 1969.
Forman, Sidney. *West Point: A History of the United States Military Academy.* New York: Columbia University Press, 1950.
Fortier, Alcee, ed. *Louisiana: Comprising Sketches of Parishes, Towns, Events, Institutions, and Persons, Arranged in Cyclopedic Form.* 3 vols. New York: Century Historical Association, 1914.
Fossier, Albert A. *New Orleans: The Glamour Period, 1800–1840.* New Orleans: Pelican Publishing Co., 1957.
Fourcy, Ambroise. *Histoire de l'Ecole Polytechnique.* 1828. Rpt. Paris: Librarie Classique Eugène Belin, 1987.
Gayarre, Charles. *History of Louisiana.* 4 vols. New Orleans: F. F. Hansell & Brother, 1903. Rpt. New Orleans: Pelican Publishing Co., 1965.
Goodrich, Carter. *Government Promotion of American Canals and Railroads, 1800–1890.* New York: Columbia University Press, 1960.
———, ed. *Canals and American Economic Development.* New York: Columbia University Press, 1961.
Green, Fletcher M. *Constitutional Development in the South Atlantic States, 1776–1860.* Chapel Hill: University of North Carolina Press, 1930.
Hachette, Jean-Nicolas Pierre. *Correspondance sur l'Ecole Impériale Polytechnique.* 3 vols. 2d ed. Paris: J. Klostermann, 1813–16.
Hemphill, W. Edwin. *The Papers of John C. Calhoun.* 4 vols. Columbia: University of South Carolina Press, 1969.
Hungerford, Edward. *The Story of the Baltimore and Ohio Railroad, 1827–1927.* 2 vols. New York: Putnam, 1928.
Kirby, Richard S. *The First One Hundred and Fifty Years: A History of John Wiley and Sons, Incorporated, 1807–1957.* New York: Wiley, 1957.
Lacuée, Jean-Gérard de. *Rapport sur l'Ecole Impériale Polytechnique.* Paris: L'Imprimerie Impériale, 1806.
Lewis, Gene D. *Charles Ellet, Jr.: The Engineer as Individualist, 1810–1862.* Urbana: University of Illinois Press, 1968.
Livre du Centenaire, 1794–1894. 3 vols. Paris: Gauthier-Villars et Fils, 1895.
Meagher, Margaret. *History of Education in Richmond.* Richmond: Works Progress Administration, 1939.
Meeks, Steven G. *Crozet: A Pictorial History.* Elkton, Va.: Meeks Enterprises, 1983.
Miller, Nathan. *The Enterprise of a Free People: Aspects of Economic Development in New York State during the Canal Period, 1792–1838.* Ithaca, N.Y.: Cornell University Press, 1962.
Munford, Robert Beverly, Jr. *Richmond Homes and Memories.* Richmond: Garrett & Massie, 1936.
Murray, Nicholas Russell. *St. James Parish, Louisiana, 1809–1900.* Hammond, La.: n.p., n.d.

Nelson, James Poyntz. *The Chesapeake and Ohio Railway*. Richmond: Lewis Printing Co., 1927.
Palmer, Robert R. *The Improvement of Humanity: Education and the French Revolution*. Princeton, N.J.: Princeton University Press, 1985.
Reed, Merl E. *New Orleans and the Railroads: The Struggle for Commercial Empire, 1830–1860*. Baton Rouge: Louisiana State University Press, 1966.
Reeves, Miriam G. *The Governors of Louisiana*. New Orleans: Pelican Publishing Co., 1962.
Rice, Harvey Mitchell. *The Life of Jonathan M. Bennett: A Study of the Virginias in Transition*. Chapel Hill: University of North Carolina Press, 1943.
Rice, Otis K. *West Virginia: A History*. Lexington: University of Kentucky Press, 1985.
Richmond Portraits: In an Exhibition of Makers of Richmond, 1737–1860. Richmond: Valentine Museum, 1949.
Sanchez-Saavedra, E. M. *A Description of the Country: Virginia Cartographers and Their Maps, 1607–1881*. Richmond: Virginia State Library, 1975.
Sanderlin, Walter S. *A History of the Chesapeake and Ohio Canal*. Baltimore: Johns Hopkins University Press, 1946.
Schama, Simon. *Patriots and Liberators: Revolution in the Netherlands, 1780–1813*. New York: Knopf, 1977.
Scott, Mary Wingfield. *Old Richmond Neighborhoods*. Richmond: Whittet & Shepperson, 1950.
Seager, Robert. *And Tyler Too: A Biography of John and Julia Gardiner Tyler*. New York: McGraw-Hill, 1963.
Sparks, W. H. *The Memories of Fifty Years*. Philadelphia: Claxton, Remsen & Haffelfinger, 1870.
Stover, John F. *Iron Road to the West: American Railroads in the 1850's*. New York: Columbia University Press, 1978.
Thirty-Second Annual Reunion of the Association of Graduates of the United States Military Academy, at West Point, New York, June 8th, 1901. Saginaw, Mich.: Seemann & Peters, 1901.
Tulard, Jean, ed. *Dictionnaire Napoléon*. Paris: Fayard, 1987.
Turner, Charles W. *Chessie's Road: A History of the Chesapeake and Ohio Railroad*. Richmond: Garrett & Massie, 1956.
Tyler, Lyon G. *The Letters and Times of the Tylers*. 3 vols. 1884–86. Rpt. New York: DaCapo Press, 1970.
Waddell, Joseph A. *Annals of Augusta County, 1726–1871*. 2d ed. Staunton, Va.: C. R. Caldwell, 1902.
Weigley, Russell F. *Quartermaster General of the Union Army: A Biography of M[ontgomery] C. Meigs*. New York: Columbia University Press, 1959.

Articles

Aldrich, Mark, "Earnings of American Civil Engineers, 1820–1859," *Journal of Economic History* 31, no. 2 (June 1971): 399–418.

Ammon, Harry, "The Richmond Junto, 1800–1824," *Virginia Magazine of History and Biography* 61, no. 4 (1953): 395–418.

Braverman, Howard, "The Economic and Political Background of the Conservative Revolt in Virginia," *Virginia Magazine of History and Biography* 60, no. 2 (1952): 266–87.

Brown, Alexander Crosby, "The Canal Boat 'Governor McDowell': Virginia's Pioneer Iron Steamer," *Virginia Magazine of History and Biography* 74, no. 3 (1966): 336–45.

———, "The Tomb of a Dream: The Marshall Tunnel and the Unfinished Portion of the James River and Kanawha Canal," *Virginia Cavalcade* 22, no. 4 (1973): 18–29.

Carter, William H., "Claude Crozet," *Journal of the Military Service Institution of the United States* 53 (July-Aug. 1913): 3–6.

Chitwood, Walter R., "Governor John Floyd, Physician," *Virginia Cavalcade* 26, no. 2 (1976): 86–95.

Coleman, Elizabeth Dabney, "Forerunner of Virginia's First Railway," *Virginia Cavalcade* 4, no. 3 (1954): 4–7.

———, "Southwest Virginia's Railroad; Lynchburg Started It, Virginia Built It, the Yankees Wrecked It," *Virginia Cavalcade* 2, no. 4 (1953): 20–28.

———, "Virginia Buys a Hole in the Ground: The Blue Ridge Tunnel," *Virginia Cavalcade* 1, no. 1 (1951): 22–27.

———, and W. Edwin Hemphill, "Boats beyond the Blue Ridge," *Virginia Cavalcade* 3, no. 4 (1954): 8–13.

Couper, William, "Colonel Claudius Crozet, 1789–1864," *West Virginia Historical Magazine* 1, no. 4 (1940): 256–69.

Délery, Simone de la Souchère, "Some French Soldiers Who Became Louisiana Educators," *Louisiana Historical Quarterly* 31, no. 4 (1948): 849–55.

Dooley, Edwin L., Jr., "Claudius Crozet: Disseminator of French Technical Education to the United States," *Proceedings of the Consortium on Revolutionary Europe, 1750–1850* (Athens, Ga., 1986), 449–59.

Druyvesteyn, Kent, "With Great Vision: The James River and Kanawha Canal, a Pictorial Essay," *Virginia Cavalcade* 21, no. 3 (1972): 22–47.

Goldfield, David R., "Marketing a Candidate: Henry A. Wise and the Art of Mass Politics," *Virginia Cavalcade* 26, no. 1 (1976): 30–37.

Goodrich, Carter, "The Virginia System of Mixed Enterprise: A Study of State Planning of Internal Improvements," *Political Science Quarterly* 64, no. 3 (1949): 355–87.

Grison, Emmanuel, "Les cours de chimie de Berthollet en Pluvoise An III," *La Jaune et la Rouge* 429 (Nov. 1987): 36–38.

Harrison, Joseph H., Jr., "Oligarchs and Democrats: The Richmond Junto," *Virginia Magazine of History and Biography* 78, no. 2 (1970): 184–98.

Heite, Edward F., "The Tunnels of Richmond," *Virginia Cavalcade* 14, no. 3 (1964): 42–47.
Hunter, Robert F., "Turnpike Construction in Antebellum Virginia," *Technology and Culture* 4, no. 2 (1963): 177–200.
——, "The Turnpike Movement in Virginia, 1816–1860," *Virginia Magazine of History and Biography* 69, no. 3 (1961): 278–89.
Imboden, John D., "Biographical Sketch of Colonel Claudius Crozet," in W. F. Switzer, *Report on the Internal Commerce of the U.S.* (1886). Rpt. *Bulletin of the Virginia State Library* (Richmond, 1914), 95–97.
Kean, Jefferson R., "The Development of the 'Valley Line' of the Baltimore and Ohio Railroad," *Virginia Magazine of History and Biography* 60, no. 4 (1952): 537–50.
Knight, John Stephen, "Discontent, Disunity, and Dissent in the Antebellum South: Virginia as a Test Case, 1844–46," *Virginia Magazine of History and Biography* 81, no. 4 (1973): 437–56.
Niehaus, Earl F., "Jefferson College: The Early Years," *Louisiana Historical Quarterly* 38, no. 4 (1955): 63–89.
Reed, Merl E., "Government Investment and Economic Growth: Louisiana's Ante Bellum Railroads," *Journal of Southern History* 28, no. 2 (1962): 183–201.
Rice, Otis K., "Coal Mining in the Kanawha Valley to 1861: A View of Industrialization in the Old South," *Journal of Southern History* 31, no. 4 (1965): 393–416.
Stanard, William G., "The Homes of the Virginia Historical Society," *Virginia Magazine of History and Biography* 34, no. 1 (1926): 1–18.
Stewart, Peter C., "Railroads and Urban Rivalries in Antebellum Eastern Virginia," *Virginia Magazine of History and Biography* 81, no. 1 (1973): 3–22.
Troubetzkoy, Ulrich, "Colonel Claudius Crozet," *Virginia Cavalcade* 12, no. 4 (1963): 5–10.
Turner, Charles W., "The Early Railroad Movement in Virginia," *Virginia Magazine of History and Biography* 55, no. 3 (1947): 350–71.
——, "Early Virginia Railroad Entrepreneurs and Personnel," *Virginia Magazine of History and Biography* 58, no. 3 (1950): 325–34.
——, "The Virginia Central Railroad at War, 1861–1865," *Journal of Southern History* 12, no. 4 (1946): 510–33.
Ward, James A., "A New Look at Antebellum Southern Railroad Development," *Journal of Southern History* 39, no. 4 (1973): 409–20.
Welch, M. L., "Early West Point: French Teachers and Influences," *American Society Legion of Honor Magazine* 26, no. 1 (1955): 27–43.

Dissertations

Brunet, Joseph, Jr., "Science and the Early Ecole Polytechnique, 1794–1806," Ph.D. diss., University of Kentucky, 1969.

Coleman, Elizabeth Dabney, "The Story of the Virginia Central Railroad, 1850–1860," Ph.D. diss., University of Virginia, 1957.

Coyner, Martin Boyd, "John Hartwell Cocke of Bremo: Agriculture and Slavery in the Ante-Bellum South," Ph.D. diss., University of Virginia, 1961.

Denton, Edgar III, "The Formative Years of the United States Military Academy, 1775–1833," Ph.D. diss., Syracuse University, 1964.

Griess, Thomas E., "Dennis Hart Mahan: West Point Professor and Advocate of Military Professionalism, 1830–1871," Ph.D. diss., Duke University, 1968.

Harrison, Joseph H., Jr., "The Internal Improvement Issue in the Politics of the Union, 1783–1825," Ph.D. diss., University of Virginia, 1954.

Hunter, Robert F., "The Turnpike Movement in Virginia, 1816–1860," Ph.D. diss., Columbia University, 1957.

Rice, Philip M., "Internal Improvements in Virginia, 1775–1860," Ph.D. diss., University of North Carolina, 1947.

Tanner, Carol M., "Joseph C. Cabell, 1778–1856," Ph.D. diss., University of Virginia, 1948.

Turner, Charles W., "The Virginia Railroads, 1828–1860," Ph.D. diss., University of Minnesota, 1946.

Index

Abingdon
  internal improvement convention at
    1831, 68
    1845, 136
  as railroad terminus, 172, 174
Abingdon *Democrat*, 173, 175
Acquia Creek, 112
All-water route to Ohio River, 37
Ampère, André, 8
Anderson, Joseph Reid, 117, 119–20, 145
Anderson, Joseph Reid, Jr., 128
Anderson, William N., 37, 39, 40, 44
Appomattox Canal, 32
Atchafalaya River, 95
Athenaeum, 135
Austerlitz, battle of, 8

Bache, Franklin, 7
Bailey, Robert T., 172
Baldwin, Loammi, 33
Ballast, 150
Baltimore & Ohio Railroad, 48, 60, 61, 114–15, 135
Bateaux, 56
Baton Rouge & Clinton Railroad, 92
Bell, John, 147
Benching and leveling, 163
Berard, Claudius, 17
Bernard, General Simon, 15, 16, 19
Berret, J. G., 169
Berthollet, Claude Louis, comte de, 6, 7
Big Sewell Mountain, 118
Black's Gap, 51
Blasting smoke (tunnel), 143, 148–49

Bliss, Captain John, 23, 26
Blue Ridge Canal, 38–39, 40, 44–45, 109–10
Blue Ridge Railroad Company, 139, 140–41
  Crozet appointed chief engineer, 141
Blue Ridge tunnel, 140–41
  hazardous midsection, 150
  "holing through," 158
  Fisk report, 165–66
Board of Public Works (Virginia), 29–30, 32
  planning for principal engineer, 40, 49, 61, 105, 122–23
  conflict with legislature, 49
  Crozet advises on successors, 69–70
  acts as Blue Ridge Railroad Company, 142
  revises Kelly & Larguey contract, 144
  and Bell petition, 147
  and financial crisis, 1855, 159
Board of Visitors (VMI), 125
  Lexington members added, 127, 130
  Crozet retires as member, 133
Bollman, Wendel, 145
Borodino, battle of, 11
Bosher's dam, 71
Bowyer's Ferry, 47
Boÿë, Herman, 138, 160–61
Brewerton, Henry, 27
Brick arching (tunnel), 143, 146, 151, 158, 159, 165
Bridges
  canal, 108
  lattice, 121–22
Bristol, 172
Brockenbrough, John, 134

Brooksville, 144
Brooksville tunnel, 142, 145, 146, 151, 153, 157, 158–59
Bryan, William H., 167–68
Buchanan, President James, 165–66
Bucholtz, Ludwig von, 160
Burgoyne, Sir John, 148
Burke, William, 135
Burr, D. I., 46
Burthe, D. L., 100

Cabell, Joseph Carrington
  reenters politics, 66
  reproaches Wright, 67
  favors canal, 73
  heads James River & Kanawha Company, 103
  hostile toward Crozet, 109
  favors all-water route, 1842, 110
  resigns, 1846, 110
Calhoun, John C., 23, 24, 26, 27
Callet, Jean-François, 4
Campbell, Governor David, 103, 105, 125, 127
Census report, 1860, 99
Charenton, 13
Charlottesville
  internal improvement convention, 1828, 54
  and Louisa Railroad, 140
Cheat Mountain, 36
Cheat River, 44
Chesapeake & Ohio Canal, 35, 37, 42, 72
Chesterfield Railroad, 60
Cheves, Langdon, 35
Cholera, 91, 156–57
Clay, Henry, 27
Clinton, DeWitt, 60
Clinton & Port Hudson Railroad, 91–93
Coal pits, 41
Coalter, John, 67
Cocke, Charles, 61–62
Cocke, John Hartwell, 39, 66, 109
Cocke, John Hartwell, Jr., 39, 46
Collège de Navarre, 2, 5

Collier's Gap, 51
Committees of Correspondence, 56–58
Couper, William, 15, 49, 69, 99, 127
Covington, 47, 118
Crawford, William H., 16, 19, 33
Crouse, William, 148–49
Crozet, Adele Eugenie, 22
  death of, 49
Crozet, Adolphus, 99, 178
Crozet, Agathe Decamp, 14, 17, 100, 124
  death of, 175
Crozet, Alfred Saint Armand, 31, 85, 124
  graduates from West Point, 132
  in Mexican War, 136
  death of, 159
Crozet, Anna, 99, 177
Crozet, Benoit, 1
Crozet, Claudia Natalia, 12, 63, 85, 124, 177
Crozet, Claudius
  birth and early life, 1
  enters Ecole Polytechnique, 2
  graduates from Ecole, 9
  commissioned, 10
  in Germany and Holland, 1810–11, 10
  service and capture in Russia, 11
  return to France, 1814, 12
  leaves army, 13
  marries, 14
  sails to America, 15
  appointed to USMA faculty, 1816, 15
  publishes textbook, 17
  appointed professor, 22
  arrested by Thayer, 24–25
  leaves West Point, 30
  obtains engineering post in Virginia, 34–36
  initial surveys, 1823–25, 35–42
    Staunton-Parkersburg route, 36
    Blue Ridge Canal, 38
    Kanawha Turnpike, 40
    James River Canal, 1825, 42

Crozet, Claudius (*cont.*)
  on James River improvement,
    1831, 58, 72
  for railroad west of Lynchburg,
    59
  surveys Lynchburg-to-Tennessee railroad route, 68
  resigns as principal engineer,
    69
  favors railroad for James River
    route, 1831, 72
  on bayou Plaquemine, 88
  urges New Orleans-to-Washington railroad, 93–94
  resigns as Louisiana engineer,
    97
  president, Jefferson College,
    100
  city engineer, New Orleans, 101
  returns to Virginia as principal
    engineer, 1837, 103–4
  urges railroad to Tennessee,
    104
  examines James River Canal,
    1840, 107–9
  Blue Ridge tunnel survey, 1839,
    113
  examines Baltimore & Ohio
    Railroad, 114
  office terminated by legislature,
    1843, 123
  president, VMI Board of Visitors, 125–28
  sells books to VMI, 133
  retires from Board of Visitors,
    133
  publishes *An Arithmetic for Colleges and Schools*, 134
  describes potential railroad
    routes, 1845, 136
  chief engineer, Blue Ridge
    Railroad and tunnel, 141
  completes tunnel work, 162
  accepts aqueduct job, 162, 167
  aqueduct job terminated, 170
  seeks teaching post, 170
  chief engineer, Virginia & Kentucky RR, 173
  seeks wartime service, 176
  writes will, 177
  death of, 178
  town named for, 179
Crozet, Eliza, 1, 99, 178
  see also Magne
Crozet, François, 1, 3, 12, 99
Crozet, Marie (Mary), 99, 178
Crozet, Pierrette Varion, 1
Crozet, William, 1, 99, 178
Culverts (canal), 42
Curran, Michael, 147
Cushaw Falls, 44
Cutoffs, 92

Danville Railroad Company, 137
Davis, Jefferson, 165, 176
Davis, L. B., 91
Dawson, William A., 92, 94
Deane, Silas, 17
Decamp, Pierre François, 14
Denton, Edgar III, 18, 26
Depression, economic, 104–5
Descriptive geometry, 5
Dettor, Joseph, 146, 151
DeWitt, Thomas H., 69, 164
Dimmock, Charles, 137
Dismal Swamp Canal, 32
Dorr and Company, 172, 175
Douglass, David B., 25, 30
Dover aqueduct, 41
Dove Spring Hollow, 142, 153, 162
Drinker, Henry S., 142
Dupuy, A. M., 146
Durand, Jean Nicolas Louis, 4

Ecole des ponts et chaussées, 5
Ecole des mines, 5
Ecole Polytechnique
  in 1805, 2
  uniforms, 3
  course of instruction, textbooks,
    4
Ellet, Charles, Jr., 149, 151, 153
Ellicott, Andrew, 22
Erie Canal, 39, 86
Estillville, 173–74
Eveleth, Lieutenant, 16
Eustis, William, 18

Index

Fairfax, Wilson, 39, 40
Falaya River, 91, 93, 95
Farrow, George A., 156
Farrow, Joseph, 147
Feeders (canal), 39, 42
Fincastle, 56
   convention at, 1845, 136
Fisk, Charles B., 165, 172
Floyd, Benjamin Rush, 172–73
Floyd, Governor John, 49, 58, 64, 69
   recommends loan, more authority for BPW, 50
Floyd, John Buchanan, 165–66, 173
Fontaine, Edmund, 149
Fording places (canal), 42
Fortress Monroe, Virginia, 15, 20
Fourcroy, Antoine François de, 4, 5, 6
Fourier, Jean Baptiste Joseph, 6
Francoeur, Louis Benjamin, 4
Franklin, Benjamin, 17
Fund for Internal Improvements
   Virginia, 32
   Louisiana, 90

Gallaher, H. L., 144, 152, 154, 167–68
Gallatin, Albert, 19
Garland, David, 44
Garland, James, committee, 58–60
Gassendi, comte de, 10
Gauley Bridge, 37, 40, 48
Gay de Vernon, Simon François, 4, 7, 23
Gay-Lussac, Joseph Louis, 7
Georgetown, 162
Giles, Governor William B., 47
Gill, E. H., 107
Gilmer, Governor Thomas W., 105
Goodloe, James, 161–62
Goodson, 172–74
Gordonsville, 113, 140
Grammaire Russe (Crozet), 12
Grande Armée, 9
Granet, Bernard, 99–100
Green, Thomas, 159

Greenbrier River, 41, 44
   bridge, 118
Greenwood depot, 149
Greenwood tunnel, 142, 151
Gregory, Governor John M., 122
Gretter, D. B., 117
Guyandotte, 47, 48, 118

Hachette, Jean Nicolas Pierre, 4, 6
Hansbrough, David, 156
Harris, Robert, 151
Harrison, Benjamin, 37
Hassenfratz, Jean Henry, 6
Hassler, Ferdinand, 33
Hawkins and Company, 172, 175
Herron, James, 69
House of Delegates, 58, 66, 127
   retrenchment policy, 1840, 106
Hughes, Robert W., 173–75
Humboldt, Alexander von, 7
Hydraulic lime, 41, 46, 71

Imboden, John D., 100
   sketch of Crozet character, 179–80
Indian Gap, 51
Ingalls, Thomas R., 101
Irish Gap, 51
Irish workers, 146–47, 157

Jackson, President Andrew, 50, 55
Jackson's River, 41
James River & Kanawha Company, 37, 103, 107. 115, 118, 149
James River Canal, 32, 42, 46, 57, 58, 135–36
   estimated cost, 1825, 42
   new survey, 1831, 62–64
   Wright opinion of, 65
   Crozet report, 1831, 70
   under construction, 104
   Crozet examination of, 1840, 107–9
   locks, bridges, 108
   cost, 108
James River Company, 37, 52
James River gorge, 38

Jefferson, President Thomas, 18, 29, 60, 98
Jefferson College, 98, 101
Joshua's Falls, 108

Kanalassi, Anthony, 160
Kanawha *Banner*, 63–64
Kanawha River, 37, 54
Kanawha Turnpike, 37, 40, 47, 55, 118
Kelly, John, 143–45, 152, 155, 159
Kelly's cut, 142, 153, 161–63

Labor relations, 146, 154–56
Lacaille, Nicolas Louis, 4
Lacroix, Sylvestre-François, 4
Lacuée, General Jean-Gérard de, 2, 3
Lafayette, marquis de, 16, 19
Languedoc Canal, 39
Laplace, Pierre, 8
Larguey, John, 143, 155
Latrobe, Benjamin H., 32
Latrobe, Benjamin H., Jr., 114
La Vergne, Huguer Jules de, 100–101
Lavoisier, Antoine Laurent, 6
Lee, Arthur, 17
Leraysse, General, 16
Lexington and Covington Turnpike, 51, 119
Lexington arsenal, 125, 127
Lexington *Gazette*, 125
Lexington *Intelligencer*, 54, 55
Lexington *Valley Star*, 136
Leyburn, Dr. Alfred, 127, 132
Literary Committee, 139
Little River Turnpike Company, 32
Little Rock tunnel, 142, 152
Lock-and-dam navigation, 36, 43
  supported by Lynchburg, 56
  Wright opinion, 65
  Crozet defends, 70–71
Locks (canal), 42, 108
Long, Stephen H., 34
Louis XVIII, 12, 13
Louisa Railroad, 113, 140
  see also Virginia Central RR

Louisiana legislature
  creates office of civil engineer, 87
  assigns tasks, 89
  incorporates Board of Public Works, 90
  authorizes slave labor, 95
Lynchburg & New River Railroad, 63, 67
Lynchburg committee of correspondence, 57
Lynchburg-to-Tennessee railroad, 68, 104
  see also Virginia & Tennessee Railroad

McComas, William, 62
McDowell, Governor James, 124, 127
McRee, William, 15, 19, 34
Madison, President James, 16, 32, 54
Magne, Eliza Crozet, 99, 178
Mahan, Dennis Hart, 30
Maiden's Adventure Falls, 38
Malus, Etienne-Louis, 9
Manchester, 41
Manchester & Petersburg Turnpike, 179
Mansfield, Jared, 22, 23, 25, 28
Map of internal improvements (Virginia)
  Crozet commissioned to produce, 1838, 1848, 137–38
  Crozet map, 1855, 160–61
Marshall, John, 47, 54, 63–64
Mason, Valentine, 54
Maupin, Socrates, 135
Maysville veto, 50, 55
Mazureau, Etienne, 100
Meagher, Margaret, 135
Mechum's River, 140, 149
Meigs, Montgomery C., 162, 166–67
  appointed to Washington aqueduct, 165
  and Crozet, 168–69
Metz, artillery and engineering school at, 10
Mézières, artillery school at, 6, 8

Midlothian, 41, 63, 175
Mills, Adele Crozet, 179
Mills, Dr. Charles S., 124, 135, 177
Mills, Nicholas, 63, 110
Mississippi River, 85–86, 92–93
Mixed enterprise system, 32, 70
Monge, Gaspard, 4, 5, 14, 134
Monroe, James, 19, 21, 26, 27, 54
Montgomery County, 46
Moore, James, 37, 40
Moore, Thomas, 33, 35, 47
Morveau, Louis-Bernard Guyton de, 6, 7
Myers, Edward T. D., 135, 146, 168

Napoleon Bonaparte, 2, 8, 9, 10, 12, 13
National Turnpike to New Orleans, 55
Neigre, Lieutenant General, 13
Nelson, James Poyntz, 179
New Orleans, 85, 96
  Bee, 92, 94, 96, 101
  to Washington railroad, 93–94
  Drainage Company, 96
  and Nashville Railroad, 97
New River, 47
Nicholas, Robert Carter, 98
Nicholas, Governor Wilson Cary, 31–32
Nicholson, Cadet Edward L., 26
North River Navigation, 110–11
Northwestern Turnpike, 48, 60, 62, 70, 116–17

O'Connor, John, 23

Parkersburg, 47
Partridge, Alden, 20–22
Pennybacker, James, 121
Petersburg Railroad, 56, 60
Peyton, Bernard, 33, 125
Pierce, President Franklin, 165
Plaquemine, 87, 93–94
Pleasants, Governor James, 35
Point Pleasant, 48
Poisson, Siméon Denis, 6
Pontchartrain Railroad, 85
Poor Valley, 173

Potomac Company, 32, 37
Preston, Governor James P., 33, 68, 138
Preston, J. T. L., 125, 127
Principal engineer, 32
  office abolished, 122
Prony, Gaspard de, 4, 6

Quinet, Baron, 16

Railroads
  Crozet's opinion of
    1826, 43–44
    early 1831, 58–59
    late 1831, 71–72
    1841, 106
  development in Virginia by 1842, 111–15
  mail contracts, 112
  tacking (switchbacks), 113, 142, 149
  Crozet describes potential routes of, 1845, 136
Randolph, Edmund, 38
Randolph, J. J., 144
Richardson, Robert, 158
Richardson, William H., 132, 133, 137, 139, 176
Richmond Academy, 134–36
Richmond & Petersburg Railroad, 112
Richmond *Enquirer*, 55, 58, 60, 62, 63, 66, 69, 134
Richmond, Fredericksburg & Potomac Railroad, 111–12, 174
Richpatch Mountain, 46
Ritchie, Thomas, 134
Rivanna Navigation, 111
Rives, Albert L., 168–69
Rives, William M., 67–68
Roanoke River, 47, 48
Robertson, Governor Wyndham, 136
Robertson's Gap, 51
Robertson's Hollow, 142, 152–53, 162–63
Rochmont, Baron Quereta de, 16
Rockfish Gap, 113
Roman, André Bienvenu, 86–87, 95, 97
  appoints Crozet, 89

Roman, André Bienvenu (*cont.*)
   heads drainage company, 96
   and Jefferson College, 98
   second term as governor, 101
Roman, Felix, 99

Saint James Parish, 86, 98–99
Sanchez-Saavedra, E. M., 138
Scott, General Winfield, 21, 33
Seaboard & Roanoke Railroad, 112
Seven Islands, 46
Sganzin, Joseph Mathieu, 4, 7
Shaw, Charles B., 70
Shenandoah River, 106
Sherman, William T., 170
Simmons Gap, 113, 140
Sizer, Mordecai, 144, 155
Slave labor, 95, 155–56
Sluice navigation, 36
Smith, Francis H., 7, 125, 128–31, 138, 170, 176
Smith, Robert P., 155
Smith, Governor William, 137
Southwestern Turnpike, 106, 136
Spaulding, Thomas M., 20
Staunton, convention proposed at, 67
Staunton & James River Turnpike, 46, 52, 119, 144, 149
Staunton & Parkersburg Turnpike, 36, 44, 48, 106, 117
Staunton & Potomac Railroad, 61
Steamboats, 43, 46
Stevens, Paul, 148–49, 155
Stewart, Peter C., 113
Summers, George W., 61
Surville, Captain, 16, 33
Swift, Joseph G., 16, 18–19, 20–22, 34, 73
Swift Run Gap, 113

Tacking (switchbacks), 113, 142, 149
Talcott, Andrew, 137, 160
Tangipahoa River, 91, 93, 95
Taylorsville, 113, 174
Temporary track (Blue Ridge RR), 142, 149, 150–51, 153, 157, 166

Thayer, Sylvanus, 15, 19, 21, 23, 26
   arrests Crozet, 24
Thénard, Louis Jacques, 7
Theodolite, 36, 138
Thomas, Pierre, 17
Thompson, William B., 113, 140, 171–72, 175
Timbering (tunnel), 143, 145, 150
Trans-Allegheny, 37, 47, 55, 61, 67, 115, 118, 122
Tredegar Iron Works, 145, 151, 158
"The True Virginian," 54
Tunnel, Blue Ridge
   survey for, 1839, 113
   flooring, 143
   ventilation, 148–50
   siphon, 150
Turnpikes, 115–22
   toll collection, 116
   width, 117
   maintenance contracts, 117
   macadamized surface, 120–21
   cost of transportation on, 122
Tygart's Valley River, 44
Tyler, Governor John, 45, 134
Tyler, John, Jr., 176

U.S. Army Corps of Engineers, 37
United States Military Academy
   early years, 17
   reform of discipline, 28
   Crozet and academic questionnaire concerning, 1860, 171
University of Virginia, 29

Vaisz, William I., 160
Valley Turnpike, 120–22, 155, 177
Virginia & Kentucky Railroad, 171–76
Virginia & Tennessee Railroad, 141, 171
Virginia Central Railroad, 145, 149, 151, 158, 174
Virginia Constitutional Convention, 1830, 55
Virginia Military Institute, 7
   act establishing, 1836, 125

Virginia Military Institute (*cont.*)
  second act establishing, 1839, 127
  and Crozet as founder, 125–30
  opening day, 130
  reinterment of Crozet at, 178

Wagram, battle of, 10
Walker, R. S., 144
Walter, Thomas U., 165
War of 1812, 19
Washington, George, 37
Washington aqueduct, 165, 169–70
Washington College, 126
Waterloo, 13
Waterways (Virginia), 107–10
Waynesboro, 52, 140
Waynesboro bridge, 144, 145, 155
Welch, D. N., 91

Westham, 38
Whitcomb, H. D., 162
White, Edward D., 87
White, William Y. C., 172–73
White's Gap, 51
Wickham, Williams C., 178–79
Williams, Jonathan, 17, 18, 20
Wilson, Josiah D., 117
Winchester, 47
Winchester & Potomac Railroad, 115
Wirt, Attorney General William, 26
Wise, Governor Henry, 55
Wood, John, 138
Wright, Benjamin, 39, 64–66, 70–72, 149
Wythe Courthouse, 58, 176

Zoeller, Christian, 17

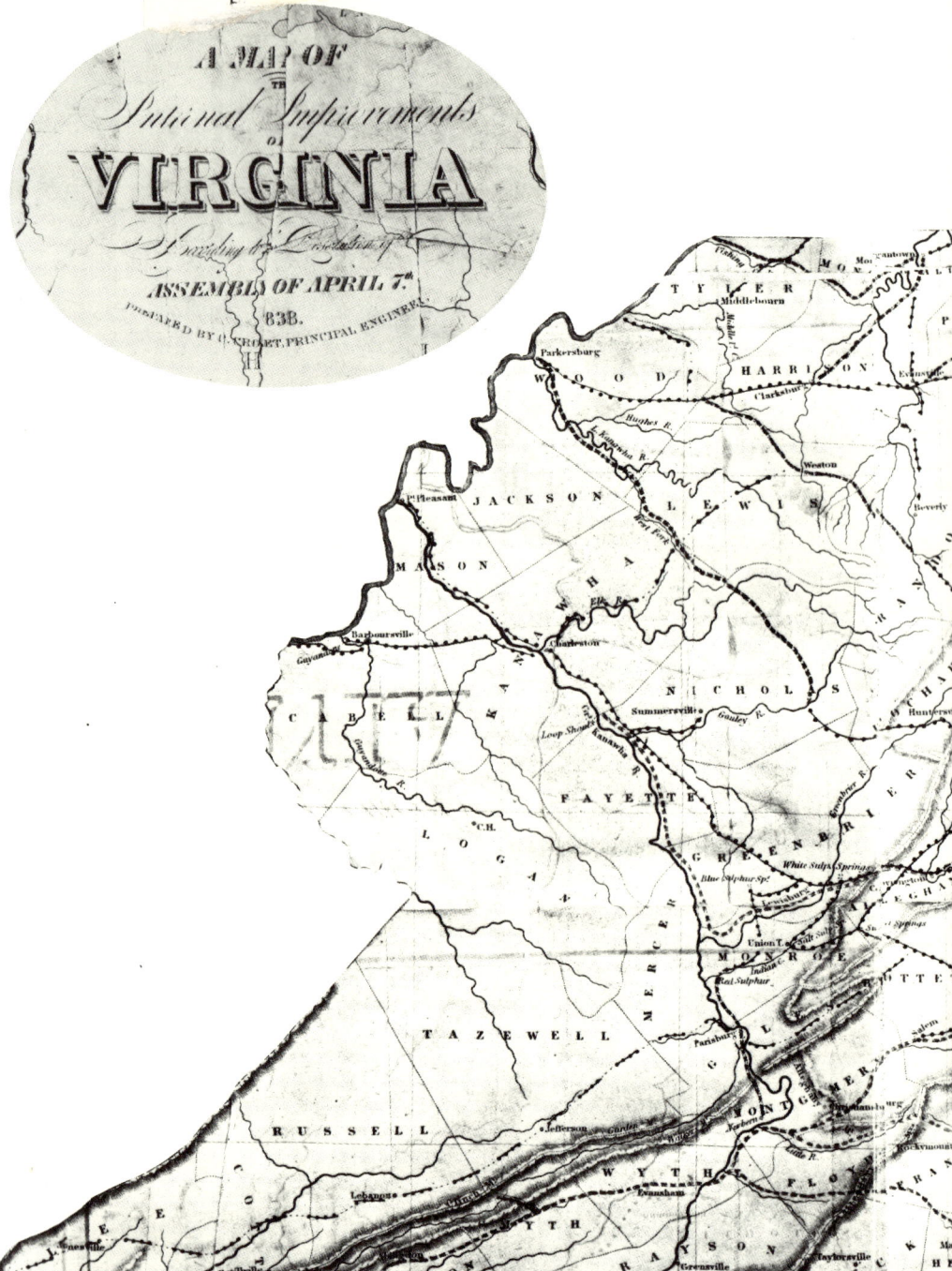